KINGS & QUEENS

About the Authors

Peter Snow CBE is a highly respected journalist, broadcaster and author. He was ITN's Diplomatic and Defence Correspondent from 1966 to 1979 and presented BBC's *Newsnight* from 1980 to 1997. He presented *Tomorrow's World* and two series of battlefield programmes with his son, Dan Snow. For many years he was an indispensable part of election nights. He has written several books on military history and he and Dan are the best-selling co-authors of *The Battle of Waterloo Experience* and *Treasures of British History.*

Ann MacMillan was born in North Wales and moved to Toronto as a child. After receiving a BA in English and History, she became one of Canada's first female news correspondents. She and Peter Snow met at a Commonwealth Conference in Ottawa in 1973 and when they married, her broadcaster moved her to its London Bureau. As CBC News London Bureau Chief she reported widely on Britain's royal family. She and Peter co-authored *War Stories* in 2017 and *Treasures of World History* in 2020.

KINGS & QUEENS

THE REAL LIVES OF THE ENGLISH MONARCHS

PETER SNOW & ANN MACMILLAN

WELBECK

Published by Welbeck
An imprint of Welbeck Non-Fiction Limited,
part of Welbeck Publishing Group.
Based in London and Sydney
www.welbeckpublishing.com

First published by Welbeck in 2022

A CIP catalogue record for this book is available from the British Library

ISBN
Hardback – 978-1-80279-003-0

Typeset by seagulls.net
Printed in the UK by CPI (UK) Ltd

2 4 6 8 10 9 7 5 3 1

Every reasonable effort has been made to trace copyright holders of
material produced in this book, but if any have been inadvertently
overlooked the publishers would be glad to hear from them.

To Royalists and Republicans alike

CONTENTS

PART I

THE HOUSE OF WESSEX

PART II

THE LAST ANGLO-SAXONS AND THE DANES

PART VII
THE HOUSE OF YORK

PART VIII
THE HOUSE OF TUDOR

PART IX
THE HOUSE OF STUART

PART X
THE COMMONWEALTH

PART XI
THE STUARTS RESTORED

PART XII

THE HOUSE OF HANOVER

PART XIII

THE HOUSE OF SAXE-COBURG-GOTHA

PART XIV

THE HOUSE OF WINDSOR

FOREWORD

They're unavoidable. I have worked on hundreds of podcasts, books and TV shows determined to tell the story of a period of history without chopping it up into episodes defined by who was wearing the crown. I failed every time. Monarchs matter.

I should have just listened to my parents.

As they point out in the pages that follow, the men and women who have ruled Wessex, England, Britain, and the United Kingdom have left a gigantic imprint. Apart from a handful of scientists, writers and artists, along with some politicians and warriors, no one else has been outstanding enough to become synonymous with a whole era of history. Athelstan's Wessex, Henrician and Elizabethan England, Williamite Ireland, Georgian and Victorian Britain ... they define our past.

Louis XIV summed up what so many of these monarchs represented when he proclaimed: "L'État c'est moi" ("I am the State"), and I suspect Edgar, William I, and many others would have agreed. There are plenty of examples of empires, states or regimes that simply dissolved once their charismatic overlord died or was deposed. Cnut ruled over a vast maritime empire from the Atlantic to the Baltic, but it did not outlast him. The first Plantagenet monarchs governed from Cork in Ireland to the Pyrenees, but that collapsed in short order once the powerful presences of Henry II, Richard and, perhaps most importantly, Henry's wife Eleanor of Aquitaine died.

Of course they mattered. They were essentially head of the legislative, judicial, and executive branches of government. They determined what language we spoke. They minted the money. They made the laws, enforced them, and settled disputes among their subjects. They were usually supreme warlords. Armies marched and fought and died on the whim of the monarch. Harold seized the throne and called up warriors to fight off at least two challengers, Harald Hardrada and William of Normandy. Kings and queens sent men to savage deaths on hundreds of battlefields. They dominated the spiritual as well as the temporal. Early rulers decided between the old gods and Christianity, later they chose between Luther, Calvin and the Pope. From Henry VIII till today the monarch has been the supreme authority in the Church of England.

Kings and queens have always set the trends and commissioned art. George IV shaped fashionable tastes. Shakespeare depended on the patronage of Elizabeth and James I. Kings appointed Chaucer and Wren to senior diplomatic and clerical positions. Royals shaped the landscape, built our cities. William I created the New Forest, raised towering castles and unleashed the gigantic forces of Romanesque architecture, which eventually saw every cathedral in the land torn down and rebuilt. Charles II oversaw the rebuilding of London after the Great Fire. The Royal Navy, Royal Observatory, Royal Botanic Gardens at Kew, the Royal Society … all the work of royal founders.

After reading this book I am forced to acknowledge that parents know best. Peter and Ann, Dad and Mum, have reminded us all why these kings and queens matter, while underlining that for all their power and reach, they were all too human.

Dan Snow

INTRODUCTION

Who needs another book on the British monarchy, you might well ask. Yet when you look behind the scenes, past the sceptres, castles, courtiers, all the pomp, power and privilege, you find human beings not so very different in character from the people they ruled. While other great monarchies – French, Russian, Chinese – have been swept away by revolution, dictatorships, and ideologies, the individuals we write about have sustained an institution for way over 1,000 years.

We tell the story of how this royal family, with all its flaws, has somehow survived, and what an extraordinary range of people have come to wield such power and given their names to so much of British history. Our aim is to look at how monarchs used their power and to what extent their lives and loves differed from or reflected those of ordinary people.

As we wrote the book we were struck by how improbable this royal story is with its parade of utterly random personalities qualified to sit on the throne only by accident of birth. Neither monarchs nor their subjects have any say in their right to the crown. They are born into it. What has now settled down as the iron rule of succession leaves no space for selection of the fittest: there's been no legendary King Arthur drawing the sword from the stone to qualify for kingship. The haphazard mishmash of gifted and flawed personalities has exposed the hereditary monarchy to both admiration and ridicule.

Exceptional kings like Edward I are often succeeded by a hopeless son. Valiant warriors like Richard the Lionheart and Henry V and exemplary standard bearers such as both Elizabeths are mingled with weaklings like Henry VI, dissolute scoundrels like Edward II, men described by contemporaries as villains such as Richard III, or zealots like Bloody Mary. Like them or not they are intriguing threads in the tapestry of Britain's rich history.

One compelling feature of the rule of hereditary succession has been how monarchs moved heaven and earth to produce an heir. It took Henry

VIII three marriages to secure a son to succeed him. That son, the child-less Edward VI, stretched the succession rule to breaking point when he insisted on transferring the crown to his pitiful cousin Lady Jane Grey. When James II produced a rightful heir who raised the spectre of a Catholic succession, it led to revolt, invasion and the end of his reign.

There have also been moments of crisis when fate or ambitious cousins upset the iron rule. Edward IV, Henry IV and Henry VII stole the throne from close relatives. Henry I's heir Matilda should have been crowned queen, but she was having a baby in Anjou when Henry died, so his nephew Stephen raced to England and claimed the crown.

An unexpected pleasure in writing this book has been coming across stories about the kings and queens that give us a glimpse of their humanity. Alfred the Great not only burned the cakes: he couldn't read until he was fully grown. Henry I never smiled again after his son and heir drowned at sea. Edward III's crown was stuffed with cotton so it wouldn't fall off his young head. Elizabeth I had a French boyfriend in late life. Charles I went off in disguise to woo the daughter of the king of Spain. When William III had an asthma attack in the middle of the Battle of the Boyne a burly soldier saved him from falling in the river. George II asked to be buried in a sideless coffin so his bones could intermingle with his wife's. Edward VII set his clocks half an hour late to be sure of extra light for his shooting parties. George V spent hours collecting stamps, and George VI, before he became king, competed in the Wimbledon tennis championships.

As we've explored these lives it's been more and more striking how their elevated position couldn't protect the royals from the frailties of their subjects. Most Anglo-Saxon kings died in their 20s or 30s. William the Conqueror found himself trembling violently during his coronation. Nothing could save all 17 of Queen Anne's children from miscarriage or death by the age of 11.

George III famously suffered bouts of madness. There were fears about Victoria's mental health when her 42-year-old husband Albert died, and Elizabeth II suffered the divorces of three of her four children.

Another strand in this story is how royal power, which once deter-mined the fate of the nation and was near absolute in the hands of William the Conqueror, has been slowly whittled away. As far back as 1215, King John was browbeaten by his barons to set his seal on the Magna Carta, a pillar of world democracy. Over the next 800 years, through a process of hard-fought give and take, a constitutional monarchy emerged. By the twenty-first century the kings and queens finally knew that their place was as figureheads not as law-makers. Yet, after all this time, Britain's constitution remains complex and imprecise. In 1939, 13-year-old Princess Elizabeth, later to become queen, spent hours poring over a book about the constitution by the scholar Sir William Anson. It is, he wrote, a "somewhat rambling structure ... like a house which many successive owners have altered".

There is still no overwhelming appetite in Britain for an alternative to the monarchy. The age-old procession of kings and queens has entrenched itself so deeply it is inseparable from British life. In the words of the author Rebecca West, the monarchy is "The emblem of the state, the symbol of our national life, the guardian of our self-respect."

The royal rollercoaster, peopled by such a disparate collection of heroes, rascals and, for the most part, human beings as mixed up as the rest of us, has somehow allowed the monarchy to persist, but we find it tantalising to imagine what would happen if the throne of Elizabeth II was occupied by a monarch like her duty-free uncle Edward VIII.

A Note on Anglo-Saxon Names

Many Anglo-Saxon names have a so-called "digraph" double-letter prefix, Æ- at the front. Thus Athelstan is correctly spelt Æthelstan. We have simplified this to the familiar way the kings are pronounced. Thus Æthelred the Unready, we have spelt Ethelred, as he is widely known, but in all other cases we have replaced the Æ with an "A" as with "Athelstan".

PART I

THE HOUSE OF WESSEX

871-978

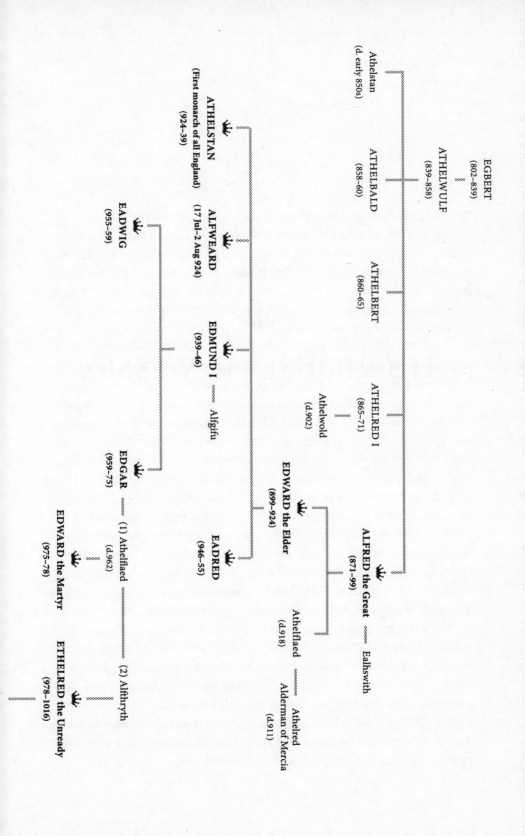

1

ALFRED

871-99

We make no apology for beginning with Alfred. Of all the monarchs in British history, he was the closest to Plato's ideal of a philosopher king. In the coarse patchwork of Anglo-Saxon England, he did much to lay the foundations of the nation: its administration, its language, the advancement of learning and the rule of law. He held off foreign marauders for long enough to consolidate Englishness as a way of life, setting in place early elements of the civilization that has lasted to this day.

And Alfred's achievements were all the more astonishing since he was at war for half his reign and only learned to read when he was an adult. He was far-sighted enough to ask a Welsh bishop and scholar, Asser, to write his life story and also commissioned the *Anglo-Saxon Chronicle*. Both works, when you allow for a pardonable dose of flattery, give us a valuable insight into England at the end of the ninth century. We have only a few images on coins to tell us what Alfred looked like, but we know that he was one of five brothers – and Asser tells us that Alfred was "more comely in appearance" than them. He was "pleasing in manner, speech and behaviour" and passionate in his pursuit of wisdom. The Wessex where Alfred was born in 849 struggled to hold off thousands of Viking invaders. Wessex, broadly today's southern counties between Cornwall and Kent, was the core of Anglo-Saxon England. Mercia in the Midlands, Northumbria in the north-east and East Anglia were constantly ravaged and sporadically occupied by the Vikings. These Scandinavian raiders, some from Norway but mainly Danes from Denmark, were lured by the wealth of Anglo-Saxon England. The first raiding party arrived in 789 and an Anglo-Saxon official who asked them their business as they disembarked was promptly cut in two. By the time of Alfred's birth, the Vikings were way beyond grabbing what loot they could. Under leaders with bloodthirsty names like Ivar the Boneless and Sigurd Snake-in-the-Eye, they seized and settled much of northern and eastern Britain.

Alfred's father Athelwulf and three of Alfred's elder brothers who succeeded their father on the throne fought – and usually failed – to hold the Vikings back. Athelwulf spotted his youngest son's early promise and took him to Rome when he was only a little fellow of six. It was Alfred's second visit; he had already been taken there as an infant, and he obviously impressed the Pope, who anointed him as a likely future king. The Anglo-Saxons had been Christians for 200 years and the Pope and his Roman Catholic church loomed large in Western Europe. Monasteries were flourishing centres of learning, and Alfred carried a book of psalms and other religious sayings in his pocket from an early age. He couldn't read them, but was an avid learner. Asser tells a touching story about how the young prince was fascinated by his mother reciting tales from a beautifully illustrated book. She promised the book to the first of her sons to learn and recite it, and Alfred won.

Alfred's father died soon after his return from Rome, and his elder brothers reigned for just five years each until the last one, Athelred, died in 871. Alfred was now 22 and, like most young male Anglo-Saxons, was nimble with the sword, the axe and the shield. He had already helped Athelred score an unusual victory over the Danes at the Battle of Ashdown. Shortly afterward, Alfred succeeded his brother and was immediately embroiled in several battles, most of which the Danes won. But Alfred was lucky. The Danes, still pagan, decided to switch their struggle for supremacy over the Christian princelings from southern to eastern and northern England. They crushed Edmund, the Anglo-Saxon ruler of East Anglia, and brutally executed him by tying him to a tree and using him as an archery target. By 875, they subdued Northumbria, and the central Anglo-Saxon state of Mercia.

While the Danes were busy up north, Alfred had a brief window to entrench his rule in Wessex. His royal capital rotated from place to place, but Winchester was his favourite. He inherited the valuable and usually sound advisory council, the Witan, from his predecessors. It met in various places and Alfred was often on the move too, well aware of the political value of being seen and recognized by the hierarchy of local officials who were the lifeblood of Anglo-Saxon governance and society.

It wasn't long before a Danish leader called Guthrum turned the invaders' greedy eyes back to Alfred's Wessex. From 875, Guthrum's hit-and-run raids had Alfred and his forces darting from one threatened point to the next. By 878, the Danes had penetrated deep into Wessex, often by using their shallow draft vessels to cause havoc way up river valleys. Early that year, Guthrum was strong enough to establish his headquarters at Chippenham, and his bands of Danes roamed with such impunity over Alfred's territory that the king felt forced to take refuge in the marshes of Somerset.

He was little more than a fugitive in his own kingdom. The famous story was inserted by a later scribe in Asser's biography – perhaps based on oral gossip passed down over the years – that Alfred sought shelter in a cowherd's cottage. It was there, we're told, that the cowherd's wife, who had no clue that her guest was the king, asked him to keep an eye on the cakes she was baking on the fire. Alfred's mind was on greater things and he was cleaning his weapons when the woman returned. The cakes were burning and, according to the medieval text, his furious host shouted: "Look here, man! You hesitate to turn the loaves which you see to be burning, yet you're quite happy to eat them when they come warm from the oven!"

Alfred was soon lying low more securely in a fort at Athelney, an island in the marshes. From there, he set out in the spring of 878 in a desperate bid to save his kingdom before Guthrum could swallow it up. Legend has it that before he embarked on this critical foray, he disguised himself as a musician and slipped into Chippenham to assess Guthrum's military strength. The story may have boosted the image of Wessex's warrior king, but Alfred would hardly have taken such a hazardous step when he could have found a willing volunteer to do it – so it's probably just another myth.

Alfred's standing army or "fyrd" was scattered over the western parts of Wessex. In May, the king dispatched a message to all the fighters he could reach and about 5,000 from Somerset, Wiltshire and Hampshire assembled somewhere just south of Warminster. Alfred marched them north and suddenly found himself facing Guthrum's so-called "Great Heathen Army" at Edington (once known as Ethandun) about three miles to the east of Westbury.

The battle fought there was one of the most decisive in British history. If Alfred had lost, Anglo-Saxon England would have collapsed. From behind their wall of shields, his soldiers fought desperately to destroy Guthrum's army. The Danes were routed. Alfred pursued the fugitives to Chippenham, where Guthrum's defences collapsed. He sued for peace and Alfred pulled off a remarkable deal. In what became known as the Treaty of Wedmore, he persuaded Guthrum to set aside his threat to

Wessex and retire to his domain in East Anglia. Guthrum also agreed to become a Christian. Alfred hosted the Danish leader's baptism and became Guthrum's godfather. At a stroke, Alfred had removed the deadliest threat to his kingdom. Although the Danish pressure on Wessex continued until Swein and Cnut triumphed a century later, Alfred and his descendants had time to make an indelible mark on English history.

Alfred built on his successful rebuff of Guthrum with a brilliant political stroke that doubled the effective size of his kingdom. He added Mercia, a large slice of the western midlands by befriending Athelred, the Mercian ruler, and marrying his daughter Athelflaed to him. The new Mercian couple formed an awesome partnership, and Athelflaed in particular, who gloried in the name of "Lady of the Mercians", became sole ruler on her husband's death in 911. England was now divided between Wessex and Mercia to the west and the so-called "Danelaw" in the east – with Watling Street the approximate dividing line.

The Danes returned with a vengeance in the 890s, but Alfred was now better prepared than before. His army, the fyrd, was divided in half, so that while the active part was ready for immediate service, the other half was off military duty and working on the land. By this time, Alfred had his stalwart elder son Edward fighting at his side, and they managed to hold back a large Danish army under Hastein in 893 by cleaving it in two and defeating each part separately.

Alfred developed his navy by building warships that were twice as long as their Danish adversaries. Each accommodated 60 oarsmen in hulls that were swifter and steadier than their opponents. They were sometimes victorious in battles with Danish ships, although the boats' deeper draughts could leave them high and dry on a low tide with the Danes running rings around them. But, the Danish threat had subsided by 896, and Alfred enjoyed three years of comparative stability before his death at the age of 50.

Even though he learned to read and write late in life, Alfred had, according to Asser, an "insatiable desire for knowledge". To share this with as many of his subjects as possible, he enthusiastically promoted the Anglo-Saxon language that was spoken by ordinary people. He supervised the translation of works written in Latin into words the king was fast establishing as "English". He boosted education by founding a school where his family and other nobles could tackle Alfred's English translations of Boethius's *Consolation of Philosophy*, the *Dialogues* of

Pope Gregory and the *Soliloquies* of St Augustine. It was Pope Gregory who, 200 years earlier, had pronounced that the people who lived in what used to be the Roman land of Britannia were "not Angles but angels". Alfred was the king who made "Angle-land" England.

Alfred also saw himself as a supremely wise judge. He revised and tabulated the whole body of Anglo-Saxon law that had been passed down to him, reserving the right to intervene in individual cases and arbitrate where he spotted a faulty judgement. He wouldn't hesitate to sack officials whose verdicts he thought mistaken. This might look like the height of authoritarian conceit, but the ever-loyal Asser assures us that Alfred had what he called the "wisdom of Solomon". In Alfred's own account of his lawgiving he admits he ordered the laws of his predecessors "which I liked" to be preserved and "those which I did not like I rejected". The king's prerogative was supreme.

Another of Alfred's measures which had a lasting effect was his introduction of more than 30 strongholds he called "burhs". These were dotted across the breadth of Wessex and Mercia, from coastal Hastings past Alfred's capital at Winchester to Worcester. The burhs provided refuges with little more than 20 miles between them where people could seek safety from the Danes. They were also administrative hubs that would become modern Britain's boroughs, each with its own core of officials. Alfred set the burhs within shires, today's counties. His curiosity also attracted him to technical issues such as timekeeping. He was so obsessed with the need to measure its passage that he arranged for the construction of a primitive clock. It consisted of candles 12 inches high, which burned down at a rate of 20 minutes an inch, each candle marking the passage of 4 hours.

By the time he approached what was, in those days, the ripe old age of 50, Alfred was seen as the father of his people. It was not until 600 years later that he became the only English monarch to be called "the Great". He was seen, rightly, as the founder of the English nation. Charles Dickens put it well, describing Alfred the Great as possessing "all the Anglo-Saxon virtues", someone "whom misfortunes could not subdue, whom prosperity could not spoil, whose perseverance nothing could shake". He loved "justice, freedom, truth and knowledge".

2

ALFRED'S SUCCESSORS

EDWARD THE ELDER
899-924

Alfred's immediate successors were some of Britain's finest monarchs. With the glaring exception of King Eadwig, who reigned for four years from 955, the seven Anglo-Saxon monarchs who ruled for 75 years after Alfred's death brought all of England under a single crown. They built on his legacy of judicious administration and the expansion of learning. It wasn't until the time of Alfred's great-great-grandson Ethelred, the so-called "Unready", that Anglo-Saxon England began to fall apart. The pity is that robust and wise as they were, few of Alfred's successors lived long, most dying in their twenties or early thirties. It's a confusing list of up to 10 names beginning with A or E or, most accurately, Æ (see earlier note), but the country thrived until the Anglo-Saxon grip on power took a nosedive under Ethelred the Unready.

Alfred's second child, Edward the Elder, who fought the Danes with his father, became king in 899. He married three times and had 14 children, three of whom sat on the throne. Edward was said to be a gentle, liberal-minded and well-read young man – but perfectly capable of baring his teeth when his realm was under threat. He had to start early. His first cousin, Athelwold, the son of Alfred's predecessor as king, had long resented being passed over as an infant, and now demanded the throne he reckoned he'd been cheated of. Edward raised an army and penned up Athelwold in Wimborne, where his rebel cousin promptly kidnapped a nun and then sneaked off to take refuge with the Danes in Northumbria. Athelwold's revolt came to a humiliating end when he and the Danes tried and failed to defeat Edward's supporters in Kent at the Battle of the Holme in 902.

From then on, unchallenged in Wessex, Edward waged a triumphant war with the Danes in close alliance with his sister Athelflaed, the "Lady of the Mercians", who was now a veritable Joan of Arc, leading her troops into battle. By 910, the Danes had been decisively defeated at the Battle of Wednesfield and brother and sister went on to advance deep into the Danelaw. She captured Derby and Leicester. He pressed on into Essex and built a fort at Maldon. When Athelflaed died in 918, Edward assumed the sole kingship of Mercia. Just to be safe, he took the prudent but heartless step of sending Athelflaed's daughter off to a nunnery in Wessex.

That same year, Edward went on to occupy all of England up to the Humber. The Danes were down, but far from eliminated. In 921, two Danish warlords, Ragnall and Sihtric, even managed to establish a short-lived regime in York and Lincoln. And Edward was not unchallenged in Mercia. There was anger at the way he had sidelined Athelflaed's daughter, and the Mercians may also have resented the imposition of the new Wessex-style shires to replace the age-old Mercian regions. All this helped promote the rebellion Edward faced in Chester in 924. But this doughty successor to King Alfred died soon after he had crushed the rebels.

ALFWEARD
17 July-2 August 924

The next Anglo-Saxon king rivalled only Lady Jane Grey 600 years later for the brevity of his reign. It lasted 16 days. Some believe that when Alfweard's father Edward the Elder died, he intended to split his kingdom – with his eldest son, Athelstan, inheriting Mercia, where he had been educated while Alfweard, Athelstan's younger half-brother, would become the king of Wessex. Athelstan, who was anything but faint-hearted, was unlikely to accept losing half the kingdom he could claim was rightly his. Conveniently, his bothersome brother died only a couple of weeks after his father and before he could be crowned. There is no evidence that he was murdered but it is certainly suspicious that he died at Oxford just as he was embarking on a first visit to Athelstan's Mercia.

ATHELSTAN

924-39

The man who was now the unchallenged king had been the apple of his grandfather Alfred's eye. Athelstan was only a young lad when Alfred died, but Alfred had sensed his grandson's promise and given him a magnificent scarlet cloak, jewelled belt and Anglo-Saxon sword with a gilded scabbard. Athelstan's father had asked Athelflaed, the Lady of the Mercians, and her husband to arrange for Athelstan to be schooled at their court. Athelstan soon accompanied his Mercian patrons in their battles with the Danes and became an esteemed warrior. He was of average height and slim build, and according to the medieval chronicler William of Malmesbury, had fair hair "beautifully intertwined with golden threads".

There was a curious gap of more than a year before Athelstan was crowned king of Wessex in 925. The Bishop of Winchester absented himself from the ceremony and there was a clear preference in some Wessex hearts for Athelstan's younger half-brother Edwin. He backed a failed conspiracy against Athelstan, and it was some time before Athelstan became widely accepted in Wessex. When Edwin was drowned a few years later, there were suspicions that it was not an accident.

Many of his subjects may have felt uneasy about Athelstan at first, but he was soon recognized as a military champion in the war with the Danes. He reabsorbed Northumbria into Anglo-Saxon England and by the 930s, he was deep inside Scotland. His greatest victory was the crushing of the Danes and Scots at the Battle of Brunanburh in 937. No one knows the exact location, but the *Anglo-Saxon Chronicle* tells us, "Never ... was a greater slaughter of a host made by the edge of the sword" since the Angles and Saxons occupied England four centuries earlier. Athelstan's prowess set him on something of a pedestal in Western Europe, where he was regarded as a major power with the whole of England at his feet. He made the most of his reputation and influence abroad by pursuing a lively diplomacy and promoting English trade and the increasingly respected national coinage. He also entrenched the Christian Church as a central bulwark of his governance. Bishops were among his most trusted advisers, and he

13

was a generous supporter of the drive to build monasteries throughout the kingdom. Athelstan's promising reign was another short one, ending with his death in 939, when he was in his early forties.

EDMUND

939-46

Athelstan was succeeded by another half-brother, Edmund, son of Edward the Elder's third wife, a forceful woman called Eadgifu. He seems to have been Athelstan's choice. They'd fought together in the great Battle of Brunanburh, and, although he was only 18, Edmund became king on Athelstan's death.

Edmund was a staunch opponent of the Danes, who maintained their pressure, particularly from one Viking stronghold – the Irish city of Dublin. Olaf Guthrifson, the king of Dublin, managed to regain the Danish lands around York but, fortunately for Edmund, Olaf died in 941. Edmund went on to ravage Cumbria and humiliate the Scots by blinding the sons of the king of Strathclyde. Alfred's successors may have inherited his love of learning and justice, but they were quite capable of abominable cruelty. Edmund himself was to die horribly in his early twenties at a banquet in Gloucestershire. An outlaw called Leofa had somehow got into the hall, and when Edmund joined others to seize him, Leofa fatally stabbed the king in the stomach.

EADRED

946-55

Eadred was the second of four kings in a row to die in their early twenties or thirties. Like his murdered brother Edmund, he had to face unrelenting pressure from the Danes. One of his most ferocious opponents was a

Norwegian warrior prince, Eric Bloodaxe, who held power for a time in York and attacked Eadred's army as it was returning from securing Northumbria. Bloodaxe's attack was so savage that Eadred turned his shattered army around and threatened to exact revenge so terrible that the northerners who'd supported Bloodaxe switched sides and banished the Norwegian.

Eadred had the good sense to retain the advisers who had provided the stability of the last half-century of government. They were now reinforced by the sagacious and energetic Dunstan, Abbot of Glastonbury, a zealous promoter of the monastic building programme. He would later become Archbishop of Canterbury and be pronounced a saint.

Sadly, Eadred's promising start was cut short by a debilitating illness which killed him in 955.

EADWIG

955-59

There has to be a low point in every dynasty, and this was it. Eadwig was only around 15 when, as the eldest son of Edmund, he became king on his uncle's death. He was, if we are to believe Dunstan's account of his disgraceful reign, an incorrigible rascal and lecher. The day after his coronation, Eadwig was to host a great celebratory feast with all the country's notables present. But the newly crowned king didn't turn up. Dunstan was sent to find him and had to drag him from his bed, where he was enjoying a threesome with his young cousin and her mother. To be fair to Eadwig, he did later marry the girl, but she was considered too close a relation to the king, and they were persuaded to part. Eadwig was so irritated by Dunstan that he expelled him from Glastonbury. The ex-abbot wisely decided to seek shelter abroad. This and other scandals made William of Malmesbury agree with Dunstan that Eadwig was "a wanton youth" who "misused his personal beauty in lascivious behaviour".

Eadwig went further to enrage the church by departing from the royal patronage of the monasteries. He seized the property of his grandmother, the hitherto influential Eadgifu, widow of Edward the Elder, and lavished money and estates on his cronies.

Popular disenchantment with their new king was soon rife in Mercia, and the kingdom was effectively split in two in 957. Eadwig held on to Wessex south of the Thames, but his younger brother Edgar was recognized in the north. Perhaps fortunately, Eadwig died at the age of little more than 20 in 959.

EDGAR

959-75

Eadwig's younger brother Edgar was cut from sterner stuff. He was only in his mid-teens, but immediately reversed Eadwig's hostile attitude to the church. He also restored his grandmother Eadgifu's estates. She had long admired Edgar and arranged for him to be educated at a Benedictine monastery. The new king recalled Dunstan and made him Archbishop of Canterbury in 960. By the end of Edgar's 16-year reign, there were 33 Benedictine monasteries throughout the country. Edgar married Alfthryth, a woman who, like his grandmother, was to become a major power at court.

Edgar was crowned with great pomp in a service in Bath that was closely echoed at Elizabeth II's coronation in 1953. Oddly, Edgar's elaborate ceremony did not take place until 973, when the king was 29 years old – perhaps because he humbly recognized he should be closer to the mature age of 30 before being formally crowned. Shortly after his coronation, Edgar called on nobles from England and rulers from Scotland and Wales to gather at Chester. All were so impressed by Edgar, or in such fear of him, that they hailed him as their ally. One highly visible feature of the great Chester concourse was Edgar's display of his large fleet on the River Dee. He was a keen proponent of naval power and had four separate fleets boasting some 4,000 ships altogether. He made a point of going to sea with them every summer.

Edgar died when he was just 31 or 32 in 975. He was widely respected, and the relative peace, stability, and prosperity of the country under Edgar earned him the nickname of "Pacificus".

EDWARD THE MARTYR

975-78

Edgar's son Edward was only 13, the youngest of Alfred's descendants, when he became king. He was of dubious legitimacy because some questioned whether his father was properly married to his mother. He owed his accession to the endorsement of the now highly respected Dunstan, Archbishop of Canterbury. This left Edgar's other surviving widow, Alfthryth, harbouring a grudge that her own son by Edgar, the mild-mannered Ethelred, should be king rather than hot-headed Edward. She didn't wait long to act. When Edward was still well short of 20 years old, his stepmother invited him to visit her in Corfe. On arrival, he was dragged unceremoniously from his horse and, though he struggled hard with his assailants, he was stabbed to death. No one admitted to or was charged with his murder, but few doubted who was responsible. Alfthryth effectively became regent when her son Ethelred succeeded his half-brother as king. He was just 10 years old.

PART II

♛

THE LAST ANGLO-SAXONS
AND THE DANES

978-1066

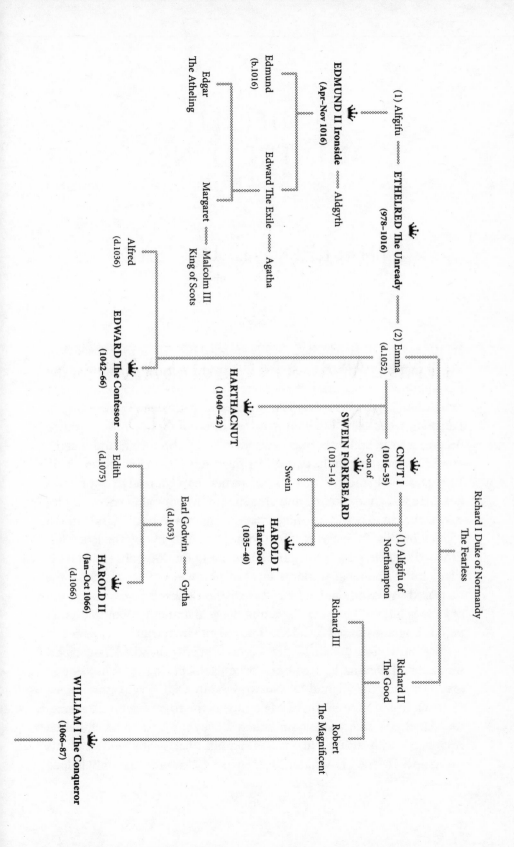

Richard I Duke of Normandy
The Fearless

ETHELRED The Unready
(978–1016)

(1) Alfgifu

EDMUND II Ironside
(Apr–Nov 1016) ∞∞ Aldgyth

Edmund
(b.1016)

Edgar
The Atheling

Edward The Exile ∞∞ Agatha

Margaret ∞∞ Malcolm III
King of Scots

(2) Emma
(d.1052)

Alfred
(d.1036)

EDWARD The Confessor
(1042–66) ∞∞ Edith
(d.1075)

HARTHACNUT
(1040–42)

SWEIN FORKBEARD
(1013–14)
Son of

CNUT I
(1016–35)

(1) Alfgifu of
Northampton

Swein

HAROLD I
Harefoot
(1035–40)

Earl Godwin ∞∞ Gytha
(d.1053)

HAROLD II
(Jan–Oct 1066)
(d.1066)

Richard II
The Good

Richard III

Robert
The Magnificent

WILLIAM I The Conqueror
(1066–87)

3

ETHELRED
AND THE DANES

ETHELRED THE UNREADY

978-1013

If Ethelred's mother, who had briskly grabbed the throne for her son, had hoped that he would be another leader in the normally robust Anglo-Saxon tradition, she and the country were to be disappointed. Bad omens had begun at his baptism, which was performed by Archbishop Dunstan, when baby Ethelred urinated in the font. In time, he was to become a weak and dithering king ridiculed by chroniclers and historians for his long and, in the end, disastrous reign. His nickname said it all. *Unraed* actually means "ill-advised" rather than "unready", but he was both. He was good-looking and elegant, but his poor judgement let him down. The country was fortunate that through his teenage years, veteran councillors like Dunstan still had some influence, but by the late 980s, Ethelred's feckless and uninspiring leadership was loosening any bonds that kept the regional warlords loyal to him. On top of this came the increased battering England faced from the Danes. It began as a series of vicious hit-and-run raids targeting the gold and other loot that prosperous England offered invaders. It was to end in outright occupation.

Swein Forkbeard, named after his bristling two-handled moustache, was king of Denmark, a country once again flexing its muscles and greedy for empire. He and his Norwegian ally Olaf Tryggvason landed in Essex in 991. The Battle of Maldon was the first of several reverses that Ethelred's shaky kingdom suffered over the next years. Ethelred responded with several ill-advised actions that neatly endorsed his nickname. He tried buying off the Danes with money that only helped them build more ships and, though they promised restraint each time, they soon came back for more. The £10,000 (tens of millions in today's values) of Danegeld – the tax paid for national defence against the Danes – handed over in 991 swelled to £36,000 by 1007.

In 1002, Ethelred was so exasperated by the Danish raids that he reacted almost hysterically by ordering the massacre of all the Danes in England. One dreadful outcome was the fate of the Danish population of Oxford. They took refuge in St Frideswide's church and it was burned to the ground with all inside it. Ethelred's next unwise move was to appoint unreliable associates to positions of power. He made his shifty son-in-law Eadric Streona, known for treachery and subterfuge, his acting viceroy in Mercia.

By 1009, Swein's marauding Danes were led by a brutal warlord, Thorkell the Tall, whose two-year rampage through southern England climaxed with the capture of Canterbury and its redoubtable archbishop, Alfeah, in 1011. His captors offered to release him for £3,000, but Alfeah refused to allow his people to pay a ransom. He was kept a prisoner by the Vikings for a whole year until, in a moment of drunken delinquency, they bombarded him with bones, ox heads and other unlikely missiles, then finally axed him to death. Even the terrible Thorkell was so appalled by this that he switched sides and agreed to commit his 45-ship navy to fight for Ethelred.

But Swein was back in 1013 with an immense force of ships and Viking warriors. For Ethelred, defeat looked inevitable. It felt as if all the masonry of his Anglo-Saxon fortress was collapsing around him. He invoked a deal he'd made with Count Richard, the ruler of Normandy (the state in north-western France created by Rollo the Viking, who had planted the Norsemen's flag there half a century earlier). Richard and Ethelred forged an alliance in the face of the great wave of Viking expansion, and Ethelred married Richard's daughter Emma. It was an alliance that offered Ethelred a refuge from the Danes. With London overrun by the forces of Swein and his fearless son Cnut, Ethelred decided to flee to Normandy with Emma and their two sons. There they were welcomed by Richard's son, Richard II, the grandfather of William, Duke of Normandy, who would be England's conqueror 50 years later.

SWEIN FORKBEARD

1013–14

Swein Forkbeard was king of England for only a few weeks. Anglo-Saxon England, his new domain, was part of an expansive empire. He had already defeated and killed his old ally Olaf Tryggvason of Norway, and his Scandinavian kingdom now absorbed England, one of Europe's richest countries. He was in his early fifties, a Christian, and by all accounts a generous and conscientious ruler. He made his home in Gainsborough, in Lincolnshire, but had no time to entrench his rule. By February 1014, he was dead, leaving his son, Cnut, as the commander-in-chief of the Viking forces in England.

ETHELRED THE UNREADY
(RESTORED)

1014–16

Anglo-Saxon England was not yet defeated. Ethelred, normally unready, was uncharacteristically agile. He sent messages home to England from his refuge in Normandy and was soon invited back by leading English nobles. They reckoned that he, with all his faults, was preferable to the Danes, whose legacy, despite Swein's promising start, remained one of belligerent savagery. Ethelred and the nobles signed a remarkable agreement, a precursor to the Magna Carta, the compact exactly two centuries later in which the English barons won important concessions from King John. Ethelred accepted minor restrictions to his power and became king again. Cnut was compelled by forces that supported Ethelred to leave England and return to Denmark.

After this shrewd step, Ethelred soon returned to his unwise ways. Rather than attempt to conciliate those who had sided with the Danes, he took revenge on them. He was complicit, with his son-in-law Eadric Streona of Mercia, in the murder of Danish nobles from eastern England. This led Edmund, King Ethelred's son by his first wife, to defy his father. Still in his early twenties, he raised an army in eastern England. Civil war looked inevitable, and Cnut seized the opportunity to return and restore Danish rule. Ethelred was now almost certainly suffering from the illness that killed him in early 1016. His former close ally Eadric Streona chose this moment to switch sides and hand over Wessex and Mercia to Cnut. By April that year, Ethelred was dead, leaving his son to try and save the kingdom.

EDMUND II IRONSIDE

April-November 1016

Ethelred's son Edmund was a sharp contrast to his father. Known as "Ironside" for his military prowess, he was clearly an inspiration to his followers and an effective military commander. He was unlucky to inherit the throne from his disastrous father when the odds were spectacularly stacked against him. Cnut was a fearsome adversary, and the fickle Eadric Streona could not be trusted to give Edmund wholehearted support from Wessex and Mercia.

Even so, Edmund won enough support to fight two battles with Cnut in Somerset and Wiltshire in the summer of 1016, and to force him to abandon his siege of London. Edmund went on to defeat the Danes just west of London and soon afterward he pushed Cnut back into Kent. It seems that the incorrigible turncoat Eadric changed sides yet again, but finally betrayed Edmund at the Battle of Assandun, fought on 18 October 1016, probably at Ashingdon in Essex. At a critical moment in a vicious melee, Eadric's men fled, leaving Cnut victorious. It appears that there was then a further battle with Cnut, and that Edmund may have been wounded. All that we know for sure is that at a meeting with Cnut, Edmund was granted control of Wessex while Cnut took the rest of the country. But Edmund was dead by the end of November. Some chroniclers wrote that he was stabbed or poisoned on the orders of the egregious Eadric, who was no doubt hoping to display his devotion to the new king, Cnut.

CNUT (CANUTE)

1016-35

Cnut had already reminded the world that he was as savage as any of his forebears by cutting off the hands, ears and noses of a group of Anglo-Saxon hostages he'd seized on a raid in 1014. He missed no tricks in securing the throne his father had briefly occupied – by luring back Edmund Ironside's brother from abroad and briskly executing him. Cnut also disposed of several other nobles he saw as untrustworthy, including the two-faced Eadric Streona: all were beheaded. The only two rivals to his claim to the English throne now lay in Normandy. Ethelred's widow, Emma, had fled there with her two sons by Ethelred, Edward (later known as Edward the Confessor) and Alfred. Cnut felt he had to neutralize any threat from them. In a brilliant stroke of romantic diplomacy, he asked Emma to marry him. She accepted, which was rather strange, since Cnut had already taken as his "consort" a well-connected woman from Northampton called Alfgifu, who had borne him two sons, Swein and Harold Harefoot. But Emma was no stranger to palace intrigues and the exercise of wifely power, and she clearly enjoyed them.

It is perhaps surprising to learn that Cnut was zealous about fostering Christianity and won respect as manager of the kingdom. He wisely preserved and even extended the hierarchy of Anglo-Saxon officials and local administrators. He was busy running two other kingdoms in Denmark and Norway, and was occasionally forced to fight to keep his Scandinavian empire together. But he gave England two decades of peace and prosperity.

Little is known about his personality, but the story that schoolchildren learn about his challenge to the tide tells us something about him. The popular version is that Cnut believed himself so powerful that he could sit on his throne on the beach and force back the waves. And when he found he couldn't, he was exposed as an arrogant fool. More likely is the account, a century later, of Henry, Archdeacon of Huntingdon, suggesting it was not at all a case of the king making an idiot of himself. He says Cnut ordered his councillors to follow him to the seashore because he was appalled and exasperated at his attendants' endless flattery and was determined to prove he was not all-powerful. The arch-deacon writes that Cnut sat on the edge of the shore and commanded the waves not to advance any further. And when they did, he jumped up with his feet soaking wet and cried out:

"Let all the world know that the power of kings is empty and worthless, and there is no king worthy of the name save Him by whose will heaven, earth and sea obey eternal laws."

When you bear in mind that Cnut was a wily old salt who had spent a lifetime at sea, there's little doubt about which story we should believe.

If this bizarre demonstration of the limits of regnal power ever took place, one noble almost certainly present was Godwin, Earl of Wessex. He was a man of sturdy Anglo-Saxon stock, typical of the English leaders that Cnut came to rely upon to run the country. And by the time of Cnut's death, Godwin was as powerful as any. He and his family would help decide the course of history for the next generation.

Cnut died in 1035. The man who had come to England as a rapacious outsider turned out to be a king who ruled ruthlessly, but well.

HAROLD HAREFOOT

1035-40

Cnut left two sons likely to succeed him: Harold Harefoot, his son by Alfgifu of Northampton, and Harthacnut, by Emma. Both men were in their early twenties. Emma was reliably reported to have insisted when she married Cnut that he could not allow Alfgifu's sons to succeed him if he and Emma had any sons. Cnut's death set the two women at each other's throats. The influential Godwin supported Emma's pitch for Harthacnut, while Alfgifu promoted Harold Harefoot. Harold had two advantages: he was strongly endorsed by the leader of Mercia, and Harthacnut was away in Denmark, where his father had sent him to help run the kingdom. Emma had to accept that Harold should be king.

Harold's predicament was sharpened by another event that took place in 1036, a year into his rule. Emma had two other older sons, Edward and Alfred, by her first husband Ethelred the Unready. They had taken refuge with her in Normandy on Swein's invasion in 1013. Now, more than 20 years later, her sons decided to risk their necks by crossing to England to see if they could win support for their claim to the throne. As Ethelred's sons, they had a case, but Alfred's was a poorly prepared and, in the end, suicidal venture. Godwin, who had sided with Emma earlier, now showed what a schemer he could be by apparently welcoming Alfred, but then delivering him to King Harold, who promptly ordered him to be blinded. So primitively was this hideous punishment carried out that the young pretender died. His brother Edward, who did much later succeed as Edward the Confessor, was either chased away or wisely abandoned his attempted return to England, briskly retreating to France. Emma was packed off into exile in the Netherlands, despairing of seeing any of her sons on the English throne while Harold Harefoot was alive.

HARTHACNUT

1040-42

Harold did not live long. When he died in 1040, Emma and her son Harthacnut made their move. Harthacnut had been in Denmark while his half-brother Harold was on the English throne, but Harthacnut now travelled straight to Bruges, where his mother had taken refuge. And when messages came inviting them to England, they sailed across the Channel with a fleet of 62 ships in June 1040. Harthacnut was proclaimed king.

He quickly showed that he did not admire his predecessor. On Harthacnut's orders, Harold's body was exhumed and dumped in a marsh. It was later recovered and buried in a church in London, possibly St Clement Danes, in the Strand.

Harthacnut's reign was relatively serene. Emma had her possessions restored and regained her important status. She may have been instrumental – though some sources deny this – in encouraging one key move by Harthacnut. He had no children of his own but, unlike his dead brother Harold, he was prepared to consider the claim of Emma's son by Ethelred, Edward (the future 'Confessor'). It was a generous act of historical importance. Edward, who had remained in Normandy, was invited to England in 1041 and the *Anglo-Saxon Chronicle* tells us that he was sworn in as the future king. Harthacnut was not well, and it was only a matter of months before his short reign came to an end in 1042. Emma's family connection with Normandy had set in motion the course of events that were to climax in 1066 with the most revolutionary change in English history.

4

EDWARD THE CONFESSOR

1042-66

It is not clear whether the new King Edward's mother Emma actually supported her son's claim to the throne. The fact that one of Edward's first acts as monarch was to confiscate nearly all Emma's possessions suggests that he burned with resentment at the fact that she'd preferred his younger half-brother Harthacnut to him. She was a formidable example of a medieval woman who exercised remarkable political power.

Another woman soon stepped into the role of a queen who made a difference. A year after he became king, Edward married Edith, daughter of the eminent Godwin, Earl of Wessex. Edith was said by her admirers to have been a woman of great beauty, highly educated and literate in several languages. She was a loyal and attentive wife who rapidly changed Edward from a nonchalant bachelor into a royal personage who enjoyed all the splendour and trappings of kingship. She also wasted no time in securing prominent earldoms for her brothers, particularly Godwin's son, Harold Godwinson, who was to succeed his father as Earl of Wessex in 1053.

Edward was tall, strong and healthy. It was only later in life when he became increasingly devotional that he was seen as frail and rather ineffective. He had spent 25 of his 40 years in Normandy and retained a natural affection for that connection. One of the few appointments he made from across the English Channel was an important one. He named Robert of Jumièges, an abbot who had befriended him in Normandy, Bishop of London and then Archbishop of Canterbury. It was an unwise decision and aroused the jealousy of his Anglo-Saxon advisers, including Godwin.

On a visit to Rome, Jumièges was reported to have made a formal alliance between Edward and the 23-year-old William, the young Duke of Normandy, the illegitimate child of Robert Duke of Normandy. Edward's mother Emma was William's great-aunt which made the two men cousins. The alliance began a chain of commitments which William claimed Edward made to him leading up to the Norman invasion of 1066. One of history's great unanswered questions is whether Edward directly or indirectly promised William the title to his English throne. The most compelling clue is the mysterious trip that Edward's brother-in-law Harold Godwinson made to Normandy in 1064 or 1065. He was shipwrecked on the coast and felt obliged to William when he was rescued and given a warm welcome by William's men. They spent some time together, and Harold appears to have been persuaded, some say forced, by William to swear that the throne of England would be his on the Confessor's death. If true, it was a remarkable surrender to a foreign power by Harold, who was, after all, brother-in-law to an Anglo-Saxon king.

The family of Godwin, Earl of Wessex, no doubt felt they had as fair a claim to Edward's throne as any Norman. Godwin's family came close to losing everything halfway through Edward's reign. A minor event in 1051 led to a crisis that shook Edward's throne. The king's French brother-in-law, Eustace of Boulogne, was visiting from France when his retinue started a brawl with locals in Dover. Godwin was sent to restore order and punish the people of Dover for reacting so forcefully, but he decided that Eustace was to blame for the fracas, and demanded the Frenchman's surrender. Robert of Jumièges leapt to the aid of his fellow country-man and declared that Godwin was plotting against King Edward. Edward's court summoned Godwin for trial but, fearing punishment, he fled and gathered a fleet to confront the king. Edward sent his wife, Edith, Godwin's daughter, to a nunnery and prepared to fight for his kingdom. Godwin and his navy sailed up the Thames to London and presented such a threat that many of Edward's supporters, including the Archbishop of Canterbury, ran for it. Edward was furious, but felt he had no choice but to negotiate. The two antagonists met in London and there was a significant reconciliation. Edward had to grit his teeth and restore Godwin and his son Harold to favour and Edith returned to Edward's side. Robert, the archbishop, was sent packing back to Jumièges. Godwin died in 1053 and Harold inherited the earldom of Wessex. His brother Tostig was awarded the earldom of Northumbria. All seemed forgiven.

Edward's reign remained relatively peaceful for the next 13 years. He had to exert a measure of ferocity to deter plundering raids from Wales. He ordered the assassination of the troublesome South Wales prince Rhys ap Rhydderch. A few years later, he sent Harold Godwinson to suppress the pugnacious prince of North Wales, Gruffydd ap Llywelyn, who spared Harold the job of executing him when he was murdered by a Welsh rival. Both heads were duly delivered to King Edward.

Edward had to endure one final family crisis before his death. Tostig Godwinson, for whom Edward had great personal affection, had been an austere governor of Northumbria and his unpopularity led to rebellion in 1065. To Edward's distress, the rebellion was successful, and its leaders demanded Tostig's exile. Edward asked Harold, Tostig's brother and his own brother-in-law, to help him suppress the rebels, but Harold refused. The king had to suffer the humiliation of banishing his good friend Tostig. All this may have contributed to Edward's decline and death in the first days of 1066. History has downplayed most of Edward's achievements. His nickname, the Confessor, was largely due to his indulgent support for the church and the monasteries. The name was also attached to him to distinguish him from his ancestor Edward the Martyr, murdered at Corfe in 978. Edward did much to strengthen England's legal code, but most of all he demonstrated his piety by the building of the magnificent abbey at Westminster. It was completed in time for him to be buried there in 1066. Edward's canonization a century after his death helped depict him as an excessively saintly and unassertive ruler, but he survived 24 years by competently managing a country which enjoyed enviable peace and stability.

As Harold and Edith, Edward's wife, sat by his deathbed, Edward is said to have indicated that he expected them to inherit his kingdom. There is no evidence that he made mention of any promise he may have made to William, Duke of Normandy.

5

HAROLD

January-October 1066

It is one of the ironies of history that the man who was perhaps England's most capable and charismatic warrior king had a reign of only 10 months. When Edward the Confessor bequeathed him the throne, Harold had almost everything going for him. He was supremely confident, fabulously wealthy, and wholly dominant at England's royal court after 14 years as its most powerful earl, the son and successor of the grand Godwin, Earl of Wessex. Harold's only English rival for the throne, Edmund Ironside's grandson Edgar, was the last of the direct descendants of Alfred the Great. But he was in his early teens, ignored both by Edward the Confessor on his deathbed and by Harold, who lost no time getting himself crowned the day after the Confessor died.

Harold's problem, which would turn out to be fatal, was that he had two other rivals for the throne. One, Harald Hardrada, king of Norway, was supported by Harold's exiled brother, the vengeful Tostig, who had never forgiven Harold for abandoning him during the Northumbrian rebellion. Even more threatening than the merciless king of Norway was William, Duke of Normandy. Known as William the Bastard, he was the son of Robert, Duke of Normandy, and his mistress, a tanner's daughter from Falaise.

William was an unashamedly fiery warlord, the product of a turbulent childhood. His father died when he was a boy, and from a young age he had to fight for his survival against family rivals who challenged his legitimacy. He had seen one of his guardians knifed in his own bedroom, another poisoned and two more murdered. He emerged an implacable fighter and a leader who became adept at winning loyal friends and allies. He proved he could be barbarous by ordering the hands and feet to be cut off men who opposed him in one recalcitrant Norman town. He was tall for his time at nearly six feet. As he grew older, he developed a paunch that became more and more pronounced. He secured his relationship with neighbouring Flanders by marrying Matilda, the daughter of the Count of Flanders. By 1066, his dukedom was as significant in France as the Anglo-Saxon kingdom was in Britain. The Normans – Norsemen who had arrived from Scandinavia only a century earlier – were now able to defy all other French kingdoms and had extended their reach as far as Italy and Sicily.

It was not only this Norman appetite for expansion that made William cast his eye across at the prosperous land on the other side of the English Channel. He believed he had a claim to the English throne, which made the newly crowned King Harold a usurper and perjurer. William had visited England at the invitation of Edward the Confessor some years earlier. It is conceivable that Edward, who owed a great deal to the Normans for the sanctuary he and his mother had enjoyed there, assured his cousin and boyhood friend William that he saw him as his successor. And then there was Harold's alleged oath after being rescued on the Norman coast which promised William the English throne. William took this as clinching confirmation that he, not Harold, should be king. It does seem unlikely that Harold would have made this offer after his rescue, because by that time his own chances of succession were very high. Whatever the truth, Harold's coronation in London was the cue for a furious William to begin plans to invade England.

William spent much of the summer of 1066 assembling a force great enough to ensure the success of a cross-Channel invasion. He managed to gather an army of around 10,000 foot soldiers and cavalry and a fleet of up to 800 vessels. Scores of horses would be crowded into his ships along with his army. It was a remarkable achievement: William was able to count on the devotion of his own supporters, and he lured other French allies with the tempting prospect of loot and the acquisition of land in their lush cross-channel neighbour. His case was boosted by the Pope's announcement in Rome that he supported the Norman claim to the English throne. The more superstitious of William's sympathizers also took it as a good omen that Halley's Comet chose to flash through the sky one night in April 1066.

William's invasion force gathered at the harbour of Dives-sur-Mer in Normandy and moved up to the mouth of the Somme in the autumn, waiting for a favourable wind. Harold was well aware of his rival's preparations, and he put his army and navy on alert along the south coast throughout the late summer. England's army, the fyrd, was now an impressive force raised from every small community in the country with legal penalties for absence. Every shire (today's "county") was divided into "hides" and "hundreds". The hide was a family group or group of families farming around 100 acres; the hundred was roughly 100 hides. These hundreds and hides had to contribute a certain a number of fighters to the fyrd for a period of two months a year. This amounted to a substantial army, particularly when the king was able to claim an emergency. Harold also had an elite band of around 3,000 "housecarls" – professional soldiers armed with swords and spears, some wielding the huge, dreaded Anglo-Saxon axes.

Harold's problem was the fyrd's two-month time limit. By early September 1066, the king felt he had no choice but to allow the fighters to go home, and he headed back to London. But no sooner had he done so than he received appalling news. Invaders were ravaging England – not Normans from the south, but Vikings from the east. Harold's estranged brother Tostig had teamed up with the man who had the most ferocious reputation in Northern Europe. Harald Hardrada, king of Norway, known as "the strongest man living under the sun", believed he had a claim to the throne as the successor to Swein and Cnut, who'd ruled England for 20 years. He and Tostig sailed their 300 Viking longboats up the Humber and threatened York and all of Northumbria. Word got about that Hardrada had unfurled his banner – a raven poised to pounce on its prey.

The English king had no choice. In an astonishing feat of military dynamism, he swept north in less than a week, gathering what he could of the fyrd on the way. He reached Tadcaster, a town 10 miles short of York on the night of 24 September. Harald Hardrada had no idea he was there. The Viking army had destroyed the Northumbrians, who had scrambled together an army to resist him, at the Battle of Fulford, near York, four days earlier. The weather was hot and, leaving their heavy armour on their ships, the invaders were resting – many sunbathing – at Stamford Bridge.

Suddenly, on the morning of 25 September, Hardrada and his men spotted a cloud of dust on the road from York. It looked to them like "the glint of sunshine on broken ice". They leapt to their feet and raced to try and form ranks. But they were split in two by the River Derwent. With Harold and his Anglo-Saxons approaching from the west, the Vikings on the west bank desperately tried to struggle across the narrow Derwent bridge and join the main force on the other side. A sense of panic spread. Tostig urged Hardrada to avoid battle and make for the ships, but Hardrada was not a man to run. Hundreds of his men were caught and killed on the west side of the river. Those who could scrambled across the bridge where a giant Viking then blocked the Anglo-Saxon onslaught. He seemed unassailable until a brave Anglo-Saxon crept under the bridge, speared upwards through a gap in the boards and stabbed him fatally in the groin. The Anglo-Saxons poured across after the Vikings and rapidly lined up to face Hardrada's fast-forming shield wall.

Harold's heralds shouted that if Tostig surrendered, he would receive his earldom back. "What about Hardrada?" the Vikings yelled back. He would get "Seven feet of English soil to be buried in", came the reply. Tostig didn't desert his ally and the Anglo-Saxons advanced. A bloody clash followed. Hardrada charged out of the Viking ranks and into the Anglo-Saxons, roaring his battle cry with a sword in each hand. Lashing left and right and drenched in blood, Hardrada was finally brought down by an arrow in the throat. Tostig was killed soon after. The Vikings collapsed, outnumbered, and outfought.

Harold's triumph was short-lived. He soon received the shocking news that William of Normandy and his army had landed on the south coast. On 28 September, the wind that had penned the Normans up in France changed. William's force sailed across the Channel and poured ashore at Pevensey unopposed. Immediately, Harold turned his army south and sent orders for the southern fyrd to reassemble. His family urged him to allow his brother Gyrd to confront William, but Harold brushed the idea aside, insisting he had to face the invader himself. By 13 October, Harold gathered his army within sight of the Channel. It was smaller than he would have liked, but he was determined to stop William's advance from Hastings to London. He was well placed, on a ridge called Senlac with his men packed tightly together, shield to shield, swords, spears and axes at the ready. The hardened steel blades of the axes were one foot long and the housecarls waved them in defiant arcs, shouting their war cries at the Normans.

William formed up his men with archers at the front, the infantry behind and horsemen in reserve. He would try to soften up the Anglo-Saxon shield wall with his arrows, throw in his foot soldiers to tear holes in it and then follow through with his cavalry. For Harold, it was critical to hold his shield wall together. Any gap would expose him and his men to the risk of being hacked to death.

At around 10 a.m., William ordered his men up the slope. The two sides were about 650 feet apart. First, the archers loosed showers of arrows and then the infantry threw themselves against the Anglo-Saxon shields. The shield wall held. William's cavalry joined the struggle, but the wall remained intact. Occasionally, a whirling Anglo-Saxon axe sliced straight through a horse's neck. Attack after attack by the Normans failed. The Bretons on the left of William's line panicked and fled down the hill. A number of jubilant Anglo-Saxons chased after them, opening up a glaring gap in Harold's all-important shield wall.

It was a dangerous moment for William too as the Bretons fled, and in the melee, a cry rang through Norman ranks that their leader was down. William was quick to react, pushing up his visor and shouting that he was alive and that, with God's help, Normandy would be victorious. He signalled to his cavalry to switch across to his left and crush the Anglo-Saxons charging down the hill after the Bretons. The Norman knights made short work of the men who had left the sanctuary of the shield wall on the hilltop. Harold may have been tempted to use the rout of the Bretons to order a general charge down the hill, but he was determined to prevent any more fractures in his tight array.

There were lulls in the battle while fighters caught their breath and retrieved any spears or other missiles that had missed their mark. But as the battle dragged on and William launched attack after attack, the Anglo-Saxon shield wall showed signs of weakening. Each Norman attack and retreat tempted some Anglo-Saxon soldiers to chase their enemies down the hill. Some believe these retreats were deliberately faked by William. Anglo-Saxons who broke ranks were surrounded and scythed down by Norman cavalry.

Harold's ranks grew thinner until gaps opened up and the Normans managed to penetrate. The decisive moment came late in the afternoon. A group of Normans broke through and surrounded Harold and his housecarls. He was then either pierced in the eye by an arrow or struck down by a Norman sword – possibly both. The Bayeux Tapestry, the remarkable 230-foot embroidery that tells the Norman version of the Battle of Hastings, shows an Anglo-Saxon figure with an arrow in his eye and, nearby, a Norman horseman dealing a death blow to another man. One or both may represent Harold.

With the king dead, Anglo-Saxon resistance folded. Some fought stoically on, but without Harold, any heart left in the English ranks faded fast and the army disintegrated. Around 4,000 corpses lay scattered on Senlac's slopes, the body of the last Anglo-Saxon king of England among them. His corpse was moved by William to a shallow grave on the seashore. At some stage, Harold's wife Edith Swanneck was allowed to transport it to Waltham Abbey for proper burial. Anglo-Saxon England's last king had shown himself a brave and resourceful leader. Had he survived, he could have proved one of the country's most popular and competent rulers. But he was outsmarted and outfought by an outsider who was to change the face of England for all time.

PART III

✦

THE NORMANS

1066-1154

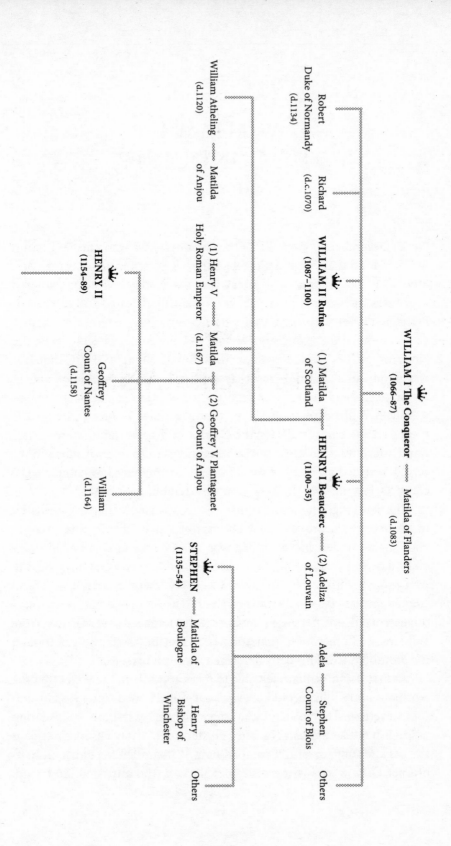

WILLIAM I The Conqueror (1066–87) ⚭ Matilda of Flanders (d.1083)

Robert Duke of Normandy (d.1134)

Richard (d.c.1070)

WILLIAM II Rufus (1087–1100)

HENRY I Beauclerc (1100–35) ⚭ (1) Matilda of Scotland ⚭ (2) Adeliza of Louvain

Adela ⚭ Stephen Count of Blois

William Atheling (d.1120) ⚭ Matilda of Anjou

Matilda ⚭ (1) Henry V Holy Roman Emperor ⚭ (2) Geoffrey V Plantagenet Count of Anjou (d.1167)

STEPHEN (1135–54) ⚭ Matilda of Boulogne

HENRY II (1154–89)

Geoffrey Count of Nantes (d.1158)

William (d.1164)

Henry Bishop of Winchester

Others

Others

6

WILLIAM I
THE CONQUERER
1066-87

On 25 December 1066, William the Conqueror was crowned William I of England in the new and glorious abbey at Westminster. Norman and other Continental knights who had won the Battle of Hastings gathered to witness the coronation along with resentful, defeated Anglo-Saxons. Perhaps it's not surprising that when, as was the custom, the congregation shouted an exuberant "Vivat!" ("Long life!") to King William, Norman guards posted outside the church thought the Conqueror was under attack. Panicking, they set fire to nearby buildings and in the smoky chaos there was a frantic scramble to get out of the abbey. A shaken William remained in place, determined to prove that he was the legitimate heir to Edward the Confessor. According to monk-historian Orderic Vitalis: "Only the bishops and clergy along with the monks stayed, terrified, in front of the altar and just managed to complete the consecration rite over the king who was trembling violently."

The new king, who would transform England more than any monarch in history, was nearly 40, a fabled warrior remarkable for his strength and single-minded brutality. He was deeply religious, attended Mass every day, and passionately believed that God backed everything he did. According to chroniclers, William was every inch a monarch with loud voice, dominant personality and red hair. "He was of just stature, extraordinary corpulence, fierce countenance … his forehead bare of hair", wrote William of Malmesbury, "majestic whether sitting or standing, although the protuberance of his belly deformed his royal person".

At first, King William felt able to relax and rule in the belief that the Normans and English could coexist peacefully. Shortly after his coronation, he returned to Normandy, taking with him "vast spoils" and a group of English nobles as hostages. They created a sensation with their elegant clothes and long, carefully combed hair. William left his Norman half-brother Odo, who was the Bishop of Bayeux, and a trusted old friend,

William FitzOsbern, to rule England. Odo became Earl of Kent and FitzOsbern was handed part of Hampshire and the Isle of Wight. There were some immediate changes. Latin replaced Anglo-Saxon English on documents and in courts, while the ruling classes and officials spoke French. Anglo-Saxon English became a third-class language. William's followers were placed in strategic locations around the country on land confiscated from English nobles. Fortified castles full of Norman soldiers sprang up at potential trouble spots. But there was continuity too. William had conquered a wealthy, united country, used to being ruled by a single king. It had an exceptionally well-organized system of government, and its citizens were used to paying taxes, traditions the king promptly adopted to increase his power and his wealth.

England's population at the time of the Norman Conquest was around 1.5 million. William brought between 10,000 and 20,000 Normans with him, and they were placed in key jobs throughout the land. It did not take long for Anglo-Saxon antagonism to grow. Odo and FitzOsbern "built castles far and wide oppressing the unhappy people", says the *Anglo-Saxon Chronicle* of 1067. That summer, there were rebellions along the Welsh border and an uprising in Kent was crushed by Odo and FitzOsbern. King William returned to England in the spring of 1068 to deal with a revolt in Exeter, home of Gytha, the mother of his predecessor King Harold. Exeter's rebels held out for two weeks, killing many of the king's troops before the town was burned to the ground. A period of calm followed, and William's beloved wife Matilda arrived from Normandy to be crowned queen.

Trouble soon started again with revolts in the Midlands, Wales and western and northern England. Then, in the summer of 1069, the Vikings returned. Supported by Anglo-Saxon rebels, the army of King Swein II Estridsen of Denmark destroyed York, killing hundreds of Norman knights. William ended that conflict by giving the Danes a fortune in gold and silver in return for their departure. All other unrest was mercilessly crushed by the king, who was becoming increasingly disenchanted with his conquered people. William stopped learning English, a clear sign that he had abandoned hope of a peaceful Anglo-Norman coexistence. From now on, he would rule England by brute force.

This was the shocking low point of William's reign. In the winter of 1069, he ordered his soldiers to lay waste to much of the north of England. He was determined to make the land uninhabitable for his opponents and unattractive to foreign invaders. In what became known as the "Harrying of the North", houses were burned, livestock killed, and crops destroyed. Amid widespread famine came reports of starving people eating insects, rats and even fellow humans. Monks at Evesham Abbey wrote of emaciated men, women and children crawling from 100 miles away, begging for food. More than 100,000 are thought to have died. William and his henchmen showed no mercy. "In their unparalleled savagery they surpassed all other peoples," noted one account. But the scorched-earth policy ended rebellion in the north.

William was now more powerful than any previous king of England. He had upended the top layer of English society. Most of the Anglo-Saxon aristocracy had disappeared, their lands and wealth confiscated by the king and given to loyal Norman lords. In return for their new wealth, these lords and their tenants were obliged to provide the king with knight service, a feudal system imported from Normandy. Each landowner, along with his designated number of knights, had to report for military duty for 40 days each year.

The embodiment of Norman strength was displayed in the hundreds of castles built all over England and Wales. From Dover to York, Windsor to Cardiff, houses were pulled down and forced labour was used to construct intimidating, impregnable stone fortresses. The newly built Tower of London had the largest keep in Western Europe. There was also a hectic programme of church-building as William put his stamp on English religion. Not a single notable abbey remained in English hands, and huge stone churches with distinctive Norman arches dominated the skyline in cities like Durham, York, and Canterbury. A new abbey was built at Battle, near Hastings, to mark the spot where King Harold had fallen and where, in William's view, God had granted him victory. Robust Romanesque and Norman architecture remains one of the glories of Britain.

In 1070, King William replaced the Anglo-Saxon Archbishop of Canterbury, Stigand, with his childhood tutor, a leading church reformer named Lanfranc. This brought England into the mainstream of Continental religious development. No longer could clerics buy religious office. The ordination of married men was banned, and Anglo-Saxon bishops were replaced by Normans. In an unprecedented second coronation in Winchester Cathedral, William was crowned by three representatives of the Pope, underscoring the legitimacy of his claim to the throne.

Five years after the Norman invasion, William faced one final uprising in Ely in the east of England, but he dealt with it in his usual brusque and decisive style. He then successfully invaded Scotland, which had been harbouring English rebels. The Scottish king agreed to recognize William's claim to the English throne, and William transferred his attention to his domains in France. Over the next 10 years, the new king of England spent 80 per cent of his time in his native Normandy, fighting neighbouring states. His family life was equally turbulent. Robert Curthose ("short pants"), the eldest of his four sons, fell out with his father probably because William refused to give in to his son's demands for more power. Robert, supported by King Philip I of France, led raids against Normandy. William was furious to discover that his wife Matilda had secretly sent Robert money.

In 1080, King William returned to England for the first time in four years and put down a rebellion in Wales. There followed what chronicler Orderic Vitalis called "a tranquil time" but, as usual, there was trouble ahead. Odo, William's half-brother and chief enforcer, was accused of plotting to become Pope. He'd been busy recruiting William's Norman knights to help him fight for the coveted job. In 1082, William ordered Odo's arrest and imprisonment. A year later, his wife Matilda died. He adored her and had long forgiven her for supporting their errant son Robert.

In 1085, William once again brought an army across the Channel as large, if not larger, than his invasion force of 1066. The enemy was once again the Vikings. There were reports that King Cnut IV of Denmark had assembled a huge fleet for a planned invasion, but the Danish fleet never set sail. With that danger averted, William turned his attention to, in the words of the *Anglo-Saxon Chronicle*, "deep speech with his councillors about the nature of the kingdom and the kind of people with which it was populated". This consultation led to one of the most striking and meticulous documents ever produced: the *Domesday Book*.

Hundreds of officials were dispatched across England and Wales to determine who owned land, what that land was worth and how much individuals paid the king in rent, tax and military service. Up to 50,000 individuals gave sworn testimony on everything from land ownership and types of crops grown to how many subtenants, peasants, ploughs, mills, animals and even fishponds were on each property.

The survey covers two specific years, 1066 and 1086, and it offers a fascinating picture of just how England changed under Norman rule. Twenty years after the Conquest, most land was held by the king, his Continental followers and the Church. Anglo-Saxon Englishmen held just four per cent. Among many other riveting insights is King William's love of hunting. Seventy forests are listed as the king's property. Forest Law, a Norman import, designated extensive areas as private hunting grounds for the king. The 20,000-acre New Forest, for example, was created by destroying houses and clearing 2,000 people off the land. Unlawful cutting of wood led to a fine. Poachers were often blinded. The *Domesday Book* also records the beginning of the end of slavery in England and Wales. Under Anglo-Saxon rule, at least ten per cent of the population was enslaved, and there was an active slave trade with Ireland. King William, at the urging of his Norman Archbishop of Canterbury, had passed a law declaring: "I prohibit the sale of any man by another outside the country." Slaves are mentioned in the *Domesday Book*, but numbers are significantly lower in 1086 than in 1066.

There has been endless speculation about why King William commissioned the Domesday survey. No doubt it was useful to know how much tax the king could raise to help fight his French wars and how many knights he could count on to keep the peace in England. The information also helped to secure his power base. For example, the king had the right to force widows to marry anyone he, the king, chose, and the survey listed all widows. The word "Domesday" refers to the day of judgement because its decisions about land ownership were final, just like those in the last judgement. William made an official record of all the information gathered to reaffirm the legitimacy of his rule.

On 1 August 1086, the king summoned landowners to Old Sarum, a castle he built in an iron age fort just outside Salisbury. They were made to swear an oath of loyalty to the king above all other men, setting a seal on William's conquest of England. Soon after this gathering, the king left England for the last time and headed back to Normandy with, according to the *Anglo-Saxon Chronicle*, "as much money as he could, obtained, as was his custom, by fair means and foul". He left behind a nation which, over 20 turbulent years, had little choice but to accept rule of an all-powerful monarch.

A year after his return to Normandy, William was locked in conflict with King Philip I of France, who controlled land around Paris. When the French king invaded the Norman city of Évreux in July 1087, William retaliated by destroying the French town of Mantes. The English king was now approaching 60 and so fat that Philip unkindly joked that he looked "like a woman who's just had a baby". As William rode through the burned-out streets of Mantes, his horse bucked, throwing him forward. His large stomach hit the hard pommel of the saddle, rupturing internal organs. William was carried to the priory of St Gervase, outside his Norman capital of Rouen. Clearly dying, he named his eldest son Robert Curthose to succeed him as Duke of Normandy. He did not specify who should become king of England, but expressed a hope that it would be his second living son, William Rufus.

William's end was surprisingly unromantic. When he died on 9 September 1087, the noblemen who had spent days by his deathbed abandoned him, rushing off to protect their property in case of unrest. When he was buried in Saint-Étienne, the abbey church which he had founded in Caen, the stone sarcophagus proved too small for his body. As his corpse was squeezed in, the intestines burst, filling the church with a disgusting smell.

William the Conqueror leaves us with one of the most controversial legacies in English history. His relentless pursuit of power and suppression of popular resistance destroyed countless lives and large parts of the country. But by building on existing Anglo-Saxon institutions and traditions, he helped persuade his subjects and the Church to support the monarchy, reducing internal feuds and deterring invasion. He could fairly claim to have left the nation stronger than he found it. The pros and cons of King William I's reign could fill this book, so perhaps it's best to turn to the *Anglo-Saxon Chronicle* for the final word: "He was a stern and violent man so that no one dared do anything contrary to his will ... Amongst other things the good security he made in this country is not to be forgotten."

7

WILLIAM II RUFUS
1087-1100

History has not been kind to King William II. Overshadowed by his legendary father and bad-mouthed by monk-chroniclers who despised his cavalier treatment of the Church, the successes of his 13-year reign are often overlooked. Nicknamed Rufus (red face) to differentiate him from his father William, the second Norman king of England was short and stocky, with a ruddy complexion, blond hair and eyes that changed colour with the light. In private, he was easy-going and loved a good joke, but in public the king was stern and intimidating. He made it clear that his will must be done. Like his father, Rufus was an impressive military leader who treated defeated enemies with respect. He did not marry or have children, and his flamboyant style of dress and royal court full of male favourites led to rumours of homosexuality.

Rufus was by his father's bedside in Normandy as he lay dying in August 1087. He heard William name the king's eldest son Robert as heir to the Duchy of Normandy. There was no mention of who should become king of England, but just before he died, William ordered Rufus to hurry to England with a letter for his trusted friend Lanfranc, Archbishop of Canterbury. It presumably named Rufus as William's heir in England, because on 26 September, less than three weeks after William's death, the archbishop crowned him in Westminster Abbey. The new king, who was in his late twenties, was not a popular choice for powerful Norman barons. Most wanted one king to rule over England and Normandy in order to protect their lands on both sides of the Channel. And they wanted Robert, Duke of Normandy, Rufus's elder brother, to be that ruler.

Less than a year after Rufus's coronation, disgruntled barons staged well-coordinated uprisings all over England. Rufus acted swiftly to win over his English subjects. His promises of money and changes to unpopular laws did the trick. When Robert sent a Norman force to England, it was defeated. The fact that Robert did not accompany his army, combined with Rufus's magnanimous treatment of the rebels he captured, convinced several nobles to change sides and support him. When the king later failed to deliver on the promises he had made to win support, Archbishop Lanfranc accused him of lying. Rufus replied, "Who can be expected to keep all his promises?"

Over the next few years, disputes with his brother Robert, military campaigns in Scotland and Normandy, building projects in London and struggles with the Church kept the king fully occupied. Rufus's youngest brother Henry (who would succeed him in 1100) repeatedly switched sides in family disputes – sometimes supporting Rufus, then backing Robert. In 1091, in retaliation for Robert's attack on England, Rufus successfully invaded Normandy. The two brothers met in Rouen for peace talks and Robert gave Rufus part of Normandy. Shortly after the Rouen meeting, news came that King Malcolm of Scotland had invaded northern England, devastating the countryside, and taking English captives back to Scotland. In a rare show of support, Robert accompanied Rufus to England and joined a successful assault on Scotland, which ended with the two countries agreeing not to attack each other. Rufus broke his word within a year and captured the (then) Scottish town of Carlisle, filling it with English colonists. The Scottish king fought back, and both he and his eldest son were killed in battle. Eventually, Rufus helped place Edgar, a half-English prince, on the throne of Scotland. Not only had he succeeded in pushing England's border north, but he also achieved an uneasy peace with Scotland.

The king's strained relationship with his brother Robert led to more fighting in Normandy, but family peace was secured after a call to arms by Pope Urban II in November 1095. The Pope had urged Christians to make a pilgrimage to Jerusalem and fight the occupying Muslims. Robert decided to join what became known as the First Crusade, but he needed money to do so. Rufus obliged by imposing a heavy tax on his English subjects to raise the required 10,000 marks (£6,700 – more than £15 million today). The king himself accompanied the three tonnes of silver to Rouen, and Robert pledged to pay him back from his Norman revenue, effectively mortgaging Normandy to Rufus.

Back in England, the king launched an impressive building programme which helped to make London the country's undisputed capital. London Bridge was rebuilt, defences added to the Tower and a cavernous hall added to the Palace of Westminster. At 240 feet long and 67 feet wide it was the largest hall in Europe. (It was later given a magnificent hammer-beam roof by Richard II, and still stands, having survived a fire in 1834 that destroyed the rest of the palace.)

The reign of Rufus was marked by growing conflict with the English Church, a struggle that would grow in intensity between future monarchs and the clergy up to the sixteenth century. The Church was exceptionally wealthy, owning 25 per cent of English land. Like his father, Rufus believed the monarch was master of the Church and he took full advantage of its riches. He sold many titles of top religious offices and claimed revenue from posts that he kept vacant. Archbishop Lanfranc died in 1089 and Rufus did not appoint a successor for four years.

The new archbishop in 1093 was Anselm, the greatest theologian of his generation. He supported Pope Gregory VII's radical reforms aimed at making the Church free of the state, with an all-powerful Pope answering only to God. In England, Church leaders argued that they, not the king, should make appointments to religious posts. Since Rufus got more revenue from the Church than he did from taxes, he rejected this proposition. In 1097, Anselm was accused of undermining the king's authority by planning to visit the Pope without royal permission. Anselm insisted that he should be subject to the Pope, not the king. After several confrontations, unable to get the king to relinquish his hold on the Church, the archbishop went into exile. Clearly distressed, he wrote to the Pope: "I have been archbishop for four fruitless years, living uselessly and in immense and horrible tribulation to my soul, so that now every day I would rather die outside England than continue to live there." The king reacted by swiftly taking over Canterbury's lucrative estates.

Given his difficult relationship with the Church, it's not surprising that the king's death was viewed as an act of God. On 2 August 1100, Rufus went stag hunting in the New Forest with a party that included his younger brother, Henry. An arrow pierced the monarch's heart, killing him instantly. Whether his sudden death was an accident or murder is unclear, since such incidents were not uncommon. The king's older brother, Richard, had died hunting in the same forest some 30 years before. It's widely believed that a Norman noble named Walter Tirel shot the deadly arrow that struck Rufus. Tirel left the scene hurriedly and headed for northern France, which left some convinced that he had killed the king on purpose. All we know for certain is that every one of the hunters rushed off, leaving the king's bleeding body to be discovered by a passing peasant. Rufus was buried in Winchester Cathedral. His brother Henry was too busy to attend the small funeral.

Rufus was mourned by his admirers but not by those he had crossed. When the tower under which he was buried collapsed in 1107, some clerics called it divine retribution.

8

HENRY I

1100-35

The timing could not have been better. Henry, youngest son of William the Conqueror, was at his brother William Rufus's side when he was killed on 2 August 1100. Whether by accident or design, the king had been fatally struck by an arrow while out hunting. Henry's eldest brother Robert, the Duke of Normandy and presumptive heir to the English throne, was far away, travelling back from the First Crusade. Henry opportunely seized the moment to gather support, headed straight to Winchester Castle and secured the all-important royal treasury. He then travelled to London and, just six days after his brother's death, Henry was crowned king of England. He was 32, stocky, dark-haired, intelligent, decisive and capable of being both cheerful and cruel. He would prove to be one of the outstanding medieval kings.

Unlike his Norman brothers, Henry was born in England. He spoke English, read Latin, and studied law so seriously that he earned the nickname Beauclerc (fine scholar). He had inherited money but no land from his father and spent many years quarrelling with his two older brothers. Both Rufus and Robert, Duke of Normandy, had confiscated land Henry had bought with his inheritance, and Robert had briefly imprisoned him. In the end, Henry wisely sided with Rufus. But after one of his staff tried to assassinate him, he took no chances and slept in a different place each night, with a sword and shield by his side.

From the start, Henry promised to be a better king than his brother. His coronation oath, the first to be written down, vowed to "abolish all the evil practices by which the kingdom of England has been unjustly oppressed". There would be more freedom for the Church and new limits to royal powers. For example, the king vowed that widows could now choose whether to remarry, and that he'd end the practice of heirs to family fortunes having to pay a portion to the king. There would also be a restoration of "the laws of King Edward" (the Confessor). The laws were unwritten, but during Henry's 35-year reign, scholars recorded and refined them, and they became the basis of English common law.

King Henry did not deliver on all his promises, but his coronation charter became a template for future twelfth-century kings and was incorporated into the Magna Carta.

Six days after his coronation, Henry made a canny match. He married Edith, daughter of his former enemy the king of Scotland, and a direct descendant of King Alfred the Great. She adopted the Norman name Matilda, but her son William was given the Anglo-Saxon surname of Atheling ("heir to the throne").

Robert, Duke of Normandy, arrived home shortly after Henry's coronation and made immediate plans to depose him. When Robert arrived in Portsmouth in July 1101, Henry was ready and waiting, riding through his camp dispensing advice about how best to beat Norman battle tactics. In the event, there was no fighting. Negotiators from both sides worked out a deal and the brothers signed the Treaty of Alton on 2 August, exactly one year after King William Rufus had died. Robert recognized Henry as king in exchange for an annual payment of 3,000 marks of silver (around £5million today). England was at peace for the rest of Henry's reign.

The two brothers fell out again in 1106, but this time Henry crossed to Normandy. He beat Robert in battle at Tinchebray and Henry took over as Duke of Normandy. He showed no mercy toward Robert, who remained Henry's prisoner for 28 years, eventually dying in Cardiff Castle. From this victory on, Henry spent half his time in Normandy fighting off attacks from the Count of Flanders to the north, Anjou from the south and the king of France from the east. While he was occupied in Normandy, Henry left his competent and cultured wife Matilda to run England with the highly efficient and loyal Roger of Salisbury, a cleric of humble birth, as her right-hand man. The appointment of Salisbury was a prime example of the king's shrewd habit of what the chroniclers called raising competent servants "from the dust".

England was run like a finely tuned machine. Under Henry's careful guidance, existing systems of taxation, local government and justice were reinvigorated. Permanent departments were set up to centralize power. The exchequer, named after the squares on a special measuring board used to make detailed calculations, collected income and recorded expenditure. Royal judges were dispatched across the country to uphold law and order. Weights and measures were standardized. The distance from Henry's nose to his outstretched thumb became a yard. A foot was based on that of a priest carved in stone on the base of a pillar in St Paul's Cathedral. There were harsh punishments for those who broke the law. Anyone found guilty of debasing the currency by using too little silver in the coins they made was castrated and had his right hand cut off. A severe dispute with the powerful English Church was resolved when the king reached a compromise with Anselm, the Archbishop of Canterbury, about the ceremonial investiture of bishops and abbots. Henry reluctantly agreed to give up his role in the ceremonial side, but he continued to have the last word in clerical selection.

Henry ran his family as astutely as he ruled England. He and Queen Matilda had two children. His son William was married to the daughter of Henry's former rival, the Count of Anjou. Henry's 12-year-old daughter Matilda wed the king of Germany and became Empress of the Holy Roman Empire. The English king also used his illegitimate children as diplomatic pawns, and there were plenty of them. Henry holds the English record for children born out of wedlock, with 22 documented births. Eight daughters were married to princes from places ranging from Scotland in the north to the state of Perche on the southern border of Normandy.

In 1120, after spending four continuous years in Normandy, Henry was ready to return to England. The king of France had been defeated in battle and Normandy seemed secure. On 25 November, Henry set sail from Barfleur, leaving his 17-year-old son and heir, William, to follow in another ship. They would never meet again. Many of the nobles – the cream of English aristocracy – who accompanied William got drunk before departure. So did members of the crew. Half a mile from harbour, his vessel, the *White Ship*, hit a rock. Prince William was quickly put into a small boat, but as he was rowed ashore, he heard his illegitimate half-sister calling from the sinking ship. He turned back to rescue her and, as desperate survivors piled into the boat, it capsized. William drowned along with nearly all 300 passengers. His cousin Stephen of Blois, who would become the next king of England, had a narrow escape: he left the ship before it sailed, as he was allegedly suffering from diarrhoea.

William's death devastated his father, who was said never to smile again. But ever the realist, with an eye on his succession, Henry came up with a plan. His wife Matilda had died, so he quickly remarried in order to produce another male heir. But his new wife, Adeliza of Louvain, remained childless. In 1126, at a council in London, the king appointed his daughter, the Empress Matilda, his heir. Although a female sovereign was highly unusual, all the nobles present swore allegiance to her. In a further move to preserve his royal line and to secure peace in Normandy, Henry looked for a new husband for Matilda, whose German husband had died. He chose Geoffrey Plantagenet, soon to be Count of Anjou. His surname was derived from the *planta genista*, the Latin name for the yellow sprig of broom he wore in his hat. Even though Geoffrey never visited England, the lion motif on his shield became the heraldic symbol for the country's monarchs. Matilda was 25 when they married, her husband just 15. They had a turbulent relationship and within months Geoffrey sent Matilda back to her father. Henry, desperate for heirs, returned her to her husband. Although the marriage remained tempestuous, the couple went on to have three sons, including the future King Henry II of England.

The final years of Henry I's life were overshadowed by disputes with his daughter Matilda and son-in-law Geoffrey, who wanted to control Normandy. When Geoffrey demanded castles which were promised as part of Matilda's dowry, Henry refused to hand them over.

The king made his final trip from England to Normandy in 1135. Like his father William the Conqueror, he loved hunting, and in late November he visited Lyons-la-Forêt, a royal lodge near Rouen. After disobeying doctors' orders and eating what they described as "a surfeit of lampreys", Henry fell fatally ill. Before he died, he made all those present renew their vow to accept Matilda as his heir. She was in Anjou about to give birth, so was unable to assert her claim. Henry's best-laid plans for his daughter were not to succeed.

9

STEPHEN

1135-54

Stephen of Blois twice vowed to respect his uncle Henry's wish that the king's daughter Matilda should succeed him. But the minute he heard that the king had died, Stephen raced straight across the English Channel to claim the throne for himself. Son of Henry's sister and grandchild of William the Conqueror, he had been a favourite of Henry and was well known in England. Londoners gave him a rapturous welcome and Stephen processed to Winchester, where he received the blessing of the bishop who was, conveniently, his brother. England had never had a female monarch, so it was easy to argue that Stephen was the man for the job. He was crowned at Westminster Abbey just 22 days after his uncle died.

Thanks to a host of contemporary chroniclers, we have a particularly clear picture of King Stephen. He was "a mild man and gentle and good", a fine warrior, handsome, charming, and easy-going. He was also enormously wealthy. King Henry had given him land in England and Normandy and his wife, Matilda, Countess of Boulogne brought him rich estates on both sides of the Channel. But the new king had many weaknesses too. He lacked resolve and was far less tough than his Norman relations. He relied on a small circle of close friends for advice and was said to turn a deaf ear to wise counsel.

The early years of Stephen's reign were relatively uneventful. Empress Matilda, King Henry's appointed heir, was far away in Anjou. (Matilda's first husband was the Holy Roman Emperor Henry V, and she kept the title of "empress" after his death.) Stephen's first challenge came from King David of Scotland, who invaded northern England and captured Carlisle and Newcastle. Stephen led a large army north and defeated the Scots, but he let David keep Carlisle, which was widely viewed as a sign of weakness.

Three years after he was crowned, Stephen made a serious mistake that alienated the powerful Church. He arrested Bishop Roger of Salisbury, who had been King Henry's able adviser. Roger's son, the

Lord Chancellor and two nephews, the Bishops of Lincoln and Ely, were also seized. They had built new, well-defended castles and increased their troop numbers which, in Stephen's view, showed they backed the Empress Matilda, not him.

Support for Empress Matilda was, in fact, growing. Robert, Earl of Gloucester, one of King Henry's many illegitimate children and half-brother to Matilda, was the first powerful baron to defect. With other disillusioned landholders, he plotted for the empress to replace Stephen. She arrived in England on 30 September 1139, but it was hardly an invasion. Accompanied by just 140 knights, she sought refuge in her step-mother Adeliza's castle in Arundel, Sussex. Stephen could have seized her and sent her straight back to Anjou, but he foolishly allowed chivalry to get the better of him. He allowed Matilda to travel and join her rebellious half-brother Robert in the west of England. This marked the start of a civil war which split England in two and caused untold destruction. The *Anglo-Saxon Chronicle* describes Stephen's reign as "the nineteen winters", saying, "never did a country endure such misery".

Most serious fighting of the civil war took place in the first two years. Stephen rushed around the country trying to crush rebellions. One observer wrote that the king started "many things energetically" but followed up "slothfully". His attack on a larger force in Lincoln in February 1141 proved disastrous. He was captured, and his cousin Matilda imprisoned him in Bristol Castle, at first comfortably but, after an attempted escape, he was put in chains. Stephen's reign would have been over if it hadn't been for his loyal wife – who outfoxed Empress Matilda.

The empress was a strong-willed, arrogant woman who "alienated the hearts of almost everyone", but she won the support of senior members of the Church by promising new freedoms for the clergy. Powerful Londoners were not so accommodating, especially when the would-be queen announced increased taxes. Four months after the capture of Stephen, Empress Matilda travelled to London to be crowned. The night before the coronation, with tables laid for her celebration feast, citizens of the city took up arms and forced her to flee. An army organized by Stephen's wife, Matilda, retook London for the king.

The uncrowned Empress Matilda first fled to Winchester but discovered that she was no longer welcome there. She had to flee on horseback, but her half-brother and key adviser, Robert of Gloucester, was not so fortunate. He was captured while covering her retreat. Matilda had no choice but to order a prisoner exchange, which proved a poor bargain. Stephen, her prisoner in Bristol, was freed in exchange for Robert. Nine months after being captured, Stephen was recrowned in Canterbury Cathedral.

A year later, the king laid siege to Oxford Castle. He knew Matilda was in residence there and that her capture would end the war, but she made another breathtaking escape. On a cold December night, she was lowered on a rope down the castle walls to the snowy ground below. Dressed in white, she and four companions hurried to safety. The stand-off between the two sides that followed soon became anarchy. The *Anglo-Saxon Chronicle* says: "Every rich man built his castles ... filled them with devils and evil men who plundered and burned and taxed and tortured without mercy." The "devils" included mercenary soldiers who raped and pillaged as they went.

The Empress Matilda remained in England for a total of nine years. She left for Normandy in 1148, after the death of her staunch ally Robert of Gloucester. Her son Henry now took up the fight. He was duke of both Normandy and Anjou. His Angevin father had taken advantage of the English civil war to capture Normandy from Stephen. Henry's marriage to the land-rich Eleanor of Aquitaine had made him master of nearly half of medieval France. In the summer of 1153, aged 20, this spirited warrior led a force to England. Twice, King Stephen marched out to meet Henry, but both times the king's war-weary soldiers refused to fight. In the end, the two sides agreed to negotiate. Stephen's son Eustace had been named as his successor and was vehemently opposed to Henry becoming king but, conveniently, he died. Nine months after Henry arrived in England, he and the king agreed that Stephen would remain monarch for the rest of his life and Henry would be his heir. They sealed their promises with a kiss in Winchester Cathedral.

Henry was lucky. Stephen died a year later, and Henry I's dream that an Angevin son of his daughter Matilda would sit on the English throne came true.

PART IV

THE HOUSE OF ANJOU
(ANGEVINS)
1154-1216

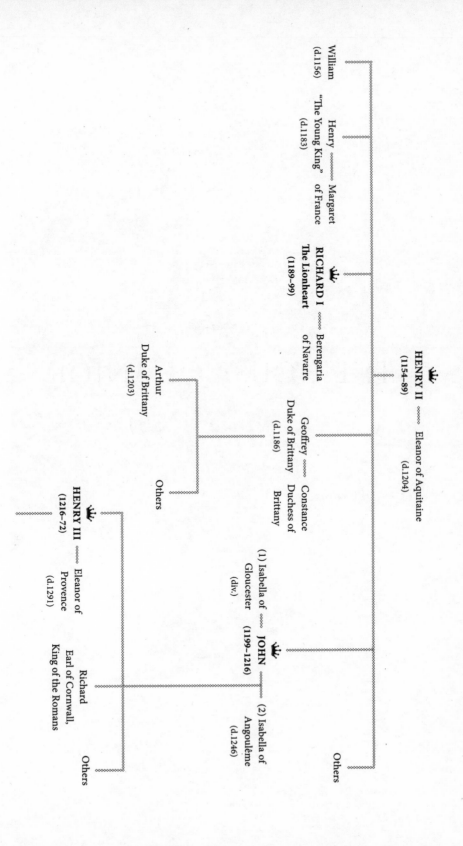

The ANGEVIN EMPIRE in France
in the 12th Century

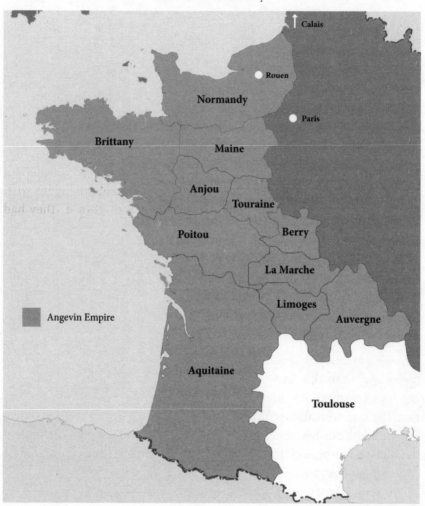

Calais

Rouen

Normandy

Paris

Brittany

Maine

Anjou

Touraine

Poitou

Berry

La Marche

Limoges

Auvergne

Angevin Empire

Aquitaine

Toulouse

10

HENRY II

1154-89

Henry II, forever tarnished by the murder of Thomas Becket, deserves to be recognized – certainly for his first decade – as one of England's most promising kings. The country he inherited was in chaos. He left it rich and secure. His rows with Becket and later with his own family led to tragedy but he left a vast realm stretching from the Scottish borders to the Pyrenees.

He was the first of three Plantagenet kings called the Angevins, after his father, Geoffrey of Anjou. He began his reign more French than English, with his education exclusively in French and Latin and his wife, the formidable Eleanor of Aquitaine, once queen of France. They had met in Paris in 1151, when he was only 18 and she 11 years older. The dark-eyed beauty was married to the lacklustre Louis VII, and she must have been struck by Henry's robust physique, as well as his sharp wit and intelligence. Most of all, she knew he was Duke of Normandy and Count of Anjou. She also knew that Henry's single-minded mother, Matilda, brought up her son to believe that the English throne should rightly be his. He was Western Europe's most eligible bachelor. So no sooner had Eleanor's marriage to Louis been annulled because she had failed to bear him a son, than this feisty and ambitious woman rode off post-haste to her own Duchy of Aquitaine in western France. She got word to Henry that she was free and, within weeks, in May 1152, they were married. She wasn't the only winner from this partnership: at a stroke, Henry had doubled his dominion. He now ruled western France from Normandy to the Spanish frontier.

It took Henry another year to pressure the beleaguered King Stephen to promise him the throne of England. Stephen conveniently died in October 1154. Henry had already made a powerful impression on English barons, who admired his tireless energy and self-assurance. He was charismatic, unpompous in dress and manner, but had, when aroused, a flaming temper. One contemporary remembers him so enraged that he began chewing his mattress. He was a striking presence and lost no time stamping his authority on the country by ordering the destruction of the forest of defensive castles that had sprung up during the mayhem of Stephen's reign.

This red-haired dynamo, who seemed to one contemporary observer like a fast-moving human chariot dragging everybody else behind him, was clearly determined to end all political infighting. And he did it by surrounding himself with gifted administrators. Most significantly, he chose as his chancellor Thomas Becket, whom the respected Archbishop of Canterbury, Theobald, viewed as a supremely competent cathedral archdeacon. Henry and Becket bonded at once. They became friends, joking and teasing each other. Becket lived lavishly and dressed much more finely than Henry. Once, in a London street Henry spotted a man in rags and suggested to Becket it would be an act of charity to give him a warm cloak. "Yes," replied Becket, "you as king should see to it". Henry promptly reached over and, after a bit of a friendly tussle, handed the man Becket's posh topcoat.

Henry's prime foreign policy preoccupation was his love–hate relationship with the country which he now owned half of. Here Becket did him proud with a flamboyant visit to Paris in 1158, spraying gold and silver gifts in all directions and negotiating the betrothal of Henry's infant son to Louis VII's daughter. Only a year later, Henry flaunted his military muscle in France by massing a large army to attack Toulouse. He only called the campaign off when Louis travelled to Toulouse to show solidarity with the local count. The French king was sadly aware that by losing his queen, Eleanor of Aquitaine, he had lost a large chunk of his country, but he made only desultory efforts to take on Henry. During his 35 years in power, in addition to his empire in France, Henry enjoyed a mainly stable and sometimes friendly relationship with the rest of the British Isles.

Eight years into Henry's reign, the death of Theobald, the Archbishop of Canterbury, prompted Henry to make the biggest blunder of his reign. In 1162, he asked his chancellor, Thomas Becket, to take the job. The Church was a powerful force in the governance of medieval England and Henry wanted to restrict its influence. Who better than Becket to do the job? His brief sojourn as archdeacon had been his only real religious job and Henry believed Becket's experience as chancellor should have convinced him to work in the nation's wider interests beyond the particular needs of the Church. Becket, deeply reluctant at first, finally accepted, but embarked on a course utterly opposed to the king's high hopes. The most extravagant and gregarious of men promptly adopted the lifestyle of a monk. He became a model of sanctity, and zealously protective of the powers of the Church.

Anxious to prove his commitment to his new calling, he rejected Henry's request to play the double role of archbishop and chancellor. From now on, Becket would manage the Church, not the state. Try as Henry would to persuade Becket to curb what the king rightly saw as the excessive reach of Canterbury's authority, Becket refused point-blank. In those days, a remarkable number of people counted themselves churchmen. Henry believed the Church's revenues should go to the national treasury, and that priests and others who claimed to come under the Church's jurisdiction should be subject to the law of the land, not tried in Church courts. A cleric who committed a serious crime should be punished like anyone else, and not allowed to get away with doing some kind of penance. Becket resisted. Time and again, the two who'd been bosom friends had terrible rows. "By God's eyes," shouted Henry, "the Church's money shall be given as revenue and entered in the royal rolls and it is not fit that you should gainsay it". In his new role as protector of the Church, Becket shot back: "By the reverence of the eyes by which you have just sworn, my Lord King, there shall be given from all my lands or from the property of the church not a penny."

This struggle climaxed in January 1164, when Henry summoned a large gathering to one of his palaces and presented the so-called Constitutions of Clarendon. This was a summary of an agreement that he believed Becket had accepted at a private meeting. It listed a number of concessions made by the Church but when Becket saw the document, he was horrified and took the desperate step of trying to escape to France. He failed and was summoned by the king to face what amounted to a trial at Northampton. In a melodramatic confrontation, Becket strutted in and out of the chamber carrying his archiepiscopal cross before him, declaring the court had no right to try him. He then ran for it and managed to escape to Flanders.

For the next five years, Henry had no Archbishop of Canterbury. This made his next move awkward. He and his queen, Eleanor, had four surviving sons: Henry, the eldest, born in 1155, then Richard, Geoffrey and John. He wanted to take the unusual step of crowning Henry as the

"Young King" in order to establish the succession. This should have been the job of the Archbishop of Canterbury, but in Becket's absence, Henry asked the Archbishop of York to carry out the ceremony in June 1170. Becket was affronted, and two fruitless meetings in France between him and the king that summer only made things worse. Their relationship took on the elements of tragedy. They even shed tears together over the rupture of their close friendship and their failure to repair it. At their last meeting, Becket told the king: "Lord, my heart tells me that in taking my leave of you now, I will not see you again in this life." He was right.

Becket returned to England in early December, sending ahead instructions that he would be excommunicating the clerics who had crowned the Young King. When Henry learned this, he exploded into one of his uncontrollable rages. Legend has it that he said, "Who will rid me of this turbulent priest?" In fact, his far less vindictive words were: "What idle and miserable men I have encouraged and promoted ... who let me be mocked by this low-born clerk!" Without telling the king, four knights rushed off to Canterbury and cornered Becket in the cathedral. Dressed in full armour, they shouted, "Where is the traitor?" "No traitor," replied Becket, "but a priest of God. What do you want?" The answer was a lethal slash by Raymond Fitzurse. He aimed his hefty sword at Becket's head and shattered it. Becket slipped to the ground murmuring – so the chroniclers reported – "I am ready to embrace my death." When Henry heard the news, he was devastated. He was condemned throughout Europe, and Becket the martyr became a saint. The king's plans for radical reforms to the powers of the Church were largely shelved.

Henry II had 19 more years to reign, and he had another tragedy to endure: his sons' jealousies. His obsession with retaining all power in his own hands was partly to blame. Even though he split his empire, giving England, Normandy, and Anjou to the "Young King" Henry, Aquitaine to Richard, and Brittany to Geoffrey, none of them were satisfied because the king insisted on remaining in charge. And to make matters worse, Queen Eleanor of Aquitaine was incensed by Henry taking an exceptionally attractive woman 20 years younger than herself as mistress. Some suggest Henry flaunted his affair with Rosamund Clifford to encourage Eleanor to agree to an annulment. She refused, turned her back on him and left for France in 1167. Young King Henry, frustrated by his father's reluctance to give him any real say in the affairs of state, cosied up to Louis VII, the king of France, and rebelled against his father in 1173, forcing Henry to negotiate a settlement with Louis. The king took the precaution of putting Queen Eleanor under effective house arrest to stop her backing his sons against him.

The Young King's death in 1183 complicated things further. Henry transferred the succession in England, Normandy, and Anjou to Richard. But Aquitaine he switched to his feckless and patently incompetent youngest son, John – who was oddly Henry's favourite. Richard would not accept the loss of Aquitaine. He was already unhappy that his father refused to surrender authority over the lands he'd given him. This left the king virtually friendless in the family. His mistress Rosamund had died. It was rumoured that Eleanor had contrived to get her poisoned or even stabbed her herself.

Henry was still all-powerful but saddened by his failure to keep his family together. He might have resolved things by returning Aquitaine to Richard and making him undisputed heir to the whole kingdom. But he disliked Richard and loved John. Henry's problems were exacerbated by the accession of Philip II Augustus to the French throne in 1180. Philip was a forceful contrast to his father Louis and was determined to win back most or all of England's French empire. The blunt reckoning came in summer 1189, when Richard, in full alliance with Philip, brought his father to his knees. The reign that had begun with such promise ended in humiliation. Henry was made to agree to a litany of concessions to both his French enemy and to Richard, who was now incontrovertibly his heir. He is said to have whispered in Richard's ear before he went off to die at his castle in Chinon, "God grant that I may not die until I have my revenge on you." The final blow to the spirit of this once towering figure came when his favourite son John joined the rebels. On 6 July, weak and exhausted, his last words were "Shame, shame on a conquered king."

11

RICHARD I
THE LIONHEART

1189-99

England's king for the next 10 years earned himself the nickname of "Lionheart" for his image as one of history's swashbuckling super-heroes. Richard I was immensely brave, no question about that. And his command of the Second Crusade was broadly successful. But his adventure in the Holy Land cost England a gigantic sum of money, and his reputation for chivalry was tarnished by the massacre he ordered after the storming of Acre.

Richard stood silent before his father's bier in July 1189. He had no reason to mourn Henry, who had kept denying him what he saw as his rightful inheritance. Now he was free to exercise the power of a real king. He was just short of 32 years old, built like an athlete and tall, with striking reddish gold hair. Richard was popular in England, where his coronation was greeted with widespread rejoicing, and feared and respected in the French dominions he'd done so much to fight for. He was also on reasonably friendly terms with Philip II of France, who had made the gesture of formally sharing a bed with him to show his peaceful intent.

Philip and Richard planned to split the command of the Third Crusade. Only two years earlier, the awe-inspiring Saracen leader Saladin had won a great battle against the Christians at Hattin and occupied Jerusalem. Richard had "taken the Cross" and was committed to contribute a large English army and navy to the campaign. His hunger for the fight was all the sharper since he knew he was behind schedule, having been outstripped by other leaders like Frederick Barbarossa of Germany, who was already on his way to the Middle East, but was to drown in southern Turkey.

Richard spent the first five months of his reign stabilizing relations with Scotland and Wales that promised calm borders in the north and west. He then threw himself into the task of assembling a force for the Crusade and raising the money for it. He was lucky that his father had already set in motion the "Saladin tithe", a tax that made the most of popular resentment at the loss of Jerusalem. He was also careful to ensure that he left England in the hands of loyal and efficient administrators, like the admirable William Marshal. Richard was worried about his shifty and unreliable younger brother, John, who had shown loyalty only to himself. The king trusted their redoubtable mother, Eleanor of Aquitaine, to keep John to heel while he was away. She was only partially successful.

One of Richard's less attractive features was his treatment of women. He was a shameless womanizer who ordered wives and daughters of his acquaintances to have sex with him. He chose to make Berengaria, the daughter of Sancho VI of Navarre, his wife because it helped guarantee the southern border of his beloved Aquitaine. This infuriated his French ally, Philip, who expected Richard to marry his half-sister, Alys.

Richard expected his new bride to come with him on the Crusade and, chaperoned by his mother Queen Eleanor, Berengaria travelled to Messina in Sicily for the wedding. The marriage to Berengaria was delayed when Richard's fleet was thrown into confusion by storms as it sailed east in the spring of 1191, and his fiancée's ship was blown all the way to Cyprus. Richard headed for the Cypriot port of Limassol and fought a brisk campaign to overthrow the ruler of Cyprus who, though a Christian, was markedly inhospitable to Crusaders. Richard won, married Berengaria in Cyprus, boosted his funds by selling the island to the Templars and sailed on to arrive in the Holy Land in June.

He found the Crusader forces besieging the town of Acre in northern Palestine. Richard was now in his element. Even though he was struck down by illness, it didn't stop him fighting in the frontline, and his enthusiastic English reinforcements helped wear down Acre's defenders. Richard had cleverly brought with him not only the newest wall-busting trebuchets but also a stock of particularly hard Sicilian stones to launch from them. Acre's battlements crumbled, and on 12 July 1191, the town surrendered. But there was tension among the allies. Philip, increasingly resentful and jealous of Richard, sailed off with his French army for home. Leopold V, Duke of Austria, who raised his flag over the walls of Acre, was deeply insulted and enraged when Richard had it pulled down. He too went home. As for Saladin, facing his worst ever defeat, he was, reported one of his attendants, "more affected than a bereft mother or a lovesick girl".

Richard was now in total command, and he could be ruthless. On the afternoon of 20 August, the man who saw himself as the embodiment of chivalry committed a crime of exemplary savagery. Saladin had failed to pay a ransom for the Muslim prisoners taken by the Crusaders as agreed at the time of Acre's surrender. Richard marched as many as 2,700 prisoners out of the city and had them executed. Some were beheaded, others slashed to death with swords. Richard's excuse, which sounds pretty thin, was that because the time limit for ransom payment had expired, "the pact which he [Saladin] had agreed was entirely made void".

With Acre secured, Richard now moved down the coast to occupied Jaffa. The advance south under constant attack from Saladin was a grisly running battle. Muslim horse archers swept in, filling the air with clouds of arrows. Richard's men responded with crossbow bolts. Casualties were heavy on both sides. At Arsuf, just short of Jaffa, a group of Richard's men, exasperated by the showers of arrows, charged headlong at their attackers. The Lionheart wheeled his horse around and led his cavalry against the Muslims, hacking his way through the centre of the melee. This battle, which he hadn't intended to fight, was a triumph. Saladin, already in poor health, feared for Jerusalem. He desperately dismantled forts that might offer Richard strongpoints on the route to the holy city. Richard pressed forward to the village of Beit Nuba. The city whose capture would have secured Richard unrivalled fame lay only another 12 miles away to the east. But his army was exhausted and, against his instinct to go for the kill, he decided to abandon the campaign for the winter.

It was not until the following June that Richard was back in Beit Nuba. Again, he stopped short, doubting he had the resources to besiege Saladin in his new capital. He worried about the length of his supply line if he laid siege to Jerusalem, and feared Saladin had poisoned wells around the city. Richard, unwell and wracked by reports of his brother John's disloyalty at home, is said to have walked to the top of a hill from where Jerusalem was faintly visible and asked that his eyes be covered so that he could not see the city he believed beyond his power to take. On 4 July 1192, he gave the order to retreat to the coast.

Ironically, Saladin was also wracked by doubt. Only two days before Richard retreated, the Muslim leader's advisers decided that Saladin should leave Jerusalem for his own safety. So the news that Richard was retreating was a welcome relief. If Richard had known that Saladin and his commanders were thinking of leaving, he might have attacked and triumphed.

The Third Crusade was not quite over, and the Lionheart was to prove himself indisputably worthy of his nickname. When Saladin attacked Jaffa at the beginning of August, Richard appeared with a fleet and personally led his men ashore. He leapt from his galley into the shallows, wielding his crossbow and his Danish axe. So ferocious was his assault that he and his knights managed to relieve the Crusader garrison. A few days later, Saladin staged a surprise attack on Richard's camp just outside Jaffa, and Richard again hurled himself at his enemies, "splitting them to the teeth", as one chronicler described it.

Greatly though this helped boost Richard's reputation for prowess, his crusade ended in a truce with Saladin. The king's health, his strategic calculations and anxiety about his brother John's disloyalty made him decide that Jerusalem would be a siege too far, and he returned to Europe. He never met his great Saracen antagonist, who described Richard as immensely brave but "reckless".

Richard had a disastrous journey home. Given the hostility of the French king, he decided to travel through Austria, where Duke Leopold still hadn't forgiven the English king for pulling down his flag at Acre. So Richard and his attendants travelled in disguise. A canny observer spotted them near Vienna, and Richard soon found himself imprisoned in Dürnstein Castle on the Danube. A charming story without foundation has it that Richard's minstrel, Blondel, discovered him by going around singing a ditty they both knew, prompting his master to sing it back from inside Dürnstein.

It took 14 months of negotiations to agree an extortionate ransom for Richard's release. Fate wasn't kind to Duke Leopold: he fell off his horse and suffered such a ghastly injury to his ankle that he ordered his foot to be amputated. Leopold held an axe to his ankle while a servant struck the axe head three times with a mallet. He died shortly afterward.

During the three years that Richard was away from home, his brother John had been up to no good. He falsely proclaimed that Richard had died which encouraged several barons to rebel. When the rebellion failed, John fled to France and allied with King Philip. Once home from the crusade, it took Richard just two months to extinguish remaining resistance and then cross to France to repair the damage his Angevin empire had suffered. When he landed in France, the treacherous John threw himself at his elder brother's feet and begged forgiveness. Remarkably, Richard kissed him saying: "You are a child and you have had evil counsellors looking after you." Richard now had to spend the best part of five years re-establishing English control in Normandy, Anjou, and Maine, as well as stifling unrest in Aquitaine. The most striking monument to his success was Château Gaillard, the sturdy fort he built way above the River Seine, within reach of Paris.

Richard was close to his goal of winning back his lands when he took a typically reckless chance outside the rebellious castle of Châlus-Chabrol in March 1199. Wearing no armour, he left his camp to examine the walls and was shot by a crossbowman on the battlements. The bolt flew so accurately into the Lionheart's shoulder that Richard actually complimented the man who'd shot him. The wound was poorly treated. Gangrene set in, and Richard died 10 days later, on 6 April 1199.

England had lost a great king. But while he was celebrated for his extraordinary martial achievements, he failed to give due attention to the country in which he spent just six months of his reign. He left England to deal with the crippling costs of his campaigns – and in the hands of a knavish successor who plunged the country into chaos.

12

JOHN
1199-1216

As Richard the Lionheart lay dead, two powerful English grandees met in Rouen, the capital of Normandy. "Who next?" the respected knight William Marshal asked Hubert Walter, the Archbishop of Canterbury. Walter replied he supported Richard's nephew, 12-year-old Arthur of Brittany, whom the king had named as his heir some years earlier. Marshal thought Arthur too young and temperamentally unsuitable. He argued that Richard had named his brother John as his successor as he lay dying. When the archbishop realized that Marshal backed John, he warned: "This much I can tell you. You will never come to regret anything you did as much as what you are doing now." He was right. Of all England's monarchs, King John was one of the most manifestly unfit to rule. He was devious, vicious, loyal to no one but himself and utterly unlovable, making a mess of almost everything he did.

John was lucky in his brother King Richard's generosity. Even though John had plotted against him and joined King Philip II of France to grab Richard's French territories, Richard forgave him and in the end left John his throne.

John was less fortunate in his alliance with Philip of France. Over the next decade, the wily and competent French king treated John with growing contempt. He soon detected the weakness of John's leadership and the frailty of his support in England. Although Philip had been John's ally in the 1190s when John was plotting to unseat his brother, he now turned into a bitter enemy determined to loosen the link between England and its territories in France. John's inept and half-hearted campaign to resist the pressures on his French empire ended in the loss of nearly all of it.

His reign began with an opportunity. He took a force to France only two weeks after his coronation and Philip, rather than fight, offered peace and urged John to come to terms with his young nephew Arthur of Brittany. John had an obsessive hatred for the mere teenager who'd been a possible heir to the English throne and was now joining Philip to grab John's land in Anjou, Poitou and Maine. The Treaty of Le Goulet between John and Philip in May 1200 was short-lived. John made no effort to befriend his nephew Arthur, who was popular in France. Even more foolishly, John made new enemies further south by luring the ravishing Isabella of Angoulême away from the man she was betrothed to. John was infatuated with Isabella, who was 20 years younger than him, and married her in August 1200. This so infuriated her former fiancé's influential family, the Lusignans, that they became allies of Philip. Together, they embarked on what soon became the unremitting erosion of England's possessions in western France.

By 1202, John and Philip were openly at war. John's mother, the venerable Eleanor of Aquitaine, by this time 80 years old, found herself besieged by the forces of Arthur and the Lusignans in Mirebeau Castle in Anjou. John was struggling to defend Normandy against Philip, and he now astonished his rivals with his one miraculous military success. In a lightning move, he raced some 150 miles south-west to rescue his mother. His army stormed Mirebeau, freed Eleanor and imprisoned Arthur. Any respect John might have gained for his military win was then promptly sacrificed when he was accused of murdering his nephew.

There are many accounts of how Arthur died, and all of them point to John. The worst story is that, in a fit of typical Angevin rage, John stomped into Arthur's cell, killed him with his own hands, and had the body dumped in the River Seine. Another version is that he encouraged one of his knights to kill Arthur, echoing his father's treatment of Thomas Becket. Certainly, at one stage, he ordered Arthur's custodian, the widely esteemed Hubert de Burgh, to blind and castrate his prisoner. What happened then is cloaked in mystery. De Burgh is said to have rejected carrying out such an atrocity, claimed that Arthur died of natural causes and secretly released him. Arthur was then rumoured to have been murdered by John or others in Rouen. Whatever happened, the stain never lifted from John, leaving him reviled at home and abroad. By 1204, John had lost to King Philip almost all of the duchy that had raised England's Norman Conqueror 140 years earlier. The extent of John's unpopularity came into sharp focus in 1205, when he abandoned another attempt to rescue his French possessions because most of his barons refused to follow him.

The next few years worsened John's predicament at home. He remained committed to restoring his control of western France, but this required vast sums of money which he had to extort by any means possible. He could no longer rely on revenue from the Continental subjects he had lost, and growing levels of taxation in England fired popular fury. The king also outraged the Church by seizing its properties when the Pope refused his choice of Archbishop of Canterbury. The rift with Rome became intolerable in 1207, when Pope Innocent III, a forthright reformer, consecrated as archbishop the respected Christian scholar Stephen Langton. When John declared Langton an enemy of the English crown, the Pope promptly placed the country under an interdict. All Church services ceased. In 1209, John was excommunicated, but far from being upset, England's incorrigible king now felt completely free to exploit the Church's ample annual income.

John, by this time impervious to his reputation for incompetence, turned into a cruel dictator. For further spoils, he singled out the Jews. There were plenty of wealthy Jewish moneylenders to persecute, and even torture, to swell funds. One Jew in Bristol refused to comply, and John ordered one of his teeth to be pulled out daily until he handed over 10,000 marks of silver (over £5 million today). After losing seven teeth, the agonized man paid up.

The king continued to lose friends among the baronial class. William de Briouze, who had personally captured Arthur at the siege of Mirebeau Castle, was one of his most loyal courtiers. John had showered honours on William in the early part of his reign, but that ended when the king heard that William's wife, Maud, had been gossiping about the murder of Arthur of Brittany. After William escaped to Ireland, John seized his wife and son, imprisoned them and starved them to death. When the door of their cell was opened, it became clear that Maud's extreme hunger had led her to start eating her dead son.

There was one brief interlude in John's disastrous reign during which he managed to strengthen England's power in the British Isles. His restless nature and delight in brandishing his military banners led to successful campaigns in Wales, Ireland and the Scottish borders, which did away with all domestic threats. By the summer of 1212, the king felt confident and rich enough to make another attempt to restore his power in France. In 1213, his navy humbled French King Philip's ships in a successful assault on the harbour at Damme, in modern-day Belgium. Two months later, John ended his conflict with the Pope by embracing Stephen Langton, the pontiff's choice for Archbishop of Canterbury.

These successes were followed by more humiliation. John's invasion of France in 1214 was a military catastrophe. He began with high hopes of winning back Brittany and Anjou, but when Philip's son Prince Louis moved forward to face him with a large army, John's followers deserted him. Shortly afterward, his other force, under the Earl of Salisbury, was roundly defeated by Philip at the Battle of Bouvines. It was the end of John's futile military ambitions.

When John returned to England, he was faced by barons he had done everything to weaken. He had fleeced them with taxation, interfered with their system of justice by insisting that he was the supreme judge and encroached on their property as an unscrupulous landlord. He had pushed them too far.

In the first months of 1215, the barons demanded that John recommit himself to the charter of his great-grandfather Henry I. The king responded by making further overtures to the Pope; by agreeing to embark on the next crusade, he sealed a new friendship with Innocent III. With the Pope on his side, John became even more stubborn and drove the increasingly fiery barons to the verge of civil war. On 17 May, rebellious barons occupied London, determined to enforce their demands. John could not ignore the obvious support they had, and negotiations followed. A document, which largely reflected the barons' complaints, was drafted by both sides. On 15 June, after days of haggling on a water meadow by the Thames at Runnymede, King John and the barons agreed on the "Articles of the Barons", a document that was renamed the "Magna Carta" ("Great Charter") a few years later. Both the king and his barons swore to observe it. It was the first time in history that an English king was forced to formally recognize that the monarch was not all-powerful. The original document of 63 clauses has long since been lost, but four of the many copies that were distributed around the kingdom are still preserved: one in Lincoln, one in Salisbury and two in London's British Library.

Most of the clauses entrench the rights of the barons and the Church. The first states: "The English Church shall be free". Others provide for habeas corpus and trial by jury, foreshadowing the evolution of citizens' rights. The Magna Carta is a foundation of Britain's unwritten constitution, representing the first agreed restriction of the power of the monarch, although the beginnings of parliament would have to wait another 50 years.

King John had no intention of sticking to his word. He persuaded his new friend the Pope to declare the Charter "null and void of all validity forever".

Philip of France now waged war on John for murdering Arthur of Brittany a decade earlier. This led to one of the rare successful landings of a foreign force on English soil. In May 1216, Philip's son Prince Louis arrived with a large French army, disembarked in Kent, marched to London, advanced as far as Winchester without encountering much opposition, and attacked the huge castle at Dover that guarded the key crossing from France. In London, Louis was proclaimed John's successor as king by a number of rebel barons and citizens of the capital, all of whom were exasperated by John's rule and desperate for a change. It is a captivating and under-reported episode in British history. Louis came close to being, for a while, king of England. He was effectively recognized as such by the king of Scotland who travelled south to do Louis homage. But Louis never captured King John or his son and heir Prince Henry, and failed to achieve a conclusive hold on all those who had the power in England.

Even so, as 1216 wore on, it did look as if this could be another 1066. As Louis continued to fight, John canvassed the country frantically looking for support. In the autumn, he was caught by the tide when crossing The Wash, a tidal estuary off Lincolnshire. He lost some of his attendants and a whole pile of belongings, including crown jewels, in the sea. He then went down with dysentery and died at Newark Castle in Nottinghamshire on 19 October. So ended the reign of England's most unworthy king, destroyed by his own tyrannous behaviour and callous indifference to his subjects. The best to be said for him is that he did leave his people one precious gift: the Magna Carta.

PART V

♛

THE PLANTAGENETS

1216-1399

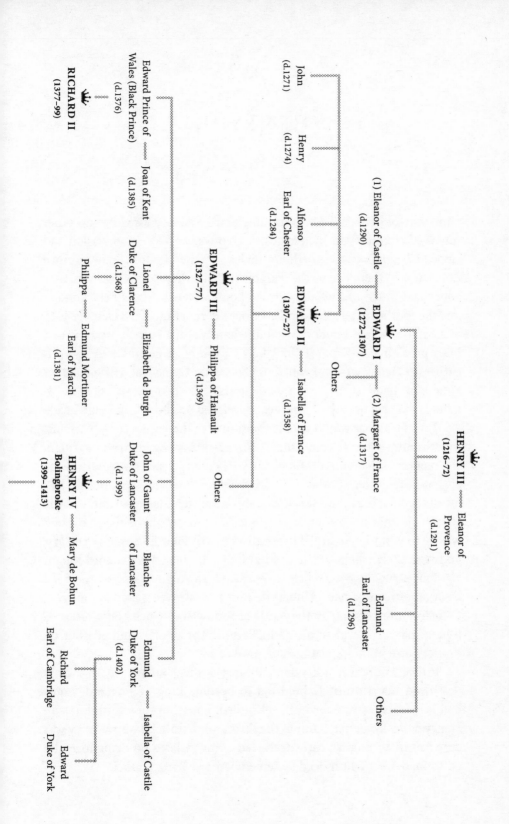

13

HENRY III

1216-72

Nine-year-old Henry III was not England's first boy king, but no other inherited a country in such chaos. A civil war and foreign invasion had ripped England apart. Rebellious nobles, who had invited French Prince Louis to help them rescue the country from the hopeless King John, now controlled much of England. Prince Louis's French forces held London and the south-east. It's no wonder Henry's coronation on 28 October 1216 was a muted affair. London was in the hands of the French prince who'd been proclaimed "King of England" by the rebel barons four months earlier, so Henry was enthroned in Gloucester Cathedral. His late father King John had lost the crown while fleeing his enemies, so a gold head-band belonging to Henry's mother was placed on the young king's head.

The battle that would decide the future of the nation took place just months after Henry's crowning. A force led by King Henry's guardian, the redoubtable William Marshal, marched on French occupiers of the city of Lincoln on 20 May 1217. Marshal, a seasoned warrior who had loyally served five kings, was now in his seventies. He hurried into battle so quickly that he had to be reminded to put on his helmet. So eager was he to win that he urged his soldiers to kill their horses, if necessary, and take shelter behind the dead animals' bodies. After a hard-fought six-hour struggle, the French surrendered. In August, a naval force led by another royalist hero, Hubert de Burgh, destroyed a convoy carrying French reinforcements in the Battle of Sandwich. Prince Louis accepted a hefty payment and returned to France. The door slammed shut on France's attempt to repeat the conquest of 1066.

Prince Louis was a brilliant military leader, but two main factors destroyed his stunningly bold bid to become king of England. Louis had been seen as saviour until John died, but from then on John's son Henry had a far better claim to the throne and, unlike Louis, Henry was crowned in an English cathedral. Had Louis insisted on being formally enthroned, he might indeed be remembered as King Louis I.

For nearly two decades, young King Henry's England was run reasonably smoothly by a team of barons, led by the exemplary Hubert de Burgh. Magna Carta was reissued in 1216 and 1217 to win public support for the monarch, but it was the 1225 version of the Great Charter that marked a crucial milestone on the road to democracy. In exchange for money to fight wars in France, the king and his advisers promised more political freedoms. From this moment on, the king was expected to discuss matters of national importance with a gathering of barons and bishops who could say "no" if they didn't get what they wanted in return. Their new assembly was called "parlement" based on the French *parler* ("to talk").

Henry did not show early promise. He grew into a man of average height with a drooping eyelid that made his face look crooked. He was well educated and deeply religious but seemed incapable of making wise decisions. The judicious de Burgh was replaced as mentor by the overbearing Peter des Roches, who was so unpopular with the Church and the nobles that the king was forced to get rid of him. Henry began his adulthood accepting that he had to respect the rules laid down by the Magna Carta. It was one of few astute moves in an ill-fated reign.

The young king's judgement soon went awry. He dreamed of restoring his family's honour by winning back land in Normandy, Anjou and Aquitaine. But he did not have the money, experience or political support to do it. He filled royal palaces with images of great kings of the past. One wall featured his uncle Richard the Lionheart in imaginary combat with his Saracen arch-enemy Saladin, a scene repeated in tiles on the floor. One extravagance the nation would be grateful for was Henry's obsession with Edward the Confessor. It led him to rebuild the Anglo-Saxon king's Westminster Abbey, transforming it into a Gothic masterpiece that rivalled the great cathedrals of France.

One of Henry's worst failings as he grew up was his choice of self-seeking advisers who did not have England's best interests at heart. His marriage to 12-year-old Eleanor of Provence landed his court with a host of relatives from her mother's powerful ruling family of Savoy. Henry gave them titles, land and rewarding marriages. One Savoyard uncle became Henry's chief adviser, another the Archbishop of Canterbury. There is no doubt Henry loved his enchanting child bride. Two years after the wedding, an assassin tried to kill the king at a royal hunting lodge, but he failed because Henry was not in his own bed. He had chosen to sleep in his wife's room that night. Their first son, born in 1239, was named Edward, after the king's adored Confessor.

The arrival of yet more foreign relatives in 1247 brought mayhem to the royal court. Four years after King John, Henry's father, died, his mother Isabella married Hugh, a member of the notorious Lusignan family from Poitou. He was the son of the man whom Isabella had jilted in order to marry King John. The Lusignans, an arrogant, violent, and uncouth lot, were suddenly back in favour. Henry unwisely invited his mother's four Lusignan children, his half-brothers, to England, and gave them titles and property. One was appointed Bishop of Winchester and, in a dispute with the Archbishop of Canterbury, sent an armed gang into Lambeth Palace. They stole everything they could get their hands on. Henry, always short of cash, relied on the Lusignans for loans and refused to take action against them – to the fury of English barons, who hated these malign interlopers.

By this time, Henry's hopes for reclaiming his ancestors' lost lands were dashed. The much richer King of France had taken Poitou and attempts to win back Normandy failed. The English king managed to hang on to Gascony, but at great expense. In 1254, he came up with a crazy project. The throne of Sicily was vacant, and Henry secretly negotiated to pay the Pope an enormous sum, just over 135,500 marks (£100,000, nearly £200 million today), to put his second son, Edmund, on it. But when Henry asked parliament for the money to pay for his Sicilian folly, he was shocked when it refused. He didn't give up. In 1257, Henry went back to parliament, this time accompanied by his son Edmund, dressed in an Italian costume. Once again it said no to him.

Henry's timing could not have been worse. 1257 had been a disastrous year for England. Sickness had swept the country. Floods that had killed the crops were followed by winter frosts, which meant spring seeds could not be planted. When the king renewed his demand for money in the spring of 1258, he provoked a full-scale political crisis. His barons rebelled. They were led by Simon de Montfort, the king's brother-in-law, a friend turned enemy. The rebel nobles swept fully armed into the Palace of Westminster on 30 April, accused Henry of not abiding by the Magna Carta, and demanded reform. The startled king cried, "What is this, my lords? Am I, wretched fellow, your captive?" The king was not taken into custody, yet he had little choice but to accept a new form of government which put unprecedented constraints on royal power. These were the Provisions of Oxford, which placed the king under the authority of a council of 15 barons headed by de Montfort. This council would

advise the king, oversee affairs of state, and choose all major royal officials. Parliament would meet three times each year, and not at the whim
of the king. Henry also agreed to remove all foreigners from his service.
When the despised Lusignans refused to leave England, de Montfort
informed them: "You will either lose your castles or your heads." They
quickly departed. The Provisions of Oxford were published in Latin and
French and, for the first time, in English.

But Henry was too stubborn to change his ways. In 1261, he
renounced the Provisions of Oxford, invited the Lusignans back to
England, and replaced key officials with his own men. Led again by de
Montfort, Henry's opponents took up arms. By the summer of 1263, they
had captured most of south-east England. The king sought safety in the
Tower of London. His wife, Eleanor, was pelted with rubbish when she
tried to leave the city. The following spring, the king ventured out to fight
a major battle at Lewes. De Montfort came under attack and, although a
broken leg meant he had to be wheeled into battle in a cart, he managed
to defeat the royalist army. The king and Prince Edward were captured;
Henry promised once again to endorse the Provisions of Oxford, and
Edward was taken hostage to ensure his father kept his word.

With the king a powerless figurehead, de Montfort moved to
strengthen parliament and created the forerunner of today's system of
government. Counties and large towns were asked to elect knights and
leading citizens. Knights had been elected to parliament before, but from
now on, ordinary citizens would be elected too.

But the royal struggle wasn't over. A year after being taken captive
at the Battle of Lewes, 26-year-old Prince Edward made a daring escape
on horseback. He was joined by nobles who had tired of de Montfort's
increasingly autocratic rule. On 1 August, a royalist force successfully
attacked Kenilworth Castle, home of de Montfort's son, also called
Simon. He was forced to escape by rowing naked across a lake. Three
days later, carrying banners seized at Kenilworth to trick the enemy, an
army under Prince Edward defeated de Montfort's forces at Evesham.
The king, who was in the custody of de Montfort's army surrounded
by his enemy's guards, was only rescued after shouting: "I am Henry of
Winchester, your king! Do not kill me!" De Montfort met a particularly
gruesome end. Normally, nobles were ransomed when taken prisoner,
but royalist soldiers chopped off de Montfort's head, hands and feet,
and hung his testicles over his nose. Sporadic fighting continued for

another year, and peace was not established until the king agreed that rebel barons could buy back confiscated land. Henry spent his final years accepting baronial power and the need to work with parliament. So, in the end, de Montfort's mark on history remains indelible.

Whatever we think of Henry, we do have to give him credit for his greatest achievement: Westminster Abbey. In the autumn of 1269, he and his sons Edward and Edmund carried the remains of Edward the Confessor to a magnificent new tomb Henry had constructed in the heart of the abbey. The king died three years later, aged 65. As his body, dressed in ceremonial robes, was carried through his great church, one witness remarked that he "shone forth with greater splendour dead than when he was alive".

Henry III was one of the longest-serving kings of England and among the least impressive. But his reign led to reforms which fundamentally changed the way the country was run. The expansion of parliament forced succeeding monarchs to recognize that their power, which was once absolute, now had to be shared.

14

EDWARD I

1272-1307

Edward I was in Sicily returning from the Ninth Crusade when he learned of his father's death. There was no need for him to rush back to England. He was the undisputed heir, a popular choice, and his exploits in the Holy Land had enhanced the reputation he'd gained as a great warrior and wise leader at the Battle of Evesham during his father's reign. The 33-year-old Edward was a towering figure. Handsome, except for the drooping Plantagenet eyelid, "Longshanks" stood a majestic six feet two. His expedition to the besieged Christian outpost of Acre had not accomplished a great deal, but Edward fought with the single-minded determination he'd shown at Evesham. He had also been exceptionally brave. When a Muslim assassin thrust a knife into his hip, Edward punched him in the head before stabbing him to death. His wife, Eleanor of Castile, allegedly sucked at the wound in case the blade carried poison.

As the new king processed through Italy, visiting the Pope in Rome and participating in French tournaments, troubadours sang that he was "the best lance in the world". In Paris, Edward paid homage to the French king as required by the 1259 Treaty of Paris. Under that agreement, his father King Henry III had renounced claims to land on the Continent – except for Aquitaine, which ran from Bordeaux to the Spanish border. Edward finally returned to England and was crowned in August 1274. He repeated the traditional oath about protecting the church and his subjects but, unlike many of his predecessors, he meant it. Despite his promise to the French king to renounce land claims on the Continent, Edward removed his crown after his coronation and swore not to replace it until he had regained the territory that his father had lost.

Edward did not repeat the mistakes of past English monarchs. He surrounded himself with clever, reliable men whose advice he took. He chose to compromise rather than to confront. He held regular parliaments that included smaller landowners and leading townsfolk – so-called "commoners" – as well as the usual nobles and bishops, a milestone on the road to Britain's two Houses of Parliament. Within three months of being crowned, Edward sent officials across England to conduct the largest survey since the *Domesday Book*. Their investigations served two purposes. The so-called "Hundred Rolls" recorded population and land holdings for tax purposes and to determine the rights of the king over land and property. But, to the delight of his subjects, they also exposed myriad abuses by royal administrators. There followed statute after statute which reformed the legal system and established Edward's reputation as one of England's greatest lawgivers.

One of Edward's important contributions to history is that he redrew the map of the British Isles. He extended English rule to Wales with iron determination. In 1277, the king led a well-organized and successful attack on the Prince of Wales, known as Llywelyn the Last. The English and Welsh had been adversaries for over 200 years, but Welsh princes were also often at each other's throats. During England's recent civil war, Llywelyn had gained control over most of his Welsh adversaries, and Henry III gave him the hereditary title of the Prince of Wales. In return, Llywelyn agreed to pay homage to the king of England. Since he had already refused several times to do this, Edward led a massive army into North Wales and forced the prince to surrender. Llywelyn kept his title but lost most of his land.

Five years later, Llywelyn's brother Dafydd started a second war. This time, Edward crushed the Welsh completely. Llywelyn was killed. Dafydd was taken prisoner and later was hanged, disembowelled, his body cut into quarters and displayed across the land, "the right arm with a ring on the finger in York; the left arm in Bristol; the right leg and hip at Northampton; the left at Hereford". His head was put on a pole in the Tower of London. English rule was imposed on Wales. To quell future uprisings, Edward ordered the construction of a menacing ring of eight castles dotted strategically across North Wales. They were built by the master French mason James of St George, whose imposing castles the king had admired on his travels to the Crusades. In 1284, Edward brought his pregnant wife, Eleanor of Castile, to the unfinished Caernarfon Castle, where she gave birth to the future King Edward II. He was later named "Prince of Wales", a title given to heirs to the English and British throne from then on.

After annexing Wales, Edward spent three years in Gascony and planned another crusade. For that, he needed money, and in 1290, he asked Parliament to impose the largest single tax of the Middle Ages. The body agreed on the condition that the king expel the Jews, England's most unpopular community. Under Church law, Christians were forbidden to lend money at interest, so Jews became the nation's moneylenders. Borrowers who owed them money became increasingly resentful and hatred was further spurred by malicious allegations based on anti-Semitic tropes, for example that Jews killed Christian children for blood as an ingredient in Passover bread. Previous monarchs had imposed restrictions on Jewish business activities and enforced Church rules that required Jews to wear yellow badges of identification. Now, barons who owed Jews money effectively bribed the king to expel them all from England, thus disposing of their debts and granting Edward the tax money he badly needed. Among the estimated 3,000 Jews who were forcibly expelled was a group on board a ship which was grounded by low tide in the Thames estuary. The ship's captain reportedly told his passengers to disembark to stretch their legs. When the tide came in and water started rising, he refused to allow them back on the ship and mockingly urged them to ask their God to save them as he watched them drown.

That same year Edward was devastated by the loss of Eleanor, his wife of 36 years and mother of their 15 children. Edward adored his wife and ordered stone crosses to be erected in the 12 towns where her body rested from Lincoln to London. Three Eleanor crosses survive. The king's adoration did not extend to his children. He had a fiery temper, and records show that in one outburst, he threw his daughter's coronet into a burning fireplace. During another argument, he's said to have pulled out a chunk of his son Prince Edward's hair.

In the autumn of 1290, another death had a momentous impact on Edward's reign. At the time, England and Scotland enjoyed good relations and the sole Scottish heir to the throne, a seven-year-old called Margaret, was betrothed to King Edward's son. Tragically, she died while travelling to England. Scottish nobles then asked King Edward to choose their next monarch from a list of 14 claimants. After two years of deliberations, John Balliol, founder of an Oxford college, was crowned in the ancient capital of Scone.

Balliol was happy to pay homage to the king of England until Edward's onerous demands led to war. In 1295, Edward ordered Scottish lords to provide troops for a battle with the French king over Gascony. The nobles refused and rebelled against both Edward and the Scottish king. They stripped Balliol of power and set up a 12-man council to run Scotland. The following year, they signed the "Auld Alliance", a treaty with England's enemy, France. Edward was furious. He assembled an army of 30,000 and marched on Berwick, Scotland's largest city, in March 1296. The town was burned to the ground and as many as 15,000 men, women and children were massacred. According to one account, "streams of blood flowed from the bodies of the slain ... so that mills could be turned round by the flow of their blood". It took less than three weeks to conquer the rest of Scotland. Balliol was captured and sent to the Tower of London. All Scotland's royal regalia were removed to London, including the sacred Stone of Scone, upon which Scottish kings had been crowned for centuries. It was placed in a shelf on the coronation chair in Westminster Abbey and was only returned to Scotland in 1996. As Edward handed over control of Scotland to its new English governor, he crudely joked: "A man does good business when he rids himself of a turd."

Believing he had sorted out Scotland, Edward transferred his attention to France, crossing to fight there in 1296. But he had underestimated the Scots. Rebels led by William Wallace, a charismatic knight immortalized by Mel Gibson in the 1995 film *Braveheart*, launched deadly attacks. In one on Stirling Castle in 1297, a leading English administrator was killed, and his skin reportedly made into a belt for Wallace's famous battle sword. Hundreds of Scots joined the rebel cause, and another war became inevitable.

The king returned to England in March 1298 after signing a truce with the French king Philip IV, agreeing to marry Philip's sister and betrothing his son Edward to the French monarch's daughter. On 22 July, his army defeated Wallace at Falkirk. England again controlled parts of southern Scotland, but guerrilla attacks continued. In 1306, another rebel hero emerged. Robert Bruce, grandson of a contender to the Scottish throne, declared himself king. Edward, now approaching 70 and in ill health, sent an army north. Bruce was defeated but not captured. Edward took grim revenge, executing the rebel's brothers and displaying his sisters in cages on castle walls.

Within a year, Bruce was back on the attack. Edward left his sickbed to head north with his army. He only got as far as the Scottish border. On 7 July, as his attendants lifted him from bed, he died in a village on the banks of Solway Firth. He reportedly asked that his bones be carried at the head of the army until the last Scot surrendered. King Edward I was buried in Westminster Abbey. Inscribed on his tomb is "Hammer of the Scots". In truth, the warrior king who had hammered Wales had fallen far short of that boast in Scotland.

15

EDWARD II

1307-27

The coronation of Edward II on 25 February 1308 should have been a cause for great celebration. Instead, it descended into farce and foreshadowed a disastrous 20-year reign, which ended with Edward becoming the first English king to be thrown out of office.

The son of the indomitable Edward I was irresponsible, lazy, stubborn, untrustworthy, malicious and he drank too much. The fact that he preferred cart driving and rowing to regal pursuits like jousting led to talk that he was a commoner who'd been switched with the real prince at birth. But Edward's major failing was that he allowed himself to become infatuated with ambitious, unscrupulous men who took advantage of his weak nature.

Normally, the noble who walked in front of the king in the coronation day procession was a distinguished earl, but Edward chose an unpopular interloper, Piers Gaveston, for that honour. The knight from Gascony, whom the king had made Earl of Cornwall, was dressed like "the God Mars" in purple silk robes covered in pearls. As he walked through Westminster Abbey carrying the sacred crown of Edward the Confessor, Gaveston was booed by members of the congregation. At the post-coronation feast, Edward ignored his new wife, 12-year-old Isabella, daughter of the king of France, and spent the evening lounging on a sofa, talking and joking with Gaveston.

Within three days of the coronation, a group of magnates including the king's disapproving cousin, the Earl of Lancaster, demanded that Gaveston be stripped of his earldom and banished from England. But it was not until Edward's father-in-law, King Philip IV of France, added his voice to the growing chorus of dissent, that Edward reluctantly agreed; however, he kept Piers close, making him Lord Lieutenant of Ireland, large parts of which were under English rule.

By 1309, Gaveston was back by Edward's side, his earldom restored in exchange for the king agreeing to legal and financial reforms. Edward's favourite caused further offence by giving leading aristocrats nicknames like "burst belly", "black dog", "the churl" and "Joseph the Jew". While the king and Gaveston were in Scotland unsuccessfully attempting to defeat the elusive Robert the Bruce, dozens of disgruntled nobles and bishops moved to limit the king's power. When Edward returned from Scotland in the summer of 1311, he was handed a document containing 41 clauses, known as the Ordinances. They forbade Edward from going to war, leaving the country, making appointments, or giving gifts without Parliament's permission. The king was also ordered to dismiss his "evil counsellors". Despite Edward's desperate pleas on behalf of the man he called "my brother", he was forced to agree to the Ordinances and send Gaveston into exile.

In January 1313, Gaveston made the fatal mistake of returning to England. The king welcomed him back and promptly revoked the Ordinances. His furious opponents threatened civil war and Edward fled north with Gaveston, leaving his pregnant queen, Isabella, behind. They holed up in Scarborough Castle, but when Edward left to round up armed support, angry nobles laid siege to the castle. Gaveston surrendered and although he was guaranteed that Parliament would decide his fate, he ended up in the hands of enemies who wanted him dead. Led by the Earl of Lancaster, they accused Gaveston of violating the Ordinances and handed him over to two of Lancaster's henchmen. One sliced his body with a sword; the other cut off his head. The bloody murder shocked previously disgruntled nobles, and some returned to Edward's side. The heartbroken king vowed revenge.

Edward soon faced another problem: Scotland. At the height of his father Edward I's reign, England effectively ruled Scotland, but by 1314, its rebel king Robert Bruce controlled much of the country. With the help of loans from the king of France, the Pope and the English Church, Edward managed to put together an army of 15,000 men. Leading a wagon train that stretched 20 miles, he arrived at the besieged Stirling Castle determined to finish his enemy off once and for all. The Scots were outnumbered by two to one, but they took full advantage of the boggy, narrow battlefield on the edge of a stream called Bannock Burn. Bruce had ordered his men to dig potholes covered by grass to make the ground even more treacherous. The main battle took place on 24 June. When overconfident English soldiers charged, they ran over the uneven ground and straight into 12-foot pikes carried by the Scots' infantry, who were tightly packed into *schiltrons*, defensive formations that looked like

ABOVE: The "Alfred Jewel". Gold, enamel and quartz, possibly depicting Alfred the Great himself. It reads, "Aelfred mec heht gewyrcan" – "Alfred ordered me made".

BELOW LEFT: Athelflaed, Alfred's formidable daughter, became ruler of Mercia and trounced the Danes.

BELOW RIGHT: Athelstan (left) paying homage to Saint Cuthbert. A fine warrior like his grandfather Alfred, he called himself "King of all England".

LEFT: Edgar presenting a new charter of Winchester to Jesus Christ.

BELOW LEFT: Ethelred the Unready's large sword flatters him. His long but dithering reign left England a prey to the Danes.

BELOW RIGHT: Cnut (Canute), England's Danish king, could be bloodthirsty but was a wise ruler.

ABOVE: Edward the Confessor (right). The Bayeux Tapestry depicts him persuading his Saxon cousin Harold (left) to offer the English throne to his Norman cousin William. If Harold did this, he regretted it later and fought William at Hastings.

BELOW: "*Harold Rex* (the king) *interfectus est* (is killed)", says the Bayeux Tapestry. It shows Harold (bottom right) falling to a sword blow – or is that him (top left), trying to pluck an arrow from his eye?

ABOVE: William I the Conqueror, illegitimate son of the Duke of Normandy, dressed for battle. His conquest transformed Britain more than any other monarch.

RIGHT: William II Rufus ruled in the shadow of his legendary father and was killed by an arrow while out hunting.

Henry I sits with bowed head above the *White Ship* where his son died. The family tree below shows his daughter Matilda and her son, later Henry II.

ABOVE: Stephen stole the throne from his cousin Matilda, plunging England into civil war.

LEFT: Matilda captured Stephen and planned a London coronation, but its citizens took up arms and forced her to flee.

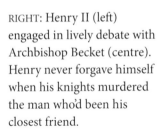

RIGHT: Henry II (left) engaged in lively debate with Archbishop Becket (centre). Henry never forgave himself when his knights murdered the man who'd been his closest friend.

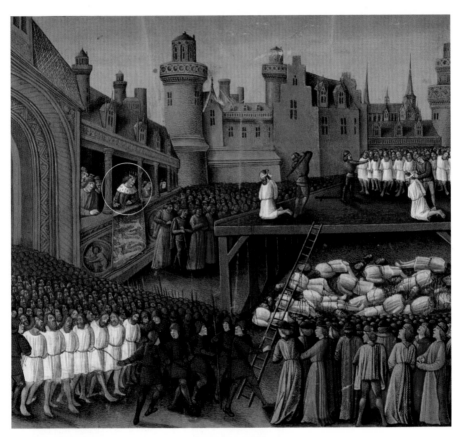

Richard I the Lionheart (circled) watches the beheadings he ordered of more than two thousand Muslims seized in the storming of Acre. Bodies are piling up beneath the scaffold.

ABOVE: John, with the crown slipping from his head, lost England's lands in France and was outfaced by his barons at home.

RIGHT: Henry III holds up Westminster Abbey which he rebuilt in Gothic style. It was one of his few achievements.

RIGHT: This is believed to be Edward I. The tall figure fits his nickname "Longshanks". He crushed the Welsh and was "Hammer of the Scots".

BELOW: Hugh Despenser the Younger, favourite of Edward II, meets his end disembowelled on a ladder for all to see.

Edward II, seated, receives the crown. He was later forced to hand it to his son.

Edward III's coronation took place when he was just 14. His long reign saw the French defeated at Crécy and Poitiers.

RIGHT: Richard II's unimpressive reign ended with his forced abdication. He died of starvation in captivity.

BELOW: Richard II looks on as the Mayor of London prepares to kill Wat Tyler, leader of the Peasants' Revolt.

LEFT: Henry IV (Bolingbroke) arrives in London to seize Richard II's throne. He reigned uneasily facing several rebellions.

BELOW LEFT: Henry V, hero of the House of Lancaster, defeated the French at Agincourt, but died before he could be crowned King of France.

BELOW RIGHT: Henry VI's feckless rule prompted the Yorkist rebellion that launched the Wars of the Roses.

RIGHT: Edward IV the Yorkist leader finally won victory for the white rose.

BELOW: Edward IV, wife Elizabeth Woodville and son Edward V, who would be smothered in the Tower, receive homage from the Duke of Gloucester (second from left), soon to be Richard III.

Richard III was a man of great courage but accused of ordering the murder of the two princes in the Tower. His reign was cut short by Henry Tudor's invasion.

Henry VII, first of the Tudors. His victory over Richard III left him haunted by fear of conspiracies for the rest of his reign.

Henry VIII, a heavyweight in every sense. Dazzling and athletic when young; after three of his six marriages, a rapacious and corpulent tyrant. He broke with the Pope and smashed the monasteries.

ANNA BOLINA VXOR- HENRI- OCTA

LEFT: Anne Boleyn, the attractive and strong-willed second wife of Henry VIII was mother to Elizabeth I. Her alleged adultery led her to the block.

BELOW: Henry VIII on his deathbed confirms his successor, nine-year-old son Edward VI, flanked by his uncle Lord Protector Somerset (standing), uncle Thomas Seymour and the arch-Protestant Archbishop Thomas Cranmer. The Pope lies crushed on the floor.

giant hedgehogs. The *schiltrons* advanced, forcing the English to retreat in shambolic disorder, crushed by their own numbers and bogged down in marshland. Hundreds died in battle or trying to cross the Bannock Burn and nearby River Forth. King Edward, whose horse was killed beneath him, was lucky to escape.

His ignominious defeat at what came to be called the Battle of Bannockburn further damaged the king's already tarnished reputation. And there was worse to come. Robert Bruce went on the rampage, launching raids further and further into England. Bruce's brother Edward invaded Ireland and ruled as king until defeated by forces loyal to England. The economy collapsed too. The Great Famine of Northern Europe, caused by successive years of torrential rain and unusually cold weather, destroyed crops and livestock. An estimated half a million English people (out of a population of six million) died between 1315 and 1322.

Throughout this period, the king tried repeatedly to get rid of the Ordinances which made him virtually powerless. His arch-enemy, the Earl of Lancaster, headed a council designated to enforce the Ordinances, but he soon tired of politics and retired gloomily to his northern lands. Into this power vacuum stepped Edward's new favourites, the Despensers, father and son. Hugh the Elder was a baron who had fought at the side of King Edward I. Hugh the Younger was a scheming, greedy bully who, it was said, "bewitched the king's mind". Like Piers Gaveston before him, young Hugh became Edward's chamberlain, controlling all access to the king. Edward and the Despensers became known as "the three kings".

When Edward gave each Despenser vast landholdings in Wales, local lords, known as Marchers, rebelled. In 1321, the so-called "Contrariants" attacked Despenser properties. Supported by the Earl of Lancaster, they demanded the banishment of both father and son. Edward was forced to agree, but the Despensers returned to England, encouraged the king to fight and put down the Marcher Lords' revolt. On 14 January 1322, Edward led a well-organized army into Wales. Within two months, his Contrariant enemies had been defeated. The Earl of Lancaster, who had tried to flee in disguise, was captured. The king agreed that his cousin, because of his royal blood, should be simply beheaded instead of hung, drawn and quartered. There followed what has been described as a reign of terror. More than 100 of Edward's noble opponents were murdered or imprisoned and their lands seized. He abolished the Ordinances "for once and for all". Hugh Despenser the

Elder was appointed Earl of Winchester and young Hugh became the richest landowner after the king.

The last two years of Edward's reign were a pathetic shambles, and the downfall of the king and the Despensers, came about in a most unexpected manner. In 1325, Edward sent his wife Isabella to Paris to sort out a quarrel with her brother, King Charles IV of France. He then dispatched their 12-year-old son, Prince Edward, to pay homage to the French king. Neither returned. Isabella, who hated the younger Despenser, issued a statement saying, "Someone has come between my husband and myself … I will not return until this intruder is removed." But the queen would soon return to England with a vengeance. Disgusted with her husband, she started an affair with Roger Mortimer, a cunning English lord who had fought against the king and famously made a dramatic escape down a rope from the Tower of London before fleeing to Paris. They sought help from William of Hainault, Duke of Holland, and after Queen Isabella promised that her son Prince Edward would marry his daughter, the duke provided money for a small invasion force. The queen and Mortimer led that force to England at the end of September 1326.

As support for Queen Isabella grew, King Edward and the Despensers fled west. Hugh the Elder was seized in Bristol and sentenced to death for treason. The desperate king and the younger Hugh tried to sail to Ireland, but the wind pushed them back to Wales, where they were captured hiding in a wood. The detested Hugh was tied to the top of a 50-foot ladder so all could see his disembowelling, hanging and quartering. His head was displayed on London Bridge.

The question now was: what to do with Edward? Never before had an English king been deposed. He was removed to Kenilworth Castle, former home of his cousin the Earl of Lancaster. In early 1327, a session of Parliament declared the king must abdicate. Edward refused. On 20 January, a delegation of 24 nobles and bishops arrived at Kenilworth and made it clear that he must step aside. An eyewitness records that Edward, "in the shock of sorrow … lost his wits and collapsed in a heap on the floor" and "with tears and lamentations", finally gave in. His 14-year-old son, Edward, was crowned king just five days later.

After failed rescue attempts, the former king was moved to Berkeley Castle, where he died on 21 September. Most chroniclers claimed that he was murdered – either by smothering or by having a red-hot poker shoved up his backside.

16

EDWARD III

1327-77

One striking feature of the Plantagenet story is the fact that strong kings were succeeded by inadequate sons who in turn, fathered successful rulers. Edward III whose father was disgraced and ultimately deposed turned out to be one of England's outstanding kings.

Edward was just 14 when his coronation took place on 1 February 1327. His crown was stuffed with cotton to prevent it slipping off his young head. At first, he was king in name only, with power lying in the hands of his mother Queen Isabella – known as "the she-wolf of France" – and her tyrannical lover Roger Mortimer. They controlled access to Edward and placed spies in his household while enriching themselves with vast tracts of land grabbed from supporters of Edward II. Their mismanagement of England made powerful enemies. Three years after the coronation, Mortimer accused the Earl of Kent, the king's relative, of treason and ordered his beheading. One of Edward's supporters, fearing for the king's safety, warned: "Better eat the dog than let the dog eat you." The young monarch clearly listened. On 19 October 1330, Edward and a dozen armed companions entered Nottingham Castle via an underground passage. They found Mortimer in Queen Isabella's apartment. Ignoring her plea to "have pity on noble Mortimer", he was seized, put on trial, and found guilty of 14 charges including the murder of Edward II. He was drawn and hanged while Isabella spent the rest of her life banished, albeit luxuriously, in a Norfolk castle.

Edward grew up a natural leader. Handsome, with a kind face, he was intelligent, charismatic, self-confident, and extremely likeable. He listened, took advice and governed by consent. A brave warrior, he created the most feared army in Europe and his battle tactics would be studied by future generations. His ability to reach out to nobles and commoners alike led to the longest period of peace in medieval England. His happy marriage to popular Philippa of Hainault produced 12 children. If he had one failing, it was that he lived too long.

The first years of his adult reign were spent having fun. Edward loved chivalry and pageantry and, like many of his ancestors, was fascinated by tales of King Arthur and his Knights of the Round Table. He set up tournaments where nobles jousted and staged mock battles – ideal training for real conflicts to come. Members of his court were treated to extravagant parties, which included dressing up as exotic animals. Nor did the king forget his other subjects. The unrest during his father's reign had led to a breakdown in public discipline; Edward encouraged reforms that brought about much-needed law enforcement.

Edward's first military challenge came from England's old enemy Scotland. In 1333, the king moved his capital from London to York, where, for the next four years, he masterminded attacks to regain the land Robert the Bruce had seized from Edward II. When former Scottish king John Balliol's son Edward challenged Bruce's son, King David II, for the Scottish throne, Edward supported Balliol and together they laid siege to Berwick, Scotland's main port. On 19 July, they defeated a much larger Scottish army at nearby Halidon Hill. Balliol, now king, handed Edward control of Berwick and much of southern Scotland. David II fled to safety in Normandy.

From now on, conflict with France would dominate King Edward's reign. In 1337, French King Philip VI confiscated Aquitaine, a territory ruled by the English for 200 years, sparking off the Hundred Years War. At first, the dispute was limited to occasional skirmishes, but in 1340, Edward raised the stakes. On a visit to Ghent in Flanders, (accompanied by his wife, who gave birth to John of Gaunt there) the king publicly announced his claim to the throne of France. His mother Isabella was the late French king's sister, so Edward was the closest male relative, but the throne had gone to his cousin Philip. After staking his claim, Edward returned to England to raise an invasion force.

On 24 June, he took an army to Flanders in 150 ships. The French were waiting in the Bay of Sluys with three lines of anchored vessels, chained together. The English headed straight for them, boarding the French ships and wreaking havoc with hand-to-hand fighting. King Edward, wounded by an arrow, sealed his reputation as a hero. Nearly the entire French fleet of over 200 ships was destroyed. There was "more blood than water", wrote one chronicler, who went on to say that if the fish who devoured the dead could talk, they would "have spoken fluent French". Edward tried to force the French into a land battle, but King Philip refused to fight. In desperation, Edward challenged Philip to single combat but that, too, was turned down.

Three months after Sluys, Edward, who had run out of money to pay his troops, reluctantly agreed to a truce, and returned to England. He angrily fired officials whom he accused of withholding funds needed to continue the fight against France. His despotic behaviour nearly provoked a rebellion, but Edward showed that he had learned from the mistakes of his ancestors and backed down.

It took six years for him to organize and finance the next invasion force. In July 1346, he landed in Normandy with 14,000 men, the largest English expeditionary force of the Hundred Years War to sail to France. Most soldiers were volunteers lured by promises of regular pay and a share of the spoils of battle. At Edward's side was his eldest son, 16-year-old Prince Edward, later known as the Black Prince possibly because of the black armour he wore. After laying waste to vast tracts of land, the English were attacked by a French force double its size near the village of Crécy, south of Calais. Edward had one major advantage: 6,000 archers, many of whom had trained from boyhood. Their longbows could shoot up to six steel-tipped arrows a minute – much faster and farther than the enemy's crossbows.

When the French advanced, the great chronicler Froissart wrote, "English archers stepped forth one pace and let fly their arrows so wholly together and so thick that it seemed snow." After mowing down cross-bowmen, the archers turned their aim on successive French cavalry charges. For the first time, canons were also used, firing metal pellets and making a terrifying noise. Around 1,500 French nobles died at Crécy, along with the blind King John of Bohemia, whose crest of three feathers and motto – "Ich dien" ("I serve") – were appropriated by the Black Prince and handed down to all subsequent Princes of Wales.

One story in particular illustrates the relationship between the two Edwards. The king adored his son but expected the best of him. The Black Prince, hard pressed in the battle, sent a messenger to his father calling for help. Froissart tells us that the king refused, saying, "as long as my son is alive ... suffer him this day to win his spurs".

After such a victory as Crécy, many commanders would have returned home, but not King Edward. He made straight for Calais, to capture the port for future landings in France. The town held out for 11 months, but on 3 August 1347, six leading citizens emerged with ropes around their necks, signifying surrender. King Edward ordered them beheaded, but after his pregnant queen begged for mercy, he relented – a scene made famous by Auguste Rodin's sculpture *The Burghers of Calais*, which stands outside London's Houses of Parliament.

King Edward returned from France in October 1347 as a triumphant conqueror. While he was away, King David, once more on the throne of Scotland, had been roundly defeated at the Battle of Neville's Cross. The Scottish king was taken prisoner and remained in English captivity for 11 years. But victorious celebrations were short-lived. In the summer of 1348, the Black Death arrived in England. Fighting with France ceased, and Edward oversaw measures which helped ameliorate the effects of the plague. Laws were passed to limit wages and food prices. Crime was controlled by the creation of local Justices of the Peace, who had the power to make arrests and try cases.

To commemorate victory at Crécy, Edward founded the chivalrous Order of the Garter at his birthplace of Windsor Castle on 23 April 1349. It included the king, Prince Edward and 24 nobles, most of whom had fought at Crécy. The Order was dedicated to Saint George, whom the king made patron saint of England. There are two explanations for the garter symbol. Either it was named after garters worn by knights at the Battle of Crécy or, more romantically, it referred to a garter dropped accidentally from a lady's leg that the king had gallantly picked up from a ballroom floor. He allegedly said, *"Honi soit qui mal y pense"* ("Evil be to him that evil thinks"). That has become the Order's motto.

In 1355, the French war resumed as Edward and the Prince of Wales launched a two-pronged invasion. King Edward landed at Calais in late October, but quickly returned home to deal with Scottish attacks on northern England. Prince Edward went to Bordeaux, and his army spent several months rampaging through southern France, grabbing enough loot to fill 1,000 wagons. On 19 September 1356, the prince's force was attacked by a French army double its size near Poitiers, in west-central France. Once again, the English were victorious. Among the many nobles captured was John, king of France. All were taken back to London and had high ransoms put on their heads. Once paid, the money would be used to build many a stately home.

Both the kings of France and Scotland were now English prisoners. Edward began peace negotiations with the imprisoned French king, but they collapsed when France itself imploded. In early 1358, an angry mob attacked the royal palace in Paris, killing several officials. There was also a turbulent peasant uprising known as the "Jacquerie". Once order was restored, the captive French king and Edward drew up a treaty that ceded nearly half of France to England. When that was rejected by officials in Paris, Edward invaded France for a third time.

An English army of 10,000 landed in Calais in October 1359 and headed south-west toward Reims, the cathedral city where French kings had been crowned since the year 812. Edward was accompanied by the Prince of Wales and another son, John of Gaunt, the Duke of Lancaster. Unusually, the English king travelled with his crown, so it was assumed he planned to be crowned King of France. After a five-week siege, it became clear that well-defended Reims would not surrender. The English army moved north to Paris but, once again, the French refused to fight. Weakened by lack of food and winter weather, the English army limped back toward Brittany. Near Chartres, a storm with hailstones so large they killed horses proved the final straw. John of Gaunt persuaded his father to start peace talks, and Edward met French negotiators in the village of Brétigny, near Chartres. Within a week, they agreed that the king of England would receive sovereignty over the duchy of Aquitaine, as it had been under Henry I, along with Calais and the county of Ponthieu in Normandy. The ransom demand for the imprisoned French king was also reduced. It was paid and he was released after four years in captivity.

Edward returned home claiming victory. He celebrated his fiftieth birthday in Westminster Abbey. With money pouring in from war bounty and ransom payments, the king's court flourished. So did the English language. The 1362 Statute of Pleading replaced French with English as the official language in Parliament and law courts. Poets like Chaucer, who worked in the royal household as one of the king's personal assistants, were encouraged to write in English. Windsor Castle became a medieval showpiece with the addition of St George's Chapel, spiritual home of the Order of the Garter. The royal sons were given new dukedoms, the first time the title "duke" had been used in England. The Black Prince moved to Bordeaux in 1363 to preside over Aquitaine.

But things soon turned sour for both father and son. In 1364, King John of France died and was replaced by his son Charles V, who had no intention of honouring the Treaty of Brétigny. The Black Prince became involved in a costly war in Castile. He bankrolled and led a force to help Prince Peter the Cruel regain the throne from his French-backed half-brother, Henry of Trastámara. In 1367, the Black Prince scored a brilliant victory at Nájera, but he paid a high price. He was struck down by an illness, possibly malaria, which left him so weak he was unable to sit on a horse. On his return to Aquitaine, he faced a rebellion over taxes imposed to pay for the war in Castile. Outraged nobles asked the French king to intervene. The Black Prince was summoned to Paris, an action prohibited by the Treaty of Brétigny. He refused to go and returned to England. The French king confiscated Aquitaine and, in retaliation, King Edward resumed the title king of France (a title British monarchs would use until 1802). The brief peace with France was at an end.

In 1369, Edward III's beloved Queen Philippa died. The Black Death struck England again. Royal funds were running low, and the French took back most of the territory ceded under the Treaty of Brétigny. Many of Edward's wise councillors had died and been replaced by corrupt hangers-on. The king's mistress, Alice Perrers, a former lady-in-waiting to the queen, scandalously appeared by Edward's side in public and helped herself to the dead queen's land. With each passing year, Edward slipped further into senility.

On 29 April 1376, a Parliament met to deal with the deteriorating situation. Known as the "Good Parliament", it sat for 10 weeks, the longest session so far. Started as a council of nobles who advised the monarch, parliaments had met regularly since the time of King Henry III. Gradually, knights and other leading citizens, or "the commons", had become active participants. By Edward III's time, the parliamentary lords met in the Palace of Westminster and the smaller commons group gathered in a separate chamber. Both groups came together for discussions of national importance with the Lords as senior partner. During the "Good Parliament", the House of Commons came into its own and led an attack on the Crown for the first time. It elected its first Speaker of the House and drew up a list of grievances against the king's councillors. The lords agreed to bring corruption charges against two of those councillors, marking the birth of impeachment. The king's mistress, Alice Perrers, was also ordered to leave his household.

The Black Prince never recovered from the illness he picked up in Castile, and he died 8 June 1376, leaving his nine-year-old son, Richard, as heir. The king was too weak to attend his funeral. A year later, King Edward, hardly able to talk, died with only a priest in attendance. His mistress Alice reportedly rushed off with rings she removed from his fingers. Edward was given a magnificent funeral, his body carried by 24 knights in a procession that lasted three days. When he was laid to rest in Westminster Abbey, the chronicler Froissart reported that "the grief of the people, their sobs and lamentations on that day would have rent anyone's heart". There is no question that his subjects adored him, but it is an irony that Edward, who spent most of his life on the battlefield, ended up losing the land which he had gained.

17

RICHARD II

1377-99

There is a pathos to the sorry story of the last of the Plantagenets. His reign began with some promise, but it ended in utter humiliation. Nine-year-old Richard of Bordeaux inherited the titles Prince of Wales, Duke of Cornwall, Duke of Aquitaine and Earl of Chester when his father, the Black Prince, died in 1376. A year later, after the death of his grandfather Edward III, he became King Richard II of England. The expectations he carried on his young shoulders were extraordinary. A leading church-man pronounced that Richard had been sent to England by God, and he was widely seen as the saviour of a troubled land. Scotland was once again on the attack and French ships threatened England's south coast. Three poll taxes were imposed in quick succession to pay for the coun-try's defence. In 1380, for the first time, every household, rich and poor alike, was required to pay one shilling. As inspectors tried to collect money in Essex and Kent, they were set upon by furious citizens, events which led to the Peasants' Revolt.

In June 1381, as many as 60,000 agricultural workers, craftsmen, landowners, and clergy marched on London carrying swords, axes, bows and arrows. They believed the king was on their side but targeted hated royal officials and their property. Their watchword was "With whom do you hold?" Anyone not answering "With King Richard and the true commons!" faced instant death. Despite the protestations of loyalty to the king, his advisers moved Richard into the well-defended Tower of London for safety. When a 12 June meeting he planned to hold with protesters was abandoned, rebels rampaged into London. They were convinced that their beloved king had been prevented from meeting with them. The rebels burned down the grand homes of nobles close to the king, among them the Savoy Palace, which belonged to his powerful uncle John of Gaunt. They ransacked lawyers' offices and burned legal documents. The 14-year-old king watched the flames from a window in the Tower. His subsequent action would be one of the few high points of his reign.

On 13 June, after a night of unparalleled violence in London, Richard, his mother Queen Joan and various other royal relations and advisers rode to the village of Mile End to meet the protesters. The king swiftly agreed to their demands for low land rents, an amnesty for death and damage caused by the riots, and an end to serfdom. While the talks took place, there was further chaos in London. Rebels broke into the Tower of London and murdered the Archbishop of Canterbury and the king's treasurer. One hundred Flemish merchants accused of taking jobs from Englishmen were dragged by Londoners from a church where they had sought sanctuary and brutally murdered. The streets echoed, says one chronicle, with "the wailings of the inhabitants of hell".

The next day, the king met with rebel leader Wat Tyler in the tournament ground of Smithfield. Tyler shocked the royal party by addressing Richard as "brother". When he called for ale and spat at the king's feet, a disgusted courtier started a fight and, in the confusion, London mayor William Walworth fatally wounded Tyler with his dagger. As the rebels prepared to attack, 14-year-old King Richard, with remarkable bravery, rode into their midst and shouted, "I am your king and leader, follow me!" To widespread astonishment and great relief, the protesters went home. But any sense of victory they felt was short-lived. The king soon reneged on all the promises he had made to Tyler and called the rebels "villeins" who would "remain in permanent bondage".

The next year, Richard married Anne of Bohemia, described by one chronicler as "a tiny scrap of humanity". She adored her tall, blond husband with "his face fair, round and feminine". As he grew older, Richard's baby face was matched by petulant, childish behaviour. The king was overly generous to undeserving favourites and horribly malign to those who crossed him. He would end up alienating English nobles and commoners alike.

One early mistake was his handing out of titles and land to unpopular advisers. The aristocracy was particularly outraged when Richard made his childhood friend Robert de Vere a marquess, a new English title which outranked that of earl. The king later appointed de Vere Duke of Ireland, making him the first duke without royal blood. Chroniclers compare de Vere's influence over Richard II with Piers Gaveston's over Edward II. One accuses de Vere of using "black magic" to control the king.

Things came to a head in 1386, when Richard asked Parliament for money to repel a possible French invasion. Parliament agreed, on the condition that he get rid of two unpopular advisers: chancellor Michael de la Pole and treasurer Sir John Fordham. Richard, in high dudgeon, retreated to a royal residence, saying he would not dismiss even "a scullion-boy" from his kitchen at Parliament's request. He also threatened to seek help from England's enemy the king of France if necessary. After his uncle the Duke of Gloucester and the Earl of Arundel threatened to depose him, Richard reluctantly agreed to Parliament's demands. A commission was set up to rule for a year, and the near powerless 19-year-old king embarked on a nine-month "gyration", a tour of his realm. He took de Vere and de la Pole with him and they plotted their revenge by enlisting soldiers, including hundreds of archers from Cheshire, for the king's private army.

When Richard returned to London in November 1387, he was met by demands to get rid of five of his closest aides, including de Vere and de la Pole. The lords who made the appeal, known as the Lords Appellant, were the Duke of Gloucester and the Earls of Arundel and Warwick. Joined by John of Gaunt's son Henry Bolingbroke and Thomas Mowbray, they threatened to force the king's hand. Fearing civil war, Richard urged de Vere to head south with the king's Cheshire army. But he was surrounded by Appellant forces at Radcot Bridge in Oxfordshire. De Vere's soldiers surrendered but he plunged into the Thames on his horse and escaped to France.

The "Merciless Parliament" in February 1388 moved to get rid of all of the king's favourites. The five men named by the Lords Appellant were sentenced to death. Various members of the royal household, including Richard's old tutor Sir Simon Burley were also executed. The king would never forgive the men he regarded as their murderers.

For the next seven years, King Richard played by the rules. He listened to his barons and to Parliament. He apparently forgave the Lords Appellant. As England's economy prospered, the royal court became a splendid centre of art and culture. Richard oversaw the installation of the magnificent hammer-beam ceiling in Westminster Hall. He commissioned the first royal cookbook and invented the handkerchief, described as "small pieces of cloth ... to carry in his hand to wipe and clean his nose". The centre of his ever-grander court was the king himself. "My lord" was replaced by "Your Majesty" and "Your Highness", and nobles were required to bow to the king if he happened to catch their eye.

In June 1394, Queen Anne died of the plague. The king was so heartbroken that he destroyed the manor in which she drew her last breath.

Five months later, Richard became the first English monarch to set foot in Ireland since 1210. He led a large army, which defeated rebellious Irish rulers and restored English lordship temporarily. In 1396, he negotiated a 28-year truce with France and married the French king's six-year-old daughter, Isabella. Considering that things were going so well, the king's next step is astonishing. In the words of a chronicler, England was "suddenly and unexpectedly thrown into confusion".

In July 1397, without warning, Richard imprisoned three of his Lords Appellant enemies. Within the space of 24 hours, he arrested the Earl of Warwick, a guest at his dinner table, seized his uncle the Duke of Gloucester, and had the Earl of Arundel thrown in jail, all charged with treason. Gloucester was murdered in a Calais prison, Arundel beheaded and Warwick exiled for life to the Isle of Man. Richard's rule now verged on tyranny. He grabbed his enemies' land or made them pay heavily for pardons. He packed Parliament with people he thought supported him, and was mocked for handing out honours to "duketti". In September 1398, the king ordered the two remaining Lords Appellant, his first cousin Henry Bolingbroke and Thomas Mowbray, to settle an argument by armed combat. In a theatrical flourish as they were about to start their fight to the death, the king abruptly shouted "Halt!", and then sent them into exile.

When John of Gaunt, who had remained loyal to the king, died the following year, Richard acted with a recklessness that would prove fatal to his reign and to his own life. He seized Gaunt's vast estate for himself and disinherited Gaunt's son Bolingbroke. It was a disastrous move. Bolingbroke was outraged. After the king took the risk of heading back to Ireland to quell further unrest in June 1399, Bolingbroke crossed from France to Yorkshire with a small force. He was soon joined by lords from the north, including one of the country's most famous fighters, Harry "Hotspur" Percy, the Duke of Northumberland's son. One chronicler estimates that a total of 100,000 men flocked to Bolingbroke's side. Upon his return from Ireland, the king found most of his "friends" had deserted him. Disguised as a Franciscan monk, he fled to Conwy Castle in Wales. Bolingbroke's men captured him and took him to the Tower of London. He complained to a visitor, the lawyer and historian Adam Usk: "This is a strange and fickle land which has destroyed and ruined so many kings."

On 30 September, a list of 33 articles of deposition was read out in Parliament along with an announcement that the king had agreed to abdicate. Since Richard was childless, his cousin Henry Bolingbroke, Duke of Lancaster, claimed the throne. Four months later, Richard died at the age of 33 in Pontefract Castle. Some said he had been deliberately starved to death. Others claimed that he killed himself by going on a hunger strike. Whatever the truth, Bolingbroke ordered the emaciated body to be put on public display in St Paul's Cathedral to prove to the nation that Richard II was dead. It was interred at King's Langley Priory. Thirteen years later, Bolingbroke's son, Henry V, conscious that his House of Lancaster had usurped Richard's throne, made the gesture of moving his body to Westminster Abbey. It was laid to rest beside his beloved first wife, Anne, in a tomb designed by Richard himself. Its inscription, written when Richard was at the height of his power, reads: "He threw down whomsoever violated the Royal Prerogative."

PART VI

THE HOUSE OF LANCASTER

1399-1461

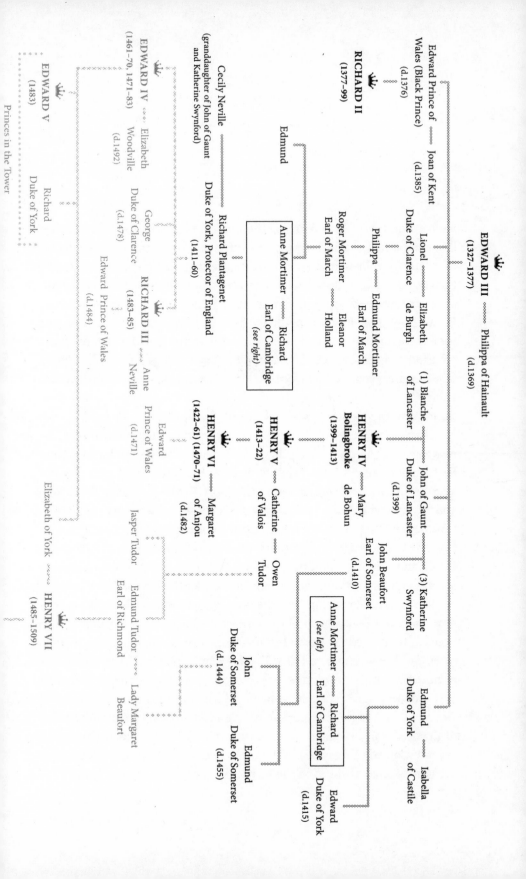

18

HENRY IV

1399-1413

Henry Bolingbroke's seizure of the crown for his House of Lancaster launched a new era in England's governance. More than two centuries of relatively robust royal continuity gave way to political uncertainty that exploded into decades of civil war. The House of Lancaster built on Plantagenet advances that were now part of the country's bedrock: Parliament, the English language and a confident and prosperous society fortified by an efficient administrative system. The system would continue to evolve for centuries, and England's kings and queens would face countless challenges before becoming the figureheads they are today. Henry IV's struggle to identify the limits of royal power is a revealing signpost to the way the monarchy would face its future.

Henry's predecessor had squandered nearly all opportunities for responsible rule, and Henry had every reason to resent former King Richard for grabbing his family's wealth. All this helped give Henry's seizure of power wide parliamentary support. But he had stolen the throne and his overwhelming weakness was his sense of insecurity. Edward II was the only king other than Richard II to be deposed since the Norman Conquest. And there were others who could claim to be closer to the throne than Henry – although the most obvious, Henry's cousin Edmund Mortimer, was only seven years old. No wonder the usurper felt uneasy.

Henry was 32 when he became king. He was well built, with a sturdy physique, and had a bushy beard and moustache. Though inclined to bouts of temper like many of his ancestors, he was a good judge of character and knew whom to trust. In his twenties, he had been a bulwark of military strategy and personal prowess, a star performer at pageants and a dependable comrade-in-arms to his demanding father, John of Gaunt. So he had no problem squashing a plot to oust him by supporters of deposed King Richard in January 1400; 22 of the conspirators were executed but he forgave 37 others. He needed friends, especially after being suspected of starving the former king to death.

This was nothing to what followed. Within a year of being crowned, Henry was returning from a show of force in the north to discourage attacks from Scotland when he learned that Wales was in rebellion. A popular guerrilla fighter named Owain Glyndŵr had proclaimed himself Prince of Wales, the very title Henry had just conferred on his 13-year-old son, Prince Henry (dubbed "Prince Hal" in William Shakespeare's plays about Henry IV and V). Under Glyndŵr's energetic leadership, Welsh raiders ravaged towns in North Wales and captured Edward I's giant castle at Conwy. Worse, in 1403, Glyndŵr was joined by the powerful Percy family of Northumberland, who had been most influential in Henry's ouster of Richard II. Indeed, Percy's son Harry "Hotspur" had earlier been Henry's right-hand man in combatting the forces of Glyndŵr. The treachery of the Percys incensed Henry, who was an energetic soldier. He marched briskly to confront Hotspur's army. It was a brilliant stroke. He caught Hotspur at Shrewsbury in July 1403, before his enemy's father or Glyndŵr could reinforce him. Hotspur was a stalwart warrior and inspiring commander. The battle appeared to be going well for him until King Henry's son, Prince Hal, the future King Henry V, by now 16, led a diversionary force against the flank of Hotspur's army. Hal was as fierce a fighter as Hotspur, and just as brave. His attack was too much for Hotspur's rebels, and in the savage struggle that followed, Hotspur himself was killed. Hal was struck in the face by an arrow and was lucky that his doctor managed to extract the arrow-head from his cheek before blood poisoning set in.

King Henry had triumphed, thanks partly to the skill and courage of his son. But the conflict with the Percys and with Glyndŵr was not over. It took another six years to defeat the Earl of Northumberland and suppress Glyndŵr's rebellion. All this military action and Henry's habit of conciliating potential opponents by dishing out property and other rewards cost a great deal of money. Henry depended on Parliament for this cash, an institution that – unlike his predecessor, Richard II – Henry accepted he had to work with. The result was constant but respect-ful negotiation conducted with Parliament through Henry's capable advisers, like Archbishop Thomas Arundel.

In 1405, when Henry was just 38 years old, he was struck by an illness that would worsen and lead to his early death eight years later. No one is sure what his virulent skin disease was. Some called it leprosy. It affected his energy and judgement. He was less and less able to campaign and his declining mobility made him grow corpulent. At the same time, his son, Prince Hal, put ever more pressure on him. In 1410, probably in response to his son's demands, Henry replaced Archbishop Arundel and other aides with friends of Prince Hal.

Henry's final years were marred by increasing tension with Hal, who complained that his younger brother Thomas was his father's favourite. Hal also believed that a burst of unrest in France gave England a chance to reclaim territory, and he called for military action, but his father was against it. The king's death in 1413 proved a welcome relief. He had been crippled by illness and in Hal he had an able and popular successor.

In his two-part play, Shakespeare casts Henry IV as a competent but haunted monarch who rarely dominates the stage. In the deathbed scene, the king notices his son, Prince Hal, who clearly thinks his father has breathed his last, trying on the crown. Henry chides him gently, saying:

"God knows, my son, by what by-paths and indirect crook'd ways I met this crown, and I myself know well how troublesome it sat upon my head. To thee it shall descend with better quiet."

19

HENRY V

1413-22

One of England's greatest warrior kings began campaigning early. The prince who would be King Henry V was 12 when he was equipped by his uncle King Richard II with a suit of full armour, knighted and taken to Ireland in June 1399 for the ill-fated expedition that sealed Richard's fate. Young Prince Henry's father, Henry Bolingbroke, landed in England while the king was away and seized the throne. After news of Bolingbroke's invasion reached Richard, he took the precaution of locking Prince Henry up in Ireland's Trim Castle. Bolingbroke sent a boat to collect his son once he had deposed the king.

Henry IV may have regretted this when he and his son eventually fell out. But the prince's precocious instinct for military leadership helped save the day at the Battle of Shrewsbury in 1403. And Prince Henry's later successful wooing of the Welsh gave his father one less front to worry about. What most divided father and son toward the end of Henry IV's reign was disagreement over France. From the day of his coronation on 9 April 1413, Henry V left no one in doubt that his prime objective as king was to re-establish a strong English presence in France. His astonishing achievement was that he was able to hand his son King Henry VI nothing less than the French throne.

Henry V was 26 when he came to the throne. His dissolute youth, which included dozens of affairs, led him to be disdained by one critic as the "servant of Venus". Kingship transformed Shakespeare's happy-go-lucky prince. As king, he aroused universal admiration. There's not a harsh word about his reign from contemporary chroniclers. He was above average height with a lean, finely chiselled face and long nose. He was athletic and could outrun almost anyone. Once crowned, he was a commanding presence with a brisk decisive manner, and he chose wise advisers. He avoided making enemies: Edmund Mortimer, Earl of March, who many believed had a better claim to the throne than Henry, was released from house arrest and made a Knight of the Bath on the king's orders. March later found himself caught up in the only major conspiracy of Henry's reign, but his courage failed him, and he confessed all to the king. The ringleaders were executed; March was spared and was loyal from then on.

Any ill feeling Henry had for his brothers also vanished after he became king. They enjoyed his trust and were given jobs. He was immensely pious, saying that God was his guide in all he did. He heaped benefits on the Church and vigorously opposed the Lollards, the followers of John Wycliffe, who despised the Pope and the trappings of the Catholic Church. A great friend and comrade-in-arms of the king's, John Oldcastle, was a Lollard. Henry tried but failed to persuade him to recant, and Oldcastle was executed.

Henry's renowned victory at Agincourt was only the prelude to his military and diplomatic triumphs in France from 1415 to 1422. He hoped to exploit the harsh dispute between followers of the powerful Duke of Burgundy and their opponents, the party of the French king, Charles VI. The French monarch was so mentally disabled that his son, the dauphin, acted as regent. Henry sent a delegation to Paris in the autumn of 1414, offering peace if the French would restore the territories they'd taken from the British since the time of Edward III's victories, some 60 years earlier. Henry also offered to seal this pact by marrying Charles's 13-year-old daughter Catherine, who was, he was told, a young woman of "beauty, grace and good demeanour". The cheeky French response – apparently the dauphin's idea – was to send Henry some tennis balls so he could play a "soft game with his friends". Henry angrily replied that he would send the French balls that would "knock down their houses".

Any contempt the French had for the cheeky newcomer to the Hundred Years War soon evaporated. On 11 August 1415, Henry crossed the channel with more than 10,000 men in a vast fleet of ships. His strategy was not just to raid French territory but to occupy it and claim the throne of France. He planned to establish his first garrison in the town of Harfleur, at the mouth of the Seine. His inspired leadership, so splendidly captured by Shakespeare's rallying call "Cry God for Harry, England and Saint George!", never faltered. He faced a resolute French garrison and an outbreak of dysentery, which struck down nearly a quarter of his men. But, helped by cannon blasting away at the walls, he secured the city's surrender on 22 September and left 1,000 men there. Since the siege took longer than he had hoped, Henry postponed further penetration into France and made for Calais. Leading 6,000 to 8,000 men, he marched north-east and was confronted by a much larger French army at the village of Agincourt on 25 October. It was Saint Crispin's Day, a day that would make an imperishable stamp on English history.

Henry placed his men in a defensive position on open ground, with woods on either side that narrowed the scope for an attacker. The ploughed, open battlefield between the woods had been soaked by heavy rain and the mud was deep underfoot. Most of Henry's men were Welsh and English archers armed with the six-foot-tall longbows that had caused such carnage at Crécy and Poitiers. Each powerfully built longbowman could shoot more than six arrows a minute to a distance of more than 300 yards, much faster and farther than the French crossbowmen could. Henry ordered his archers to plant 6-foot-high pointed stakes in front of their lines to stem French cavalry charges. The longbowmen stood four ranks deep along Henry's front and flanks, backed up by soldiers with swords drawn, ready for hand-to-hand fighting.

The French attacked and the air was instantly filled by a dense swarm of English arrows. In one minute, 5,000 archers could loose more than 30,000 shafts. The effect on the charging French cavalry and infantry squelching through the mud was devastating. Dead and wounded horses and men piled up in the mire all along the front. The two forces met in a lethal clash, but most of the damage had already been inflicted by the longbows. The English king fought in the middle of the battle. The French suffered thousands of dead and wounded, the English little more than 100. It was a stunning victory against the odds, marred only by Henry's personal order to kill unarmed French prisoners in order to pre-empt any interference with his onward march. With winter approaching, Henry's small force could not do more damage, so they sailed home from Calais in November.

Henry received an ecstatic welcome in London. Crowds cheered, choirs sang, banners waved. The king was anxious to appear modest and to ascribe the victory to God. He sent his brother John, Duke of Bedford, to reinforce Harfleur in 1416 and to inflict another defeat on the French at the Battle of the Seine. But in August 1417, Henry himself returned to France, and for the next five years, he met with unqualified success. Caen and Falaise fell within months, and he regained the title of Duke of Normandy, which King John had lost in 1204. He went further and claimed the throne of France and Catherine's hand in marriage.

It took another two years of slow but unerring campaigning before his claim was recognized and his empire in France enlarged. Rouen, the Norman capital, fell to Henry in early 1419; Pontoise, only a few miles short of Paris, was captured in June. Henry's military success was matched by the implosion of French leadership when the Duke of Burgundy was murdered by an overzealous supporter of the dauphin. The next Duke, Philip the Good, became the dominant power in France. He persuaded the feeble king Charles VI to disinherit his son the dauphin and recognize Henry as his successor. The Treaty of Troyes on 21 May 1420 made Henry heir to the throne of France. Within two weeks, he was married to Catherine.

For a man who was generally fair and generous, Henry shared one common trait with many other medieval rulers: he did not hesitate to use massacre as a weapon of war. He ordered the slaughter of prisoners after the Battle of Agincourt, and his forces killed thousands of civilians after the sieges of Caen and Meaux. It is said that he told his soldiers to halt the slaughter in Caen only after spotting the headless corpse of a woman clutching her baby. Apart from these blots on his record, Henry V's triumph was complete. He was welcomed to Paris by King Charles. Catherine was received enthusiastically in London and crowned queen in Westminster Abbey. In December 1421, Henry and Catherine rejoiced in the birth of a son, another Henry.

The last act of Henry's triumphant reign ended in tragedy. The dauphin fought on, and Henry besieged the town of Meaux, east of Paris. He was so infuriated by the staunch defenders who resisted for seven months that, in another outburst of innate ruthlessness, he had them all slaughtered. This was the unhappy prelude to a fateful summer. When Henry's queen, Catherine, crossed France with their new baby, she was shattered by the sudden collapse of her husband's health, probably caused by an attack of dysentery. After they'd enjoyed only a few weeks together, Henry died in Vincennes on 31 August 1422.

It was the end of an extraordinary episode in the story of English monarchy – rich in its military success but, as time would show, ultimately futile. Henry's masterly leadership, coinciding with French disarray, had allowed him to realize a lifetime's ambition of gaining the French crown. His tragedy was that it all came to nothing when his son, the new king, allowed the House of Lancaster to collapse in chaos.

20

HENRY VI

1422-61

On 1 September 1422, the world woke up to the astonishing news that a nine-month-old baby had inherited the thrones of England and France. The child's father, one of the greatest warrior kings of all time, had died overnight. The kingdom Henry V passed to his son stretched from Shetland to the Pyrenees – all of England and a third of France. When that son, Henry VI, died 50 years later, England's only foothold in France was the town of Calais. It would be wrong to blame Henry alone for the loss of his French dominions, but he was – of all the English kings – the least inclined to exercise power. He was pious, generous to his friends, and without malice or pomposity, but he was also listless, with no flair for decisive government.

Inevitably, because Henry VI had such a feeble appetite for command during his long reign, the names of the officials who ran the country for him stood out in high profile: dukes and earls such as Gloucester, Suffolk, the Somersets, and Warwick "the Kingmaker". Disputes and jealousies would turn these nobles into warlords and plunge the country into a disastrous civil strife: the Wars of the Roses.

For his first decade, the country was run by two of Henry's uncles: John, Duke of Bedford, a fine military commander and wise statesman, and his younger brother Humphrey, Duke of Gloucester, arrogant, intemperate and envious of John. Bedford built on England's alliance with Burgundy and enlarged Henry V's empire in France. Gloucester, ambitious and pugnacious, was the dominant figure in England, but was not nearly as well respected as his brother Bedford.

The young king was popular. He was crowned to great public acclaim in 1429 just short of eight years old, and at that early stage, there were hopes that he would build on his father's heroic image. But events soon began to darken the horizon. In 1429, Bedford's luck in France ran out. The inspired leadership of Joan of Arc, whose "voices" urged her to rescue her beleaguered country, forced the English to lift the Siege of

Orléans. Suddenly, prospects for the French royal family were revived by their wars with England and Burgundy. The English army was routed at the Battle of Patay. The city of Reims opened its gates to Charles, the dauphin whose father had recognized England's Henry V as his heir nine years earlier. Ignoring this, the dauphin, in the presence of Joan of Arc, was crowned Charles VII of France in Reims Cathedral.

England's fortunes looked up briefly when it captured Joan and – shamefully – burned her at the stake as a heretic in King Henry's Norman capital of Rouen in 1431. Seven months later, 10-year-old King Henry VI of England was crowned king of France in Paris, in a blatant assertion of his father's claim to the French throne. But the French had now lost any taste for English rule as the new French king continued to claw back territory. And a downturn in the English economy prompted calls for peace with France. All dreams of empire crashed with the death of Bedford in 1435 and the shock decision of England's ally Burgundy to switch support to Charles VII of France. Over the next 20 years, English rule was beaten back, and Normandy and Aquitaine were lost.

England's lacklustre king had little influence on events around him, leaving his nobles to struggle for power. One after another they rose, wrangled and lost as they competed to rule in Henry's name. Gloucester fell foul of rivals and was executed. The Earl of Suffolk, who became Henry's chief adviser in 1434, was so despised for his incompetence and corruption that Henry agreed that he should be put to death for treason in 1450. More importantly, Suffolk and the increasingly prominent dukes of Somerset were instrumental in promoting a marriage that propelled rivalry between the descendants of Edward III into open warfare. They persuaded the king to marry Margaret, the beautiful 15-year-old daughter of the ruler of Anjou, in 1445. Henry was 23 and she was 15. Ambitious and forceful, Margaret was to emerge as the main power in the land – the key defender of King Henry's House of Lancaster against the fast-emerging House of York.

Richard, Duke of York, could trace his lineage back to Edward III through two branches of descendants. He could indeed claim to have a right to the throne. But through the 1440s, York was a loyal servant of Henry's regime even though he was no admirer of some unpopular courtiers who surrounded the king. York enjoyed vast wealth, a widening circle of friends and won public admiration for his military service in France. York was no handsome, charismatic hero. He was short and stocky, and his determination to reform a flawed and near bankrupt government made him popular with many in Parliament. His competence provoked the jealousy of Suffolk and Edmund, Duke of Somerset. They and other cronies of the king began to deny York the financial and political support he deserved. He was outraged at the loss of Normandy, which he blamed on his rivals diverting funds he had requested to Somerset's failing campaign further west.

In 1450, resentment among ordinary people at the country's governance and the state of the economy prompted a widely supported army of rebels, led by Jack Cade, to march on London. It was a posher version of the Peasants' Revolt that had confronted Richard II's government 69 years earlier. The rebellion that included people of all classes was successfully put down and Cade executed – but it inspired a popular movement that would back the Duke of York in the upcoming civil war.

Initially, York's campaign was focused on pressing Henry to accept his advice instead of that of councillors like Somerset, who he felt was leading the king astray. On 29 September 1450, he strode into The Palace of Westminster, brushed aside the flunkies and hammered on the king's private door. When a timorous Henry admitted him, York delivered his demands for reform, the dismissal of Somerset, and his own appointment to the ruling council. Henry accepted, but then refused to dismiss Somerset on the insistence of Queen Margaret who was close to Somerset. Over the next months, it became clear to Richard of York that the only way to bring about change was by force.

In February 1452, York issued a manifesto. He proclaimed that it was not his intention to displease the king, but "seeing that the said Duke [of Somerset] ever prevaileth and ruleth about the king's person, [and] that by this means the land is likely to be destroyed" he, York, needed to act. He marched an army of some 20,000 men to confront the king's army in Kent. York offered not to fight on the condition that the king name him as heir, since Henry and Margaret had, as yet, no children. He also demanded that Somerset be punished. There followed a rowdy meeting between York and the king and queen, in which Margaret made it clear she refused to unseat Somerset. The king took her side and York could see he was getting nowhere. He would have to bide his time.

In August 1453, the king suffered a complete mental and physical collapse. He became effectively unconscious of all that was going on around him. He remained that way throughout the final stages of his wife's first pregnancy and failed even to acknowledge his young son, Prince Edward, upon his birth in October. It was soon rumoured that Edward's father was not Henry but Somerset. In any case, the birth immediately eclipsed Richard of York's claim to be the natural heir to the throne.

In 1453, York acquired his most influential ally, the immensely rich Earl of Warwick, a fearsome warrior who was exasperated by the treatment he had received from Henry over ownership of Welsh land. The balance of power shifted sharply. Warwick owned a great cluster of castles and properties in western England. He was a more inspiring leader than York and could assemble a powerful army. York's power and popularity led Parliament to appoint him Lord Protector while the king was indisposed. He and Warwick seemed unassailable until – as unexpectedly as he had collapsed – the king recovered. In February 1455, he marched into Parliament and announced that York was no longer needed as Lord Protector. Civil war was now inevitable, a struggle dubbed the "Wars of the Roses", after the red rose of Lancaster and the white rose of York. The story, probably apocryphal, goes that the roses were plucked by Somerset and York in London's Temple Gardens during a final meeting before the fighting began.

On 22 May 1455, York and Warwick fought a grim battle with the king's forces in the town of St Albans. The marketplace ran with blood as Warwick's soldiers slashed their way through Henry's army. The king did not play a prominent role in the battle, although he was wounded by an arrow. Somerset was killed in a terrible tussle that ended with decisive victory for York and Warwick. The king was captured, and York promised that he would not seek to dethrone him as long as Queen Margaret was forbidden to come to London. York was reappointed Lord Protector only to be dismissed again by the volatile and impressionable King Henry in February 1456.

Three years of fragile peace followed as Margaret, with Henry in tow, retained enough support to deter York from taking decisive action. But conflict was unavoidable, and in September 1459, at Blore Heath in Staffordshire, a Yorkist victory left 3,000 dead, most of them Lancastrians. Richard of York's success was reversed a month later when he faced a far superior force of Lancastrians at Ludlow and chose to abandon the field. The normally inept king Henry had actually donned armour and provided his troops with a flash of leadership. Until the summer of 1460, the Yorkists sheltered abroad, gathering strength for a countermove. Then, led by Warwick, the Yorkist forces landed in Kent, joined up with supporters and defeated the Lancastrians at Northampton on 10 July. King Henry was captured and brought to London. York now made no secret of his claim to the throne, but arrogantly overplayed his hand by demanding that Parliament depose Henry.

That proved too much for the king's loyalists, and York had to settle for being declared heir apparent to the throne and another stint as Lord Protector. York's best-laid plans ended gruesomely when the redoubtable Margaret raised a large army in the north. It won a crushing victory over the Yorkists at Wakefield, leaving York and one of his younger sons, Edmund, dead. The heads of York and Edmund were displayed on the gates of the city of York.

It looked a near final crushing of the Yorkist cause, but the resolute Warwick was still alive and Richard of York's elder son, 18-year-old Edward, now succeeded as duke. He was as able a fighter as his father, but more personable and with an even greater flair for command. At the beginning of 1461, Edward busily recruited followers to his Yorkist cause. On 2 February, he faced his first big challenge, confronting a Lancastrian force at Mortimer's Cross in the Welsh Marches. Edward's leadership did much to win the battle for the Yorkists, but the carnage was dreadful, leaving many thousands dead. One of the Lancastrians executed after the battle was Owen Tudor, a Welsh warlord married to the widow of Henry V, Catherine of Valois. Two of their sons would have a powerful impact on history: Jasper, who added military muscle to the Lancastrian cause, and Edmund, who would go on to father Henry Tudor, Earl of Richmond, who was to launch the Tudor dynasty as King Henry VII.

The war continued swinging to and fro, favouring one side after the other. Margaret, irrepressible as ever, agreed to give up the English border town of Berwick to the Scots in return for military support. She now moved south with a large force. Her Lancastrian army advanced toward London, collecting allies, and entered St Albans on 17 February. Warwick raced to meet it with his Yorkist army. He had lost valuable time assembling his fighters and many of them were poorly trained. The queen's army soundly beat Warwick, and captive King Henry was discovered sitting under guard beneath a tree. He was released and, at the queen's request, he promptly knighted their seven-year-old son

Edward. But foolishly, Margaret and her army stayed around St Albans, with her soldiers running amok, looting, and destroying property.

It was a fatal error. Londoners, afraid that the queen would march on them after her victory in the Second Battle of St Albans, shut the gates of the city in fear of suffering a similar fate. Warwick met up with Edward of York, and they seized the opportunity to march their Yorkist forces directly to London, where they knew they would be welcomed. The result was a triumph for the young Yorkist leader. He was feted by enormous crowds dreading a Lancastrian return. On 4 March 1461, Edward was proclaimed King Edward IV by an enthusiastic throng, led by the Archbishop of Canterbury, nobles, and parliamentarians at Baynard's Castle, the Yorkist residence on the River Thames. But Edward refused to be crowned until Henry VI and his queen had been removed from power. He knew he had to score a quick, decisive victory to entrench his kingship.

While Margaret, Henry and their son withdrew their large army northwards, Edward of York ordered his army to assemble. He dispatched Warwick to the Midlands to mobilize forces there. Edward headed north on 13 March, gathering further support. In an initial skirmish with Lancastrian cavalry on 28 March, Warwick was wounded in the leg. Shakespeare tells us the perhaps embellished story that, sensing that this had dented morale, Warwick killed his horse and, with his Yorkist soldiers looking on, proclaimed he was happy to continue the fight on foot and die with his men rather than retreat. The following day, Warwick was in the middle of the bloodiest battle of the Wars of the Roses, the Battle of Towton in Yorkshire. With a howling wind blowing snow, sleet, and rain in their faces, more than 60,000 men fought and around half of them died. It was a clear victory for the Yorkists. It still ranks as the costliest battle fought in Britain. "Many a lady lost her beloved", wrote a contemporary chronicler. Henry, Margaret, and their son fled to Scotland, leaving Edward of York incontestably King Edward IV of England. The ghastly pendulum of slaughter had stopped swinging – but not for long.

PART VII

THE HOUSE OF YORK

1461-1485

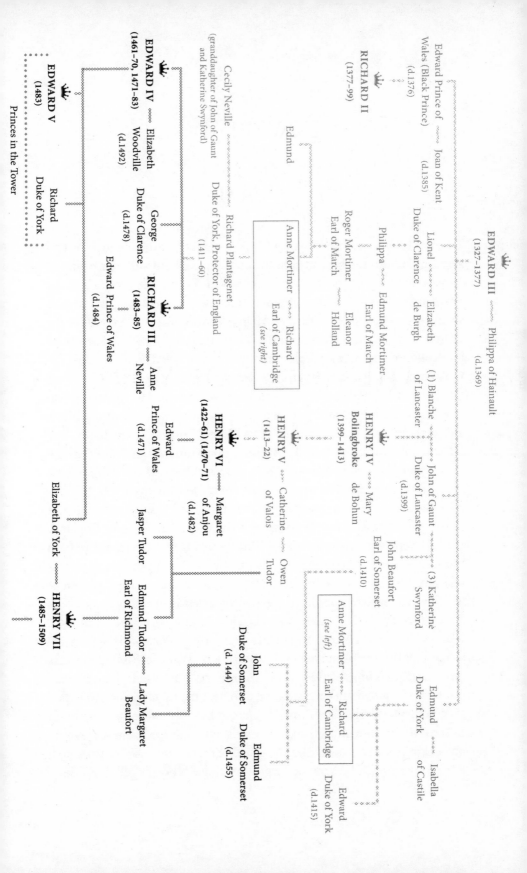

21

EDWARD IV

1461-70
(Henry VI restored 1470-71)

The new king was a fine-looking fellow, over six feet tall, handsome and assured. He did his best to rule the country well but suffered from the divisive rancour of the country's nobles, fuelled by the rivalries of the Wars of the Roses. He also suffered from the awkward fact that he was sitting on someone else's throne. Henry VI was still at large, under the thumb of his implacable wife and queen, Margaret of Anjou. Supported by Scotland, the royal couple remained a constant threat, raiding the north of England and capturing castles.

Edward IV had one major weakness – women. He was an obsessive Lothario. No female, married or unmarried, was safe at his court, although he was said never to have forced himself upon them. The fact that the king thought of "nothing but women", according to one contemporary, landed him in a serious crisis that was both diplomatic and political. His key supporter and comrade-in-arms in the victory over the Lancastrians, the Earl of Warwick, was now at the pinnacle of his power, tasked by the king with the overall defence of England. He believed that Edward trusted him so much that he would remain the king's supreme confidant. One of Warwick's main concerns was relations with France. He was determined to secure a royal marriage for Edward, which would set the seal on friendship with King Louis XI of France, rather than with Louis's rival regime in Burgundy. Warwick's eye alighted on Princess Bona, the French king's sister-in-law. A marriage between her and Edward was, Warwick thought, a wise move that the king should accept. But Edward had other ideas. He had become infatuated with a charming and beautiful young woman called Elizabeth Woodville. She initially rejected his approaches and was said to have drawn a knife on him at one stage. She told him she would not share his bed unless they married. Edward was aware that such a marriage would be frowned upon by those who judged her family far too common for royalty. But he was so carried away by his love for Elizabeth that he secretly married her in May 1464.

Warwick, knowing nothing of this, continued patiently negotiating Edward's marriage with the French princess. He was hoping to persuade the king to proclaim his engagement to Bona at a September Council meeting. When Edward realized he could no longer keep his secret, he told Warwick that he had already been married for six months. The earl was furious that Edward had made a fool of him. The wider public also viewed the marriage as a terrible misstep by the king. He had, without seeking advice, married into a family which had fought alongside his Lancastrian foes.

This was the first crack in the intimate alliance between Warwick and the Yorkists. It was to get much worse. Warwick persisted in pressing for friendship with France, but Edward preferred an alliance with Burgundy. Edward excluded Warwick's brother George Neville from the chancellorship, and Warwick began to feel he was being edged out of power. Edward unashamedly elevated the Woodville family by marrying five of Elizabeth's sisters to noblemen. The Woodvilles' influence at court was increasingly resented by Warwick and other nobles.

Up in the north, Edward's allies had finally thrown the Lancastrians out of England. Margaret fought to retain a foothold in Northumberland with Scottish support, but by 1463, the Scots had tired of her and Henry. She sought refuge with loyal Lancastrian retainers in her father's castle in north-eastern France. Her husband Henry, the ousted king of England, remained a fugitive in the north until July 1465. He was staying at the house of a loyal Lancastrian named Sir Richard Tempest, in Lancashire. Tempest's brother, John, who lived nearby, was no friend of the Lancastrians. So when he was tipped off that Richard was harbouring the deposed king, he and armed friends burst in during dinner and seized Henry. Henry's neighbour at the table, a faithful friend, leapt up and dragged the king away from his attackers and out into the forest. But they didn't get far. Henry was captured and taken to the Tower of London, where, for the next five years, he was the prisoner of the man who had taken his place as king.

Henry was not to remain in the Tower forever. The disgruntled Earl of Warwick became one of history's most notorious turncoats, setting the seal on his title of "Kingmaker" by switching sides from the white rose to the red. He threw his decisive weight behind the House of Lancaster.

One of the final links of trust between Warwick and Edward had been shattered when Edward ignored Warwick's advice to align England with France rather than Burgundy. When Edward signed a treaty with the Burgundian Duke in 1468, Warwick decided that the king, who owed his throne to the earl, had so marginalized Warwick's influence at court that he would desert him. In what Yorkists saw as an astonishing act of treachery, Warwick contacted Margaret of Anjou. In another remarkable act of disloyalty, Edward's brother, the Duke of Clarence, joined Warwick. They made one last attempt to force the king to sack his advisers and restore good government. King Edward refused and managed to retain the support of enough nobles to keep his throne. Warwick and Clarence went to France and made a formal alliance with Margaret of Anjou in the summer of 1470. Warwick sealed it by marrying his daughter Anne to Margaret's son – and Henry VI's heir – Prince Edward. The Kingmaker was now inescapably a Lancastrian. In September, Warwick and Clarence, accompanied by the faithful Lancastrian warrior Jasper Tudor, sailed to Devon with a large army in 60 ships. The popular Warwick soon won a flood of new support, and Jasper Tudor's name led many Welshmen to join his ranks. Warwick's brother John Neville, hitherto a staunch Yorkist, switched sides too. King Edward's luck had run out. He raced across to Norfolk and found a couple of barges to carry him and his supporters to Holland, where he was given shelter by Burgundian allies.

Warwick was now supreme. On 6 October 1470, he led a throng of nobles to the Tower and knelt before Henry VI, who was restored to the throne of England. The poor man must have been utterly bewildered by this turn of fortune. After five years of captivity, he was described as "a mere shadow". He had just seven months to live.

Then, Warwick overplayed his hand. He tried and failed to persuade Parliament to start a war against Burgundy. He grew steadily less popular and, within months, faced invasion by a reinvigorated Edward IV, who was backed by the power of Burgundy. Edward landed in Yorkshire on 14 March 1471, determined to re-establish his power once and for all. His return proved popular, and his army swelled as he moved down through the Midlands. Warwick did not have the forces to confront him. He hoped to be joined by Queen Margaret, who proved in no hurry to land with her own force from France. She wanted to be sure of Warwick's success before she arrived; bad weather also held her up in the Channel. Worse, Edward's brother, the fickle George, Duke of Clarence, was persuaded by another brother, crafty Richard of Gloucester, to rejoin the family cause. Edward, greatly heartened, made it to London unopposed and promptly declared that he was once again king. He briefly met Henry, who, not realizing he had been deposed, welcomed Edward and said he hoped that he would be safe in his cousin's hands. Edward's response was to send him back to the Tower of London.

The restored King Edward IV was reunited with his wife, Elizabeth, who had just given birth to their son Edward, later King Edward V. The king then marched out of London to meet Warwick's army at Barnet on 14 April. Although his Yorkists were outnumbered by Warwick's men, Edward, with steadfast help from his 18-year-old brother, Richard of Gloucester (later King Richard III), slashed through Warwick's forces and put them to flight. Edward ordered Warwick's life to be spared, but a group of Yorkists hunted Warwick down, slaughtered him, stripped off his armour and abandoned his naked corpse.

That same day, Queen Margaret landed in Devon hoping to reinforce Warwick. She quickly learned she was too late. She marched slowly north, gathering support, and was forced into battle with Edward and his brother Richard at Tewkesbury in Gloucestershire on 4 May. Her army was defeated, and Margaret captured. Her son Prince Edward fought bravely but was seized and paraded before the king and his brothers. The king asked Prince Edward why he had taken arms against him. "I came to recover my father's heritage," replied the 17-year-old prince. The king, piqued, slapped him across the face; Gloucester and Clarence finished him off with their swords.

Queen Margaret, distraught at her son's murder, was brought before newly restored King Edward in Coventry a week later. She screamed in fury at him, but he pardoned her and packed her off to house arrest and eventually to France, where she died in poverty.

The final act of King Henry VI's wretched life was played out in his cell in the Tower of London the night Edward returned to the capital. On 21 May 1471, the dreaded Richard of Gloucester entered Henry's room, almost certainly on the orders of his brother the king. In Shakespeare's play, Henry calls Gloucester a "deformed lump" and taunts him: "Teeth hadst thou in thy head when thou wast born to signify thou cam'st to bite the world". Gloucester pulled out a dagger and stabbed Henry to death.

Shakespeare's history – as always – has to be taken with a pinch of salt. The Yorkists claimed that Henry VI died of "pure displeasure and melancholy", but the fact that he disappeared completely on the very night of Edward's return to London is damning evidence for the prosecution.

It was the end of one of the sorriest chapters in the history of England's monarchy. Henry was a pathetic figure, but he did leave the country with one inestimable gift – the chapel of King's College, Cambridge, which, together with the chapel at Eton College, is perhaps the greatest glory of Perpendicular Gothic architecture. King Henry VI, who in every other way failed to make his mark, deserves to be remembered for this.

22

EDWARD IV

1471-83

Edward IV of York, champion of the white rose, was still, at 30, in the prime of life. He appeared invulnerable, with the House of Lancaster swept away and no rival claimant to the throne. As time went on, however, there were signs that the comfort and luxury of palace life was breeding self-indulgence. He grew a paunch and became noticeably lazier.

He made a half-hearted jab at the French king. Hoping for support from Burgundy, he crossed the Channel with an army in 1475. But this alliance fizzled out, and rather than do battle, Edward agreed to a truce with King Louis XI, who would pay him a handsome annual pension.

At last, England was at peace. Even family problems posed no serious threat. The king's unreliable brother George, Duke of Clarence, who had made the mistake of briefly siding with the Lancastrians in 1470, was both unwise and hopelessly impetuous. He lost a bitter dispute with his younger brother, Richard of Gloucester, the future King Richard III, over land ownership in the Midlands. He was then irritated when his elder brother, King Edward, blocked his plans to marry the daughter of the Duke of Burgundy. With the same naïve recklessness that had led him to conspire against Edward, he mixed with the king's critics in 1477 and he found himself arraigned for treachery. He failed to appear at his own trial and at the king's bidding the court found him guilty of treason. The unfortunate Clarence was rumoured to have been drowned in a butt of malmsey, or fortified wine. Clarence's timely removal had one dire consequence: it brought Richard of Gloucester one step closer to the throne.

Another family headache for Edward was the haunting presence in France of the young man who was destined to be the founder of one of England's most illustrious dynasties. Henry Tudor was the grandson of Owen Tudor, the man who had married Catherine, the widow of King Henry V. Henry's parents had been strong supporters of the Lancastrians, and Edward was probably relieved that Henry and his strong-willed mother, Margaret Beaufort, preferred exile in France to the possible danger of arrest in England. Henry, a teenager, chose to wait until Edward's reign was over. That reign ended unexpectedly in April 1483, when the king caught a chill while fishing and died.

Edward left behind a country bustling with the trade that he'd done much to promote and glorying in the literary treasures of William Caxton's new printing press, which began turning out books from 1476. He also left two sons who he hoped would carry on his good work.

23

EDWARD V

April-June 1483

The three months between April and June 1483 is one of the most tragic, shameful periods in English history. What happened during the short reign of 12-year-old King Edward V is a tale of sickening inhumanity.

When Edward IV died, his son and namesake was with the boy's uncle Earl Rivers at Ludlow Castle in Shropshire. Rivers was the brother of Edward IV's queen, Elizabeth Woodville. Her family had been promoted by the late king to some of the top posts in the land and their preferment was deeply unpopular with aristocrats who regarded them as jumped-up commoners. When the Woodvilles', patron and benefactor, Edward IV, died on 9 April, they naturally feared for their future and threw a protective shield around young Prince Edward. Elizabeth, her brother Rivers and the rest of the family immediately used their influence to persuade the King's Council to proclaim the prince King Edward V and set 4 May for his coronation. Once crowned, they believed that he would be secure on the throne.

This brisk initiative sent shockwaves through a group of nobles who felt threatened by the prospect of the Woodvilles pushing them aside. The family's hold on the young king had to be loosened. Three key nobles were viscerally opposed to the Woodvilles – Richard, Duke of Gloucester, the late king's younger brother, admired for his competence but feared for his cruelty, William, Lord Hastings, the widely respected and popular Lord Chamberlain, and the powerful and famously wealthy Henry Stafford, Duke of Buckingham. All were determined that they had to prevent the new king from becoming a puppet of the Woodvilles. That, at least, is the most generous interpretation of their motives.

Some believe that these nobles had much darker intentions, and that Gloucester plotted to seize the crown for himself from the moment his brother died. The dying king did ask Gloucester to be Prince Edward's protector, but most contemporary historians offer damning judgements about how Gloucester proceeded to "protect" the young king.

On 24 April 1483, the newly proclaimed Edward V was accompanied on the road to London by two of his mother's family: his uncle Earl Rivers, and half-brother, Richard Grey. They had only got halfway when Gloucester and Buckingham rode up and saluted the young king. Edward initially welcomed his uncle Gloucester, but soon expressed dismay when Gloucester told him that for the king's own protection, he was arresting Rivers, Grey and two other royal attendants. Edward, deeply upset, objected but, in the end, felt his only choice was to let Gloucester and Buckingham escort him to London. He never saw his four family friends again. They were taken away and later executed.

With Edward in tears, Gloucester and Buckingham expressed their loyalty to him as king and were careful to acknowledge him as their sovereign. They treated him with due deference as they rode into London on either side of him. Gloucester sent a letter to the Royal Council explaining that he thought it wise to assume control, and his assurances were supported by his close ally, Lord Hastings, who was also determined to pre-empt a takeover by the despised Woodvilles. The Royal Council, either impressed or intimidated by Gloucester's exercise of power, praised his sense of duty in protecting the new king.

Edward's mother, Elizabeth Woodville, on the other hand, was convinced that Gloucester had evil intent. She quickly sought sanctuary with her other son, Edward's younger brother Richard, Duke of York, at Westminster Abbey.

The coronation was postponed until 22 June, and the Duke of Buckingham assured Edward that the most appropriate accommodation for a monarch about to be crowned was in the Tower of London's luxurious apartments.

By early June, many began to suspect that Richard of Gloucester had ambitions beyond acting as Protector to Edward V. Dominic Mancini, an Italian diarist and resident in London, wrote that Gloucester had brought his nephew "not under his care, but into his power, so as to gain the crown for himself". Gloucester knew that once Edward was crowned, his reign would be unchallengeable. He began to suspect that some of his previously reliable henchmen, like Lord Hastings, were too loyal to young Edward to support any move to supplant him.

In the Tower on 13 June, Gloucester staged an astonishingly savage piece of theatre. He called together his top magnates, including the unsuspecting Hastings. He then coolly asked Hastings what should be done with someone plotting the destruction of the king's Protector. Hastings replied that anyone doing something so frightful should be severely punished. Gloucester then leapt up and accused Hastings of treachery. "By Saint Paul," shouted Gloucester, "I will not to dinner till I see thy head off". The wretched Hastings was removed by the guards and instantly beheaded for putting loyalty to the king before his friendship with Gloucester.

No sooner had Gloucester disposed of Hastings than he dismissed all the beleaguered young king's loyal staff from the royal apartments and replaced them with his own men. One of the last of Edward's servants to be removed said that he left the boy deeply distressed and in prayer, believing that he was about to die.

Richard of Gloucester now quickened his pace. The coronation was still set for the next week. The king's younger brother, Richard of York, remained in sanctuary with his mother at Westminster, and Gloucester worked to separate them. When the queen refused to part with the nine-year-old lad, Gloucester sent the Archbishop of Canterbury to persuade her. The cleric told her as gently as he could that the child would be perfectly safe and Elizabeth, only partly trusting him, complied. She had little choice, knowing that Gloucester would use force to snatch her son from her if necessary. By 16 June, both the king and his brother were in Richard's power, locked up in the Tower, away from public gaze.

Richard postponed Edward's coronation until November and then made another outrageous move. He spread rumours that his brother King Edward IV had not been legally married to Elizabeth and so their sons – the princes in the Tower – were illegitimate. It was a relatively simple step from here for the Duke of Buckingham to appeal to the people of London on 22 June to accept that neither Edward V nor his brother had a legal right to the succession, and that therefore the person next in line, the dead king's brother, the Duke of Gloucester, should be proclaimed King Richard III.

Two days later, Buckingham made a wider appeal to a gathering of lords and commoners who had come to London expecting to attend Edward V's coronation. The duke's words, embellished with extravagant praise for Gloucester, left his audiences spellbound with surprise and disgust. They were powerless to express any serious opposition because Gloucester had summoned a large armed force to London to hammer home his claim. On 26 June, he allowed himself to be persuaded – with a feigned show of reluctance – to accept the crown of England. Richard III's reign had begun. Edward and his brother were never seen again.

What happened to them is lost in the fog of legend, rumour and counter-rumour. Few doubt that Richard ordered the two boys murdered in the Tower. This was certainly the view of most contemporary chroniclers and, unsurprisingly, of later Tudor writers, who had good reason to want to discredit the previous Yorkist regime.

Accounts of how the boys died vary. Most claim that the princes were suffocated, and their bodies buried deep in the stonework of the Tower. Some write that the bodies were thrown into the River Thames, at sea or elsewhere. We believe the likeliest account is that of Thomas More, a man of such intellectual integrity that he probably preferred truth to Tudor anti-Yorkist propaganda. His detailed account states that King Richard told a trusted knight, Sir James Tyrell, to kill the princes. Tyrell arranged for two brawny ruffians – John Dighton, who More describes as "a big broad square strong knave", and Miles Forrest – to visit the brothers' cell at midnight. The two men silently crept up on them and "suddenly … so bewrapped them and entangled them keeping down by force the featherbed and pillows hard unto their mouths, that within a while smoored [smothered] and stifled, their breath failing, they gave up to God". The two murderers then called in Tyrell, who ordered them to hide the bodies at the foot of the staircase.

This account draws credence from evidence that emerged in 1674. A wooden chest containing the skeletons of two children was discovered buried beneath a stone staircase in the Tower. The skeletons were reinterred but later recovered on the orders of King George V in 1933. They were pronounced by experts to be the remains of two children – their sex could not be identified – of around the ages of King Edward V, and Richard, Duke of York when they disappeared.

24

RICHARD III

1483-85

Richard of Gloucester has a strong claim to be one of the English monarchy's worst villains. Whatever his committed supporters, the Ricardians, and others who discern some noble qualities in him say, his actions in securing the throne for himself by organizing the detention, disappearance and, though it cannot be proved, the probable murder of the rightful 12-year-old king and his younger brother are – to us – indefensible. Historians today rightly point out that Shakespeare's image of a devilish hunchback is a grossly exaggerated piece of theatre, echoing the Tudors' drive to blacken the name of the man from whom they stole the throne. Richard was a man of great physical courage and his brief Parliament of 1484 revealed his awareness of the need for legal reform. But in his personal exercise of power Richard III was a malevolent tyrant.

Richard of Gloucester spent the first 31 of his nearly 33-year life admired for his competence, piety and loyalty to his brother, King Edward IV. He was an effective military commander in the Scottish campaign of 1480 to 1482. He was no more ambitious or self-serving than other English aristocrats in building up his wealth and power. But once Edward IV was dead, the evidence from a whole range of sources – and not just the ones who may have had an interest in discrediting him – is that he spared no scruple in deposing his nephew, King Edward V.

Whether or not the two young princes, Edward and his brother Richard, were killed on Richard's orders, we shall probably never know for sure, but it does look very likely. They disappeared without trace within weeks of King Richard III's coronation on 6 July 1483, and he did nothing to investigate or explain. And in the violent world of medieval England it is hardly surprising that a man with Richard's uneasy claim to the throne could have reigned securely with the two princes still alive, a powerful focus for discontent. Henry IV and Edward IV made short work of their deposed predecessors.

From the time of his coronation, Richard III was deeply unpopular. Most believed the man who had been named Protector of the boy king seized the crown for himself. Although Richard maintained the loyalty of supporters in the north and some other nobles whom he was careful to reward, he had too few followers to counter mounting disaffection. And there was plenty of that.

It began with a failed plot to rescue the princes in the Tower and intensified when Margaret Beaufort began energetically pressing the case for her son Henry Tudor's right to the throne. His Lancastrian sympathies had made him seek refuge in Brittany while the Yorkist Edward IV was on the throne. Henry Tudor could trace his lineage back in two ways to the royal line. Henry's mother was Edward III's great-great-granddaughter, and his paternal grandfather had married Catherine of Valois, the widow of King Henry V. This was hardly a convincing claim to Richard III's throne but added to the rumour that Richard had murdered the two princes, Margaret Beaufort believed it would be enough to encourage rebellion. She was a forceful and persuasive woman and was delighted when Henry Stafford, Duke of Buckingham, threw his weight behind her son, Henry Tudor.

In August 1483, Buckingham, now apparently outraged by rumours that two princes that he'd helped to disentitle had actually been murdered, began gathering support for an invasion by Henry Tudor. Henry's first plan to unseat Richard was to use Buckingham's break with the king to land in England and join the duke's rebellion. But the unpopular Buckingham had failed to win support and was captured hiding in a farmhouse, disguised as a peasant. King Richard ordered his beheading in Salisbury on 2 November. Henry Tudor's ships returned to Brittany.

Richard now made an abortive attempt to have his Tudor enemy captured and brought to England. But Henry fled from Brittany to France, where he was received enthusiastically by King Charles VIII, no friend of the Yorkists.

In the course of 1484, it became clear that it was only a matter of time before Henry Tudor's army invaded. There was increased popular sympathy for him, reinforced by his promise that once king he would marry Princess Elizabeth of York, daughter of Edward IV and Elizabeth Woodville, in order to end the York/Lancaster divide. The same idea had occurred to King Richard. In order to pre-empt Henry Tudor, he too began to pursue Elizabeth of York. There were reports that Richard seduced her and persuaded her to marry him once his wife, Anne Neville, succumbed to the serious illness that threatened her life. Some said Richard had Anne poisoned in order to clear the way for a marriage that would have put his right to the throne beyond dispute. But when Anne died in March 1485, whispers that Richard had killed her became so rife that the king announced he had no intention of marrying Elizabeth who now wanted nothing to do with Richard. She waited – in hope – for the other man who had pledged himself to her: Henry Tudor.

She didn't have to wait long. Henry's determination to invade was hastened by reports of King Richard's plans to marry Elizabeth. He sailed from Harfleur on 1 August 1485, landed at Milford Haven in Wales six days later and, gathering support from his natural Tudor allies in Wales, was in Shrewsbury by 15 August. The king was in Nottingham when he received news of the Tudor landing. He immediately sought help from his allies in the north of England, and the two armies clashed at Bosworth Field, near Leicester, on 22 August. Richard's force was larger than Henry Tudor's but far less reliable.

When the battle started, the forces of two grand families on which Richard was counting, the Stanleys and the Percys, stayed off the field until they could see who was winning. At the last moment, they joined Henry Tudor, and Richard's troops were defeated. The king demonstrated his undoubted bravery by making one last charge straight at Henry's banner. He was about to tackle Henry himself when he was cut down, still wearing his coronet. His battered body was buried at the church at Greyfriars in Leicester and discovered beneath a modern car park there in September 2012. It was carefully examined, identified as Richard's and reburied in Leicester Cathedral in 2015. The body's spine was slightly bent, suggesting an ailment known as scoliosis, which may explain why he was said to have walked with one shoulder higher than the other. Shakespeare may have been putting drama before truth when he has Richard describing himself as "deformed, unfinished ... lame and unfashionable". What is not in doubt is that he was one of England's least attractive monarchs.

PART VIII

THE HOUSE OF TUDOR

1485-1603

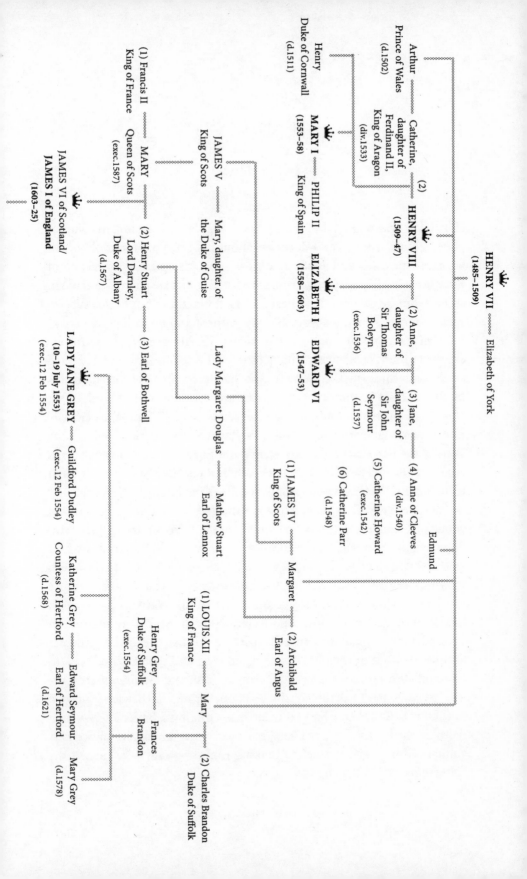

25

HENRY VII

1485-1509

Henry VII was indeed the "dark prince" that Francis Bacon, his biographer, depicts. There was a darkness about his grim paranoid obsession with conspiracies and plots to unseat him. The glamorous victor of Bosworth, unifier of the two roses, declined into a suspicious and mean recluse. But he gave England peace and left his illustrious Tudor successors a country which enjoyed able government and budding prosperity.

Henry's problem was that, like Henry IV, his seizure of the throne exposed him to challengers who questioned his legitimacy. The new king owed everything to the woman who had prompted his rebellion: his mother, the single-minded Margaret Beaufort, widow of Edmund Tudor. She was a Lancastrian, but she urged her son to marry a Yorkist, specifically Elizabeth, daughter of King Edward IV. It would, they both hoped, put the Wars of the Roses behind them. Henry and Elizabeth came to adore each other, and he was devastated by her death in 1503. They had seven children including Prince Henry, who would become King Henry VIII in 1509.

But Henry VII's neat marriage of the red and white roses was not enough to deter plotters who would haunt him for more than two decades. The first was Lambert Simnel, a 10-year-old boy from Oxford who claimed to be the Earl of Warwick. Henry had locked up the youth who was the real Warwick in the Tower as a precautionary measure when he became king. After a rumour that young Warwick had died in the Tower, a group of conspirators claimed he'd escaped in the person of Simnel and joined up with a disgruntled Yorkist, the Earl of Lincoln. Simnel travelled to Ireland, was crowned king and then crossed back to England with Lincoln and a small army of Irish and German mercenaries. He managed to drum up some support from northerners opposed to the king. But Henry had no trouble assembling a larger army which defeated the enemy force at East Stoke near Nottingham. He showed his contempt for young Simnel by making him a servant who turned the spits in his royal kitchen.

The next Yorkist pretender claimed to be none other than Richard, Duke of York, one of the princes assumed murdered in the Tower by Richard III. He was Perkin Warbeck and was actually Dutch. His claim seemed so plausible that it convinced several Yorkist nobles, including Sir William Stanley, who had switched to Henry's side at Bosworth and helped to clinch the defeat of Richard III. That did not stop Henry having him and other conspirators beheaded. The king's army finally outsmarted Warbeck's and he was sent to the Tower and hanged in 1499.

Another unlucky victim of Henry's anxiety was Edward, Earl of Warwick, who'd been kept locked up in the Tower since Edward's early teens. He was walked up Tower Hill and beheaded just a week after Warbeck's hanging. It was a shameful act on the king's part, since Warwick's only crime was that he was the last of the Yorkist Plantagenets. Henry didn't feel secure until he had secured the arrest of Lincoln's brother the Earl of Suffolk, who was eventually beheaded by Henry VIII in 1513. The Yorkist threat to the Tudors cast a long shadow.

Henry's reign was also marked by some productive moves. Like all medieval monarchs, his diplomacy was in large part energized by foreign marriages. He sealed friendship with King Ferdinand and Queen Isabella of Spain by inviting them to betroth their daughter Catherine of Aragon to his eldest son, Prince Arthur. When Arthur died in 1502, the widowed Catherine went on to marry Arthur's brother and the king's second son, Prince Henry, just two months after he was crowned King Henry VIII in 1509. Henry VII also suggested that his daughter Princess Mary marry the Habsburg heir, Charles of Ghent. These gestures helped to ensure that, apart from a brief military adventure in France, Henry kept England at peace. The Spanish ambassador in London wrote that England had never been so "tranquil and obedient".

From 1502, Henry VII's health declined. It is sobering to write today that the most privileged man in England struggled to survive diseases like smallpox and tuberculosis. Henry had TB and, while more fortunate than many of his forebears, he began to fade at the age of 45. For seven years, he grew physically weaker, shattered by the loss of his son Prince Arthur and his own devoted wife, Elizabeth, within months of each other. At least he could derive some cheer from the exuberance of Prince Henry, who was showing all the signs of emerging as a lively and able successor.

Henry VII's England was a nation in transition. The feudal system was being replaced by a fast-evolving society where increasing numbers of people were "yeomen", independent from the overlords who'd been their "masters". More people than ever before owned or rented property and shared in the fruits of booming trade and local industry. Wool and textiles were just one field in which England was a major international player. And for much of this growing prosperity, Henry could claim credit. The king created a so-called Star Chamber, which became a sort of Supreme Court that reinforced the rule of law. The anarchy, incompetence, and greed of baronial-run England of the fifteenth century was being swept away by capable administrators appointed on merit rather than rank. Henry's court boasted shrewd, talented managers like John Morton and Reginald Bray, a development continued by Henry VIII, with Thomas More and Thomas Cromwell.

Morton's judicious running of the economy was replaced after his death in 1500 by two men Henry trusted to extort every penny of tax out of as many people as possible. Richard Empson and Edmund Dudley tightened the screws of taxation and fines with a greed and heartlessness that saw their reputation and the popularity of the king, huddled away in his privy chamber, sink to an all-time low by the time of Henry's death in 1509.

Whatever his subjects felt about Henry, he left a sumptuous royal exchequer for his successor, Henry VIII. The chapel which Henry VII built to house his and Elizabeth's tomb in Westminster Abbey is another of the glories of Perpendicular architecture. As England emerged from the Middle Ages under King Henry VII, its horizons were expanded by adventurers like the Cabots, father and son, who discovered Canada and its art and thought inspired by the Italian Renaissance. The son of the "dark prince" would inherit an England bursting with vitality and opportunity.

26

HENRY VIII

1509-47

No single monarch glares at us out of history as intensely as Henry VIII. He is the big beast of the English monarchy. He made an impact on the country as telling as that of King Alfred the Great, seven centuries earlier. But Alfred is remembered as "Great" not only for what he did for England, but also for his personal integrity. Henry VIII will never be called "the Great". The evil he did was as great as the good. During his nearly 40 years on the throne, we see two Henrys: first, an athletic, immensely popular and generous young king, and by the end, a corpulent tyrant.

Henry's early years promised a reign that would outshine all others. He was well educated by an enthusiastic tutor named John Skelton, who made the young prince fluent in French and Latin. Henry's studious vitality impressed the Dutch scholar Desiderius Erasmus when he visited London, and the young lawyer and intellectual Thomas More became a friend of the prince. Henry's energy was infectious. He loved tennis, archery and, most of all, jousting. He made a name for himself as a fine horseman and star of the festive tournaments. He thought nothing of donning armour and charging at opponents in the lists. His family worried about the gusto with which he threw himself into things. He was boisterous, an extrovert and full of mischievous charm. At the wedding celebrations of his elder brother Arthur, who was the apple of his father's eye, 10-year-old Prince Henry stole the show by tearing off his plush jacket and performing a wild dance with his sister Margaret. Six months later, tragedy struck when Prince Arthur, heir to the throne, died, leaving his 16-year-old wife, the winsome Catherine of Aragon, a widow. Prince Henry's father, Henry VII, betrothed her to young Henry, anxious to maintain the valuable link with the Spanish royal family. A dispensation procured from the Pope allowed them to marry.

Henry was 17 when his father died in 1509. He was welcomed as a joyful contrast to the austere Henry VII. The new king quickly removed his father's dreaded tax collectors, Empson and Dudley. His marriage to Catherine was celebrated on 11 June, and 13 days later, they were crowned in a dazzling ceremony in Westminster Abbey. Young Henry was stunningly different from the bulky king painted by Hans Holbein years later. He was 6 feet 2 inches tall and powerfully built. His hero was his ancestor Henry V, the victor of Agincourt a century earlier, so it came naturally to the new king to flaunt his prowess in a battle with England's old enemy, France. And off he went in 1513 and won the Battle of the Spurs against the French cavalry, who tried to break Henry's siege of the town of Thérouanne, just east of Boulogne. Henry then joined his ally Maximilian I, the Holy Roman Emperor, to besiege and capture the town of Tournai in modern Belgium.

These modest successes were hailed as major triumphs when Henry returned to England, but the war achieved little. England was still a minor player in the broader European struggle between France and its rival, the Holy Roman Empire. By 1516, Henry watched as the two powers squared up to each other under new leaders, both Henry's age: the French king, Francis I, and the Emperor Charles V, soon to rule a gigantic Empire that stretched from Spain through Italy to Germany and Holland. Each would reign as long as Henry VIII, but he could not field an army to match theirs. Charles was seven times richer than Henry, and France's population greatly outnumbered England's.

What Henry could do was bolster his navy, and he did so with relish. Giant warships like the *Great Harry* (*Henry Grace a Dieu*) and the *Mary Rose* were the forerunners of vessels that made England's navy the most feared in the world under Henry's daughter, Queen Elizabeth I. He also built a string of forts along the south coast to ward off Continental invasion.

One man making his mark in Henry's court was Thomas Wolsey, a fiercely efficient administrator and cleric who proved a genius at extracting the tax to finance Henry's campaign. He shot up the ladder in the Church to become Archbishop of York in 1514 and a cardinal in 1515. Henry rewarded Wolsey's loyalty generously, allowing him to become wealthy enough to build the spectacular palace of Hampton Court on the River Thames.

By 1520, Wolsey and Henry swapped war for diplomacy and hosted Charles V and Francis I at lavish peace conferences. The most exotic was the Field of the Cloth of Gold, with the French. It was held near Calais, with days of feasting and jousting in which the two kings struck up a rumbustious relationship. True to form, Henry challenged Francis to a wrestling match, which Henry, to his chagrin, lost.

But it was Henry's attitude to women that was to transform English history. He was fond of his wife Catherine, but by 1520, she had only borne him one child, a daughter, Princess Mary. Catherine was six years older than him, and Henry had his eye on other women. By 1519, Elizabeth Blount, who was just 20, had presented Henry with an illegitimate son, aptly named Henry Fitzroy. When Elizabeth was pregnant, Henry turned to Mary Boleyn, the daughter of one of his leading courtiers. But by 1525, he had fallen deeply in love with Mary's sister, an attractive and lively young woman called Anne.

Anne Boleyn was a dark-eyed brunette who had strong ideas of her own. She was well educated and stirred by the doctrine of Martin Luther and others like him who objected to the hold the Pope and his Catholic Church had over the Christian faith. She was also wise enough to refuse to sleep with Henry until he promised to marry her. The king's passionate letters to Anne show how he was completely enraptured by her: "My heart shall be dedicated to you alone, greatly desirous that my body could be as well." Like his predecessors, Henry was determined to secure his succession and he felt sure that his wife Catherine, now in her mid-thirties, would not give birth to a son. In those turbulent days, no king, Henry figured, could be sure that a female heir like Princess Mary would succeed to the throne, so he had to marry again.

Wolsey was now tasked with the job of persuading the Pope to annul Henry's marriage to Catherine. Earlier in his reign, Henry had been a devout Catholic who earned the title of Defender of the Faith for arguing that the power of the Pope be respected. The Pope had granted him a dispensation to marry Catherine, his brother's widow, 20 years earlier. But now the head of the Catholic Church was being asked to declare that dispensation null and void so Henry could marry again.

It was the beginning of a tussle with Rome that would explode into a complete break between the English monarchy and the Catholic Church. Wolsey tried every stratagem to persuade the Vatican to agree to Henry's divorce, but the issue remained undecided. It could not have been a worse time for Henry to ask the Pope for help. In 1527, Emperor Charles V took control of the Pope when his troops invaded Rome – and Charles was the nephew of Henry's wife. Despite this setback, Henry still expected Wolsey to sort it out and twice Wolsey presided over court hearings about the royal marriage.

At the first, when Henry insisted to Catherine that their marriage was over, the queen dissolved in tears and begged him to think again. He refused, but she would not accept his decision and, at a further trial in 1529, she passionately argued her case before Wolsey and a papal legate as Henry sat on a raised dais above her. When Henry demanded a quick judgement, Catherine made a brave and moving plea for their marriage to continue. Kneeling in front of the king, she said: "I beseech you for all the love that hath been between us, and for the love of God, let me have justice and right." Fixing Henry with her gaze, she continued, "I have been to you a true, humble, and obedient wife ever comfortable to your will and pleasure ... Therefore is it a wonder to me what new inventions are now invented against me, that never intended but honesty." Finally, she stood up proudly and walked out of the court while officials vainly commanded her to return. The trial went on without her, but when Wolsey made it clear that he could not pronounce Henry free of his wife without the Pope's agreement, Henry's patience ran out. He despaired of Wolsey, sacked him as chancellor and replaced him with Thomas More. In November 1530, Wolsey was hosting a well-attended dinner. Two nobles strode in and one of them addressed him in front of all the guests: "My lord, I arrest you for high treason." Wolsey was shattered and speechless. His health collapsed and he died three weeks later. Henry promptly seized Hampton Court Palace for himself.

By this time, the king had lost patience with Rome. The devotion he'd shown to the papacy 10 years earlier was exhausted. His court was now split between traditionalists loyal to Rome and a fast-growing group who urged him to break links with the Vatican. Those who argued for reform were led by three critical figures: Anne Boleyn, who proved a persuasive manipulator, Thomas Cranmer, the new Archbishop of Canterbury, a zealous advocate of change, and, most importantly, the shrewd and immensely capable Thomas Cromwell. Supported by Anne, he had risen quickly through the ranks and was now the king's personal secretary.

All three knew the king well enough to understand it was not theology that motivated his row with the Pope. It was not Lutheran passion for revolutionary reform but downright determination to divorce Catherine and marry Anne. So they backed his astonishing move to wrench the Church of England away from its allegiance to Rome. Henry declared that he, not the Pope, was supreme head of the Church, second only to God. The schism was entrenched in English law in 1534 by Parliament in its Act of Supremacy. Henry had secretly married Anne in January 1533 when she was already pregnant. Cranmer proclaimed that the king had never been lawfully married to Catherine and declared that his marriage to Anne was legitimate. This led inexorably to a clash with conservatives like Sir Thomas More, who refused to take the oath that recognized Henry as head of the Church. He was executed in July 1536. As the executioner lifted his axe, More said he died "the king's good servant, but God's first".

Thomas More was the most celebrated of the many victims of Henry's reformation. John Fisher, the devout Bishop of Rochester, also refused the oath and Henry was infuriated when the Pope promptly made Fisher a cardinal. He ordered Fisher's execution, together with several elders of the Carthusian order who were indicted for treason after refusing the oath. Each had to watch the others being hanged, one by one, then cut down and torn into quarters, which were then displayed on long spears.

Although he was relentless in pursuing his ends, Henry stopped short of radical reform. He maintained the celibacy of priests and other Catholic rituals, but those who hoped that he would return to the Catholic fold after marrying Anne were disappointed. He soon found the new power of being the head of the Church an attractive asset, a useful expression of the king's supremacy.

Anne, who had so much to do with the birth of the Church of England, survived only three years of marriage. She bore one healthy child, Princess Elizabeth, in September 1533. But no baby boys survived infancy. Henry grew impatient and then resentful. After she'd miscarried a son, he strode into her bedroom and callously chided her with: "God will not give me a boy." Callous inhumanity became a marked feature of his behaviour. Now 44, and despite showing signs of middle age, Henry was still inclined to be reckless. He suffered a crushing blow to his head when he fell off his horse at a joust in January 1536.

The king still had a roving eye, and it soon settled on Jane Seymour, in her mid-twenties when they first met, a demure contrast to the feisty Anne Boleyn. When Anne discovered the king had given Jane a locket, she exploded in a frenzy of jealousy. Thomas Cromwell sensed that Henry was tiring of his temperamental second wife. He moved with surefooted guile in April 1536 to incriminate the queen by alleging that she had sexual entanglements with friends and acquaintances, including her own brother. Mark Smeaton, a court musician, confessed under torture that he too had made love to Anne. It was not difficult to persuade Henry of her guilt, and she was tried and condemned by a kangaroo court that included Thomas Cranmer, who largely owed his position to her.

Queen Anne was dispatched to the Tower and allowed the special concession of being beheaded by an expert French executioner with a very sharp sword. Before he ended her life with one sure stroke on 19 May 1536, Anne prayed to God to grant the king a long reign, saying "for a gentler and more merciful prince was there never". Eleven days later, Henry married Jane Seymour. It was a happy 17-month marriage which ended unhappily with Jane's death only two weeks after bearing Henry the son he so desperately desired – the future King Edward VI.

Henry's other main preoccupation while waiting for Jane to give him an heir led to an immense display of greed and destruction. In the mid-1530s, England's economy and the government's bank balance were in serious decline. The Church, which owned up to a third of England's land, was far richer than the king. With Cromwell as his broker, Henry dissolved the monasteries and seized their wealth. The great medieval contribution of the country's monks to learning, writing and trans-lating was largely complete, and it was not difficult for Cromwell to claim that these jaded institutions had grown idle and corrupt. For four years, from 1536 to 1540, Cromwell's agents filled the royal coffers by destroying one monastery after another and selling their property and riches to nobles. As for the abbots and other monastic leaders, they were indicted for all sorts of sexual and financial abuses, and many of them executed. The most notorious victim was Richard Whiting, the venerable 78-year-old Abbot of Glastonbury who was accused of treason in 1539. Horses dragged him up Glastonbury Tor, where he was hung, drawn and quartered. His body parts were exhibited publicly in neighbouring Somerset towns and his head was stuck above the gate of the abandoned Glastonbury Abbey.

The monasteries' plight won sympathy from local people, particularly the pious community in northern England. The abbeys were still valued for their contribution to employment and education, as well as religion. In the autumn of 1536, Henry received news of a gathering storm: a great march of outraged Catholics, the Pilgrimage of Grace, was heading south. They were protesting against damage to the monasteries and the rising taxes that Henry had imposed at a time of growing inflation and hardship. The king was alarmed but played it as craftily as his ancestor Richard II had done with the Peasants' Revolt. He promised to pardon the rebels and fairly consider their demands, but like King Richard, he soon went back on his word and had the ringleaders arrested and executed.

This use of naked terror as a deterrent to disorder became the pattern of Henry's last few years. He also suffered increasing physical and sexual decline. He married three more times. Thomas Cromwell, in the interests of a useful foreign alliance, urged the king to marry Anne, the daughter of the Duke of Cleves, a state in modern Germany. Henry sent the artist Holbein to paint her, and so flattering was his picture that the king said yes. The marriage was not a success. Henry complained, "She is nothing fair and hath very evil smells about her." After fumbling attempts to make love to Anne, Henry divorced her. The enemies of Thomas Cromwell – and there were many – now saw their chance and cooked up charges of treason against him. Cromwell begged for mercy, but Henry was not moved, and the king's former right-hand man was executed in the summer of 1540.

The next few years were as grim as any period of the English monarchy. The ebullient and hardy young Henry grew massively overweight. His waist expanded from a trim 30 inches to over 50. He married the vivacious and flighty teenager Catherine Howard, and had her beheaded when, disgusted with him, she had an affair with a courtier named Thomas Culpeper. Henry spent his last four years with his sixth wife, the more mature and prudent Catherine Parr. She was in her early thirties when she married him, and they remained on good terms for the rest of his life. Henry's ex-wife Anne of Cleves joked that Catherine was "taking a great burden on herself", a jab at Henry's bulk.

Henry launched himself on one more adventure in 1544. He had made a series of on–off alliances with Francis I's France and Charles V's empire, and he now sided with Charles in a campaign against France to expand England's fragile foothold in Calais. He only managed to add Boulogne, which remained English for just eight years.

The king also reversed an earlier decision, a reversal which did much to enrich English history. He revoked the bastardization of his daughters Mary and Elizabeth, which allowed them to become heirs if the future King Edward VI died childless.

Increasing infirmity and ill health finally caught up with Henry. Clearly dying, he summoned his daughter Mary to say goodbye. He asked her to be a mother to her nine-year-old half-brother Prince Edward, "for he is very little yet". The king died, at the age of 55, in the early hours of 28 January 1547.

Henry VIII was one of the grandest and most flamboyant of England's kings. His palaces at Hampton Court and Nonsuch rivalled any built by his European contemporaries. He took great pride in endowing the great colleges of Christ Church, Oxford and Trinity College, Cambridge. His actions left an indelible mark on English society: his separation from Rome, his dissolution of the monasteries, his expansion of the navy and his respectful use of Parliament. He was able to exercise more power than any of his successors. His tragic flaw was that he didn't have the judgement to always use it wisely.

27

EDWARD VI

1547-53

Edward VI was a pale shadow of his father, Henry VIII – pasty-faced and impassive, a child of nine when he was crowned, a sickly youth of 15 when he died. But King Edward was far from empty-headed. Painstakingly educated and an eager student, he was soon enveloped in the fervour of radical church reformers. Henry VIII's religious practice had been Catholic practice, without the Pope. His son wanted to go further. He backed the eradication of any remaining trappings of Catholic ritual.

Edward's six years on the throne fell under the shadow of two powerful grandees who succeeded one another as single-minded protectors of the young king. First, his dead mother's brother, Edward Seymour, Earl of Hertford, who became Duke of Somerset. Second, John Dudley, Earl of Warwick, who assumed the title Duke of Northumberland. Both were remorseless opponents of the Catholic Church. Both ended up with their heads on the block.

Somerset neatly browbeat all the other members of the Regency Council that Henry had intended to mentor Edward and became Lord Protector. He and Archbishop Thomas Cranmer, Edward's godfather and another arch reformer, ran the country without a peep from Edward, who was largely preoccupied with his studies of Cicero and Aristotle. They bolstered Henry VIII's severance from the Pope and took further measures to abolish Catholic ritual. Priestly celibacy was scrapped, conveniently for Cranmer, who was married. Churches were stripped of relics, rosaries and all the trappings of the mass. Stained-glass windows were destroyed, mural paintings of saints whitewashed over. Emphasis was placed on the truth of the gospels. The English Bible was already in widespread use, and in 1549, Cranmer produced a new English Book of Common Prayer.

At Edward's coronation service, Cranmer proclaimed the new king accountable to God, not the Pope. Now was the time, he said, to "banish the tyranny" of the Pope of Rome and to see "idolatry destroyed". A more open-minded Edward might have felt torn between his half-sister Princess

Mary's devout Catholicism and his uncle's and Cranmer's virulent Protestantism, but the young king never doubted which side he was on. He was a convinced Protestant from the start. As early as Christmas 1550, when he was 13, he had a spirited confrontation with Mary, who was more than 20 years older than him. Edward and his councillors tried to persuade her to change. She refused, and with the forthright support of her powerful Spanish cousin, the Holy Roman Emperor Charles V, chose to ignore Edward and his uncle, the Lord Protector.

And Mary wasn't alone. The actions against the traditional Catholic Church angered large sections of the population, particularly outside London. Cranmer's new prayer book provoked widespread rumblings of discontent and in the south-west there was a rebellion that had to be forcibly suppressed. Somerset ordered John Dudley, Earl of Warwick, to cope with the unrest and Dudley launched a savage military clampdown that left many dead. He emerged with such prestige and authority that he challenged Somerset's position. Somerset was packed off to the Tower of London for reacting to the crisis too slowly and incompetently. Dudley was left in command and promptly assumed the title of Lord President of the Council. Edward's laconic entry in his diary suggests he was not particularly upset to see his uncle Somerset disgraced and beheaded in 1551. He wrote: "The Duke of Somerset had his head cut off on Tower Hill."

Somerset was the second of the young king's Seymour uncles who was beheaded. His brother Thomas had suffered an equally summary execution after he'd engaged in all sorts of plotting in the court. He even tried to involve King Edward himself. Thomas had secretly married Henry VIII's widow, Catherine Parr, only four months after Henry died. He then inveigled his way into King Edward's private quarters to win his support for mischievous schemes designed to undermine his brother Somerset and gain influence at court. Even more outrageously, soon after marrying Catherine Parr, Seymour, an inveterate lady-killer, tried to work his charms on Princess Elizabeth, who was living in their house. The princess was only 14.

Thomas Seymour's abusive behaviour caused ribald gossip in Edward's court, but his actions were judged intolerable when he was caught in January 1549 apparently breaking into the king's rooms at Hampton Court. He was executed for high treason two months later.

The Seymours' deaths opened the way for John Dudley, the self-appointed Duke of Northumberland, to wield unchallenged power. With the king an enthusiastic teenage spectator, Northumberland and Cranmer pressed home their vigorous campaign against the Catholic Church. They felt strong enough to face down widespread unease about their actions as long as the king was on their side. But in the summer of 1552, Edward's health began to fail. By early 1553, it was clear that his worsening sickness due to lung failure was incurable. The prospect of who would succeed to the throne after his death provoked panic in the court.

Northumberland, at the pinnacle of his power, feared that if Edward died, he would be succeeded by his half-sister, Princess Mary. A fervent Catholic, she looked certain to overturn the entire Protestant revolution, brusquely reversing all of the reforms introduced by Henry VIII and Edward VI. Northumberland, Cranmer and the whole Protestant establishment would be doomed. In order to preserve the religious reforms, it became a matter of life and death for them to change the line of succession. Edward – with Northumberland no doubt at his side – wrote down his strategy, calling it "My device for the succession". It was simple. Edward would scrap his father Henry VIII's plan, which was established by parliamentary statute and named Mary, then Elizabeth as his heirs. Instead, Edward named his cousin, Lady Jane Grey, the granddaughter of Henry VIII's sister, as his successor. She was a modest, very studious 15-year-old, already a zealous Protestant. She would certainly stick to Edward's reformist path. In order to ensure that Jane would secure the royal line, preferably with a son, Northumberland arranged her hasty marriage to his son Guildford Dudley in May 1553.

But before the pair could have children, the king died on 6 July. Edward had intended to put his "device" to replace his father's will before Parliament, but he died too soon. All he managed to get was his Council's endorsement. At the age of only 15, the terrible illness he had suffered from for nearly a year finally overcame him. Surrounded by a small group of attendants in his bedroom at Greenwich Palace, he died with the words, "I am faint; Lord have mercy upon me and take my spirit."

If Edward had lived longer, he might have emerged from the shadow of his two powerful protectors. His passion to secure the future of the Church of England and his urgent move to switch the line of succession would now depend on a 15-year-old girl.

28

LADY JANE GREY

10-19 July 1553

Jane Grey's claim to the throne was fragile. She was named heir by the dying Edward VI though she was only his first cousin once removed. Edward's action in choosing a Protestant to succeed him was an undisguised attempt to exclude from the throne the fervent Catholic Princess Mary, Henry VIII's eldest daughter. Henry had legally nominated Mary to succeed his son, so Edward's scheme would work only if Jane won immediate support from members of the political establishment. It would be helpful if she were popular with the public and strong enough to hold off the likely challenge from Mary who was known to be both determined and fearless. Jane Grey's tragedy was that she was none of these things.

Jane had been brought up a devout Protestant with close ties to the Seymour family. She showed early promise as a diligent student and, like her cousin the king, she was taught the classics. Until shortly before Edward's death, she had not dreamed she would be called upon to be queen. It's true that she had been suggested as a bride for the young king, but never, until it became clear that Edward was dying, as queen in her own right.

When news of Edward's death broke, the Duke of Northumberland, who had played a key role in naming Jane as the successor, ordered her to be escorted to the Tower of London and proclaimed queen. It was 10 July 1553. Heralds blew a great trumpet fanfare. Accompanied by her new husband, 18-year-old Guildford Dudley, Northumberland's son, Jane was paraded as England's new monarch. In a short address, she warned that if Catholic Princess Mary took power, she would "bring this noble, free realm into the tyranny and servitude of the Bishop of Rome".

Jane knew very well what a huge risk Northumberland had persuaded her to take. Everything now depended on the support of the Council and the public. It was essential to neutralize any threat from Mary. But Northumberland had made a fatal blunder. He had failed to restrict Mary's whereabouts. The 37-year-old daughter of Henry VIII, still Edward's legally established heir, had reacted swiftly to her brother's death by steering well clear of London. She took shelter where she could count on popular support – in Framlingham Castle in East Anglia – and assembled a military force.

Northumberland moved, but too late. On 12 July, he offered Londoners 10 pence a day to join the ranks and defend Queen Jane. The response was unenthusiastic. Two days later, the duke led a small force north to intercept Mary. But Mary was winning allies even as Northumberland advanced, and she had already sent a messenger to the Council in London to announce that she was queen and that any who supported Jane would be treated graciously. On 19 July, Jane asked the Earl of Pembroke, whose loyalty she had counted on, to lead another force northwards to quell the opposition. Pembroke did nothing of the sort, telling a meeting of key nobles that he would proclaim Mary queen. He then proceeded to the Tower for a showdown with Jane and her family. Jane's father urged her and her attendants not to resist. By the evening of 19 July, Jane was a prisoner in the Tower. Northumberland abandoned any attempt to confront Mary, returned to London and, in a desperate attempt to avoid execution, publicly adopted the Catholic faith. Mary showed Northumberland no mercy and sent him to the block a month later.

Mary appeared to be ready to blame the whole attempted coup on Northumberland and spare Jane, even though she and her husband, Guildford Dudley, were condemned to death at a trial in November. Unlike her father-in-law, the Duke of Northumberland, Jane showed no sign of recanting her Protestant belief. She was prepared to die for it. From her prison cell, she sent a letter to her younger sister Katherine Grey, urging her not to accept the Catholic faith because: "God will deny you and yet shorten your days. As touching my death, rejoice as I do … for I am assured that I shall for losing a mortal life, find immortal felicity. Fare well good sister … your loving sister, Jane Dudley."

Jane's fate was sealed seven months later, when her father became involved in a rebellion against Queen Mary early in 1554. On 12 February, she saw her husband Guildford led to the scaffold on Tower Hill. Minutes later, she watched his body, wrapped in a bloody cloth, be wheeled past her window before she was led to the block on Tower Green. She was blindfolded and couldn't see where to lay down her head on the block. "What shall I do? Where is it?" she cried out, and a bystander had to guide her neck into place. Seconds later, she was dead, having spent just nine days as proclaimed queen of England.

29

MARY I

1553-58

Mary's reign like that of her half-brother Edward VI is, at first sight, an unhappy interlude in a century dominated by Henry VIII and Elizabeth, who between them ruled for 83 years. But Mary, like Edward, made an indelible mark on English history. Edward VI had done even more than their father, King Henry VIII, to banish Catholicism. Mary's work to claw it back earned her the nickname "Bloody Mary". Her burning of nearly 300 Protestants from 1555 was a dreadful crime, but the Church of England, saved by the shortness of her reign, managed to bounce back.

Mary was devoted to her Spanish mother, Catherine of Aragon, and from early childhood, was an ardent Catholic. Until her late teens, she was happy, with loving parents, and enjoying all the luxury of being a royal princess. But she suddenly found herself demoted by Henry VIII to "Lady Mary", as the king, obsessed by his need for a male successor, sought to divorce her mother. Mary's life and her relationship with her father underwent a shocking change when Henry set eyes on Anne Boleyn, a forthright Protestant who strongly disliked Mary and all she stood for. Throughout her father's and half-brother Edward's reigns, Mary stuck rigidly to her faith. Relations with her Protestant half-sister, Elizabeth, daughter of Anne Boleyn, were uneasy. Both Mary and Elizabeth inherited Henry's strong-willed stubbornness. After Anne Boleyn's execution in 1536, Mary was treated less callously by her four subsequent stepmothers, and in his final years, Henry restored her wealth and privileges. After Edward VI's death, Mary was quick to block Lady Jane Grey's vain bid for power.

Her accession in July 1553 at the age of 37 proved popular, and she was careful not to press for an abrupt restoration of the Catholic liturgy. Her changes began gradually. First, she released the conservative bishop Stephen Gardiner from prison, to preside over the reimposition of Catholic practice in English churches. Next, she set out to secure a Catholic heir. This led to her first dangerous mistake. Her choice of a potential husband was not an Englishman, as Parliament wanted, but no less a person than the heir to the Catholic throne of Spain and son of her cousin, Charles V, Holy Roman Emperor. The young Habsburg, soon to be King Philip II of Spain, responded eagerly, anxious to gain England's support against his rival France. When news of Mary's plan to marry a Catholic Spaniard leaked out, it was immensely unpopular. Even Stephen Gardiner tried to dissuade her; nevertheless, with true Tudor tenacity, Mary insisted. No one, she asserted, would have dared object to her father's choice of spouse and they would have to accept hers.

Mary's stand horrified committed Protestants like Thomas Wyatt, who became a figurehead for rebels who marched on London. Mary reacted with a fighting speech at London's Guildhall on 1 February 1554. When she became queen, she said, she was wedded to the realm, put her "spousal ring" on her finger and would never take it off: "If the subjects may be loved as a mother doth her child, then assure yourselves that I, being sovereign lady and queen, do as earnestly and tenderly love and favour you."

Her words were enough to close the gates of London against Wyatt, and he was finally forced to surrender. Another rebel who surrendered was Henry Grey, Jane Grey's father, leading Mary to abandon her earlier inclination to spare Jane and her husband, Guildford Dudley. All were beheaded.

England's new queen spent a nerve-wracking few weeks struggling to widen her appeal. She now felt seriously threatened by her half-sister, Princess Elizabeth. Henry Grey, questioned before his execution, had revealed that he and Wyatt intended to replace Catholic Queen Mary with Protestant Elizabeth. The princess was living in some trepidation at the royal court in London, and soon learned she was in mortal danger. In March 1554, she was ordered to be imprisoned in the Tower of London. She took so long composing a letter to Mary denying that she had any connection with the plotters that the tide in the Thames fell too low for a boat to carry her to the Tower, winning her one more day of freedom. Her "Tide Letter", sent off the next day, concluded with the words that she was Mary's "most faithful subject that hath been from the beginning and will be to my end, Elizabeth". The letter did not stop Mary from having Elizabeth rowed with her attendants to the Tower's Traitors' Gate. As she walked up its steps, she exclaimed "I come in as no traitor, but as true a woman to her Queen's Majesty as any as is now living." Elizabeth spent two months in the Tower, looking out at the green where her cousin Lady Jane Grey had been beheaded only weeks before. Queen Mary stopped short of the unimaginable step of executing her own far more popular half-sister.

Ignoring public disapproval, Mary went ahead with her plan to marry the Spanish husband she had chosen. She recognized that Parliament had to approve the marriage and, in the end, a compromise was reached: Philip would have very limited executive power and could only call himself king of England during Mary's lifetime.

On 17 July 1554, Philip arrived in England and wed Mary at Winchester a week later. He stayed in England for a year, and it seems that he and Mary were a devoted couple. Within months, Mary appeared to be pregnant. But hopes of an heir began to wane when it was clear that it was a false pregnancy. In August 1555, Philip left for the Continent as his father, Charles V wanted to retire and leave Philip his vast empire. Mary was left childless and increasingly nervous that Elizabeth, next in line to the throne, would succeed and restore the Protestant faith. From this time on, Mary presided over the most ruthless persecution of Protestants in English history. Up to 300 were burned at the stake, some of them leading reformists like former bishops Hugh Latimer and Nicholas Ridley.

Another victim was Archbishop Thomas Cranmer, who had served both Mary's father and half-brother, but most of those killed were local preachers, teachers and ordinary working people found guilty of heresy. Their stories are told in graphic detail by contemporary writer John Foxe in his *Foxe's Book of Martyrs*. He recounts, for example, that Archbishop Cranmer, hoping to escape death, signed a recantation and adopted the Catholic faith. After being forced to repeat his renunciation in a special Oxford church service, he stunned the congregation by standing up and retracting what he had signed with the words: "As for the Pope, I refuse him as Christ's enemy and Anti-Christ with all his false doctrine." He was immediately bundled out of the church straight to the stake. As the flames moved up his body, Cranmer stretched out the hand that had signed the document of recantation and, as Foxe put it, "held it unshrinkingly in the fire till it was burnt to a cinder".

The doomed cavalcade of Mary's martyrs didn't stop there. The burnings reached their height in the summer of 1555 amid increasing public horror. And even old Bishop Gardiner is said to have tried to stay Mary's hand before he died that year at the age of 72.

Mary's husband, Philip, returned to England briefly in the summer of 1557 and Mary, delighted to see him and more than ever anxious to conceive an heir, agreed to support his latest conflict with France. It was a fruitless commitment of English troops that ended to her shame with the loss of England's last foothold in France, the harbour fortress of Calais. She spent her last year the object of growing popular derision as she pathetically stuck to the delusion that she was again pregnant. Mary died during an influenza outbreak, aged 42, on 11 November 1558 with, she was later said to have lamented, the loss of Calais engraved on her heart.

30

ELIZABETH I

1558-1603

Elizabeth I is the glittering star in the royal portrait gallery. The second Elizabeth's reign has been no less successful – but for pomp and power, her flamboyant namesake has no rival. The first Elizabeth's long reign of 45 years was a masterful exercise in establishing a peaceful and prosperous English society. Wise governance and inspiring leadership steadied the ship of state after a turbulent century. Elizabeth presented the country with a welcome pause between the rollercoaster ride of the earlier Tudors and the chaos of the Stuarts that followed.

Elizabeth's reign was not all plain sailing. She faced as many plots and challenges as her predecessors. The religious divide bequeathed by her father, half-brother and sister carried the constant threat of civil war. Dealing with the looming powers of France and Spain demanded astute diplomacy and, in 1588, the dispatch of every available warship against the Spanish Armada. Most of all, Elizabeth was preoccupied by the challenge of her gender – what to do about marriage, children and her succession.

Elizabeth triumphed because of her skill and her luck, which secured her survival. She underwent a succession of nerve-wracking ordeals from childhood onwards. Before she was three, her mother, Anne Boleyn, was beheaded, and she was declared a bastard. Her half-brother Edward VI excluded her from the royal succession, and she narrowly escaped execution by her half-sister Mary. Her shrewd defence under interrogation after the Wyatt Rebellion of 1554 testified to her powerful intelligence and enlightened education.

Elizabeth was 25 years old, walking in the park at Hatfield House, when a messenger on horseback brought her news of Mary's death. "This is the Lord's doing," the new queen exclaimed, quoting Psalm 118, "and it is marvellous in our eyes". Almost the first thing she did was to appoint as her principal secretary William Cecil, later Lord Burghley, the man who had been her level-headed adviser for many years. He would remain the pillar of her administration for most of her reign – the wise and decisive power behind the throne, ably seconded by the crafty Francis Walsingham. Elizabeth was fortunate in the loyalty of these two men, who effectively ran the government of the country. They worked with the Council and Parliament, but always accepted that the queen had a final veto. They frequently despaired of Elizabeth's reluctance to make quick decisions, but if she was slow to make her mind up, it was due to her natural caution and a preference for doing nothing rather than acting impetuously.

Even before she was queen, Elizabeth was pursued by a flock of suitors from home and abroad. Her lively charm and vibrant personality – to say nothing of her royalty – drew men to her. She was only 14 when she caught the eye of the incorrigible Thomas Seymour, who married Henry VIII's widow, Catherine Parr, within six months of Henry's death. Elizabeth appeared to enjoy Seymour's advances and Catherine reportedly saw her husband "romping" with her young stepdaughter on Elizabeth's four-poster bed. When Seymour later paid with his head for other treasonous misdeeds, Elizabeth observed that he was "a man of much wit but very little judgement".

As the assured heir to the English throne, Elizabeth was wooed by foreign princes from Sweden to Austria and Spain. Philip II of Spain made approaches to her even before his wife, Queen Mary, Elizabeth's half-sister, succumbed to her final illness. The moment she became queen, Cecil urged her to marry as a matter of critical importance. The lesson of every recent reign, he advised, was that the absence of a (preferably male) heir was a major threat to the monarch and to the security of the country. Elizabeth thought otherwise. She had watched the unwise marriages of Lady Jane Grey and Mary lead to deep division and feared that the existence of an heir could be a future threat.

Besides, there was someone she loved passionately very close to home: Robert Dudley, later Earl of Leicester, the heart-throb of her court. Childhood friends, they had long enjoyed galloping off together at breakneck speed on horseback. The gossipy Spanish ambassador Count de Feria claimed Elizabeth "visits him [Dudley] in his chamber day and night". Her intense love for Dudley was stymied by the awkward fact that he was already married. And the prospect of any royal partnership with him faded decisively when his wife Amy was discovered dead one morning at their home. He wasn't there at the time, but was an immediate suspect and, although Elizabeth remained enraptured by him, she told Cecil she recognized she could never marry him.

When the House of Commons sent her an appeal to look for a husband in the first year of her reign, Elizabeth replied that she was happy to remain unmarried and would enjoy being remembered as a queen who "lived and died a virgin".

Cecil's pressure for a royal marriage was tempered only by his fear that Elizabeth might give birth to a Catholic heir. He was, like many of the queen's key advisers, a convinced Protestant who feared that any Catholic succession would spell disaster for him and ruin for the country. England had been riven by religious division ever since Henry VIII's Act of Supremacy in 1534. On Henry's death, first Edward VI and then Queen Mary had tried to sway the Church from one extreme to the other.

Elizabeth and Cecil drove a middle course, anxious not to provoke civil war, adopting features of both Catholicism and reform. Just a year into Elizabeth's reign, her government passed the Act of Uniformity, entrenching Edward's English Book of Common Prayer and moving away from the Catholic Mass. Wisely, they chose compromise rather than confrontation. Parishes were allowed latitude, although Elizabeth expressed the wish that priests should remain celibate and church vestments preserved. This led to protests and sometimes violence from zealots of either side. The two extremes shouted "papists!" and "Puritans!" at each other, but Elizabeth had majority support and can claim credit for establishing the Church of England as a permanent feature of British life.

The queen also had to deal with a series of personal threats. From the beginning of her reign, she was obsessed with the need to neutralize rival claimants to the throne. Anyone who looked like a convincing heir could quickly become a focus for opposition. One of her first victims was Katherine, sister of the hapless Lady Jane Grey. She secretly married the Earl of Hertford in 1560, and when Elizabeth heard that Katherine was pregnant, she threw the couple into different rooms in the Tower of London. They adored each other, and Hertford managed to steal into his wife's bedroom and conceive a second child. The unfortunate Katherine died in her late twenties in 1568, still under effective house arrest.

Elizabeth's more lasting worry was the arrival in Scotland in 1561 of Mary, Queen of Scots, widow of the king of France. She was an attractive, dark-haired 18-year-old, and a devout Catholic. She was Elizabeth's cousin, and granddaughter of Margaret Tudor, who had married the king of Scotland. Their son, Mary's father, was James V of Scotland. He died when Mary was an infant, making her queen of

Scotland. From the throne in Edinburgh, she insisted that she also had a claim to rule England. Cecil and many of his colleagues saw Mary as a serious danger as long as Elizabeth remained unmarried. Since Mary's claim to the succession was strong, she needed to be stopped one way or another. To avoid a Catholic succession, they urged Elizabeth to marry and have children. But again, she refused.

Relations with Mary grew even more tense when, in 1565, she married Henry Stuart, Lord Darnley, another descendant of Margaret Tudor, and gave birth to a boy, later James VI of Scotland and James I of England. Mary's life from then on was a sorry tale of misjudgements and failed plots. Darnley turned out to be a shameless drunkard and wastrel. Suspecting that his new wife was having an affair with her secretary, David Riccio, he burst in on them at dinner with a group of friends, dragged the wretched Riccio away from Mary and stabbed him to death.

A year later, to Mary's relief, Darnley was murdered, apparently on the orders of the Earl of Bothwell, who then married her. Mary's marriage to a man of such dubious reputation proved too much for her Scottish subjects, who rose against her and Bothwell. Mary ended up in prison, then escaped, lost a battle with the rebels and, in desperation, fled to England, throwing herself on Elizabeth's mercy. For two decades, without ever meeting her, Elizabeth kept Mary closely watched under house arrest, and resisted her advisers' demands to get rid of her. It was typical of Elizabeth's habit of exasperating her closest advisers by refusing to take action when faced with a serious decision in the hope that the problem would just go away.

Occasionally, Elizabeth was forced to react. In October 1569, a year after Mary arrived in England, a group of Catholic northern earls won support from some of Elizabeth's councillors – not including Cecil – for the idea of marrying Mary to the powerful Duke of Norfolk. Elizabeth responded unusually promptly by slapping Norfolk in the Tower. The earls of Northumberland and Westmoreland retaliated by urging the northerners to rebel and replace Elizabeth with Mary, Queen of Scots. Their shambolic rebellion was quickly crushed by Elizabeth's army, and she ordered bloody reprisals. At least 450 rebels were executed in a campaign as savage as any the country had seen under Henry VIII or Queen Mary. Norfolk foolishly allowed himself to become involved in yet another conspiracy to make Mary queen in 1571. The so-called Ridolfi Plot was foiled, and Norfolk beheaded but, once again, Elizabeth refused to act against the woman the plotters wanted to replace her with, her cousin Mary.

It was another 16 years before Elizabeth's Machiavellian secretary of state, Francis Walsingham, managed to convince the English queen that Mary was involved in another plot to kill and replace her. Still, Elizabeth hesitated to sign Mary's death warrant – even after her trial and conviction for treason. In the end, she did sign it, but left Cecil to put the warrant in the hands of a messenger, who took it to Fotheringhay Castle in Northamptonshire where Mary was held. Dressed like a martyr in a red petticoat, Mary laid her head on the block in the castle hall and exclaimed, "Into your hands, O Lord, I commend my spirit" before the executioner brought down his axe. As he lifted her severed head, it dropped to the floor, leaving her wig in his hand.

Mary's execution triggered an open clash between Protestant England and the dominant Catholic power in Europe, the Habsburg empire of Philip II of Spain. Elizabeth and Cecil, both naturally cautious and pragmatic, had been anxious to keep out of growing religious conflict abroad. Walsingham and others, like her long-time favourite Robert Dudley, now Elizabeth's Chief Steward and Master of the Horse, believed England should throw its weight behind the Protestant Dutch rebellion in the Spanish-controlled Netherlands. The situation became more volatile when intrepid English naval buccaneers such as Francis Drake and Richard Hawkins, lured by the glitter of Spanish gold from the Americas, unashamedly seized Spanish ships. Elizabeth, initially reluctant to provoke open war, found herself swept along by events.

In 1585, she sent an army led by Dudley on a campaign to the Netherlands that was so unsuccessful it left Philip's Duke of Parma and his large army rampaging through the Low Countries. Meanwhile, Philip won the backing of the Pope for what they saw as a holy war against Protestant England to avenge the death of Mary, Queen of Scots. The final straw was Drake's audacious attack on Spanish ships in Cádiz harbour in 1587. In the spring of 1588, King Philip waved off the Spanish Armada of 130 ships carrying 20,000 men to link up with Parma's 30,000 troops in Calais. Together, they would invade and conquer England.

Elizabeth rose magnificently to the greatest challenge of her reign. She was not able to fight, but she could inspire. As beacons along the south coast signalled the arrival of the Spanish fleet off Lizard Point in Cornwall, the queen alerted her army to prepare to defend the coast.

While her admirals Drake, Lord Howard of Effingham and Martin Frobisher sailed out of Plymouth to harry the Armada, Elizabeth prepared the speech of her life. Faster English ships and better gunnery wore down the Spanish at the Battle of Gravelines, and in early August, Elizabeth rode to Tilbury to play her part. By this time, the 54-year-old queen was disguising her advancing age with all the tricks of wigs and make-up of the period. We know from her astonishing Armada portrait that she dressed with a flamboyance that outdid any other monarch before or after.

In the first week of August, as the Spanish fleet headed north, still a potential danger to England, the queen mounted a white horse. Accompanied by Dudley and an escort of pipers and drummers, she paraded before her troops. "I am come amongst you as you see this time," she famously told them, "not for my recreation and disport but being resolved in the midst and heat of the battle to live or die amongst you all … I know I have the body of a weak and feeble woman, but I have the heart and stomach of a king, and of a king of England too, and think foul scorn that Parma or Spain or any prince of Europe should dare to invade the borders of my realm".

In the next few days, the Spanish fleet was driven by stormy winds and heavy seas up the east coast and around Scotland and Ireland. The weather and the fighting cost Spain at least 45 ships and 11,000 men. England lost 100 men and no ships. It was a national triumph, although Elizabeth and her admirals did little afterward to reward the sailors who had fought so bravely. Drake's naval foray to punish the Spaniards the following year ended in failure, but none of this detracted from the glittering image of a British queen trouncing the awe-inspiring Armada.

Elizabeth's advisers never despaired of persuading her to marry. The last serious suitor was the French Duke of Alençon, whom she met in her late forties. Although too late for children, a French husband would still boost England's clout in the Europe-wide power struggle with Spain. Elizabeth was charmed by Alençon, who was shorter than her and spotty, but very affectionate. She continued addressing him as "My Dearest" for some time. Her age did little to deter her from flirting with English favourites too. Her Lord Treasurer, Sir Christopher Hatton, was so enamoured of the queen that he wrote her effusive letters: "Would God I were with you but for one hour. My wits are overwrought … I love you." She was keen enough on her long-time admirer Robert Dudley to become deeply jealous when he remarried. She was also furious when another romantic daredevil, Walter Raleigh, her favourite at the time of the Armada, took her lady-in-waiting Bess Throckmorton as his wife. In a fit of petulance, the queen sent them both to the Tower.

From 1585, all talk of marriage faded away and Elizabeth proudly bore the title "The Virgin Queen". There has always been debate about whether Elizabeth actually was a virgin. She was certainly never pregnant.

The last of her favourites was the reckless Robert Devereux, Earl of Essex, immensely handsome, but foolish enough to be insolent when he didn't get his way. He was sent to Ireland to fight a rebellion in 1599 and was indignant at Elizabeth's lack of sympathy when he failed. On the morning after his return from Ireland, he barged into the queen's bedroom to protest about his treatment. She forgave him, but his impetuous nature drove him to a fruitless rebellion against the queen two years later. He was arrested and executed.

By the 1590s, Elizabeth had enjoyed her most glorious years and her team of loyal advisers began to thin. Dudley and Walsingham died in 1588 and 1590, respectively, and Hatton in 1591. Elizabeth's last decade saw the country suffer an economic decline with rising unemployment and taxation. William Cecil, Lord Burghley, who had managed government with a steady hand for 40 years, died in 1598, leaving his able son Robert Cecil in charge. One of the younger Cecil's notable achievements was to lay the ground for a smooth succession to James VI, the first of the Stuart kings.

Elizabeth's health had always been good. Except for a bout of smallpox in 1562, she had never been seriously ill. In her sixties, the keen-eyed French ambassador described her as "nimble in body and mind" but he found her face long, thin and "very aged", under "a great, reddish-coloured wig", her teeth "very yellow and unequal", with many missing. Those flattering paintings of her in later life tactfully concealed any flaws.

Seven months before her seventieth birthday, Elizabeth suddenly declined. Sick, depressed and unable to eat, she wasted away and then died at Richmond Palace on 24 March 1603. The woman who had seen off so many challenges and lived so gloriously left a glow over the end of the Tudor dynasty. Ably backed by her top ministers, Queen Elizabeth gave England a real taste of what wise monarchy could achieve.

PART IX

THE HOUSE OF STUART

1603-1714

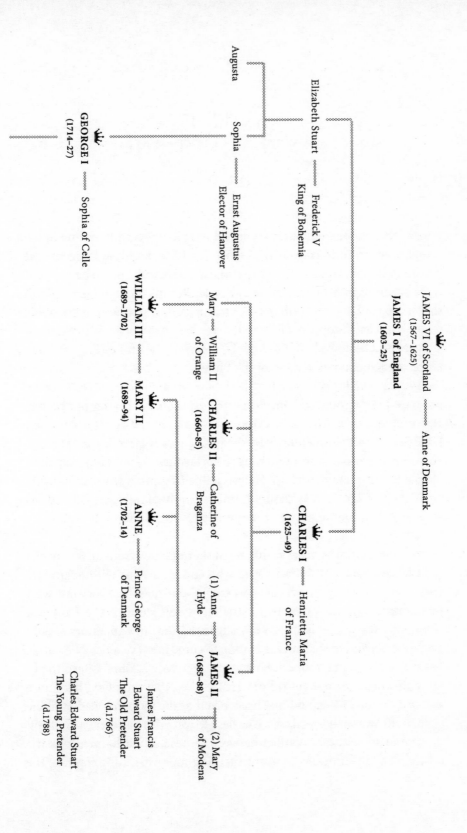

JAMES VI of Scotland
(1567–1625)
JAMES I of England
(1603–25) ∞ Anne of Denmark

Elizabeth Stuart ∞ Frederick V
King of Bohemia

Augusta

Sophia ∞ Ernst Augustus
Elector of Hanover

GEORGE I ∞ Sophia of Celle
(1714–27)

CHARLES I ∞ Henrietta Maria
(1625–49) of France

Mary ∞ William II
of Orange

CHARLES II ∞ Catherine of
(1660–85) Braganza

WILLIAM III ∞∞ MARY II
(1689–1702) (1689–94)

ANNE ∞ Prince George
(1702–14) of Denmark

JAMES II ∞ (1) Anne
(1685–88) Hyde
∞ (2) Mary
of Modena

James Francis
Edward Stuart
The Old Pretender
(d.1766)

Charles Edward Stuart
The Young Pretender
(d.1788)

31

JAMES I
(JAMES VI of SCOTLAND)
1603-25

James Stuart appeared better equipped to rule England than any of his recent predecessors. He was in the prime of life, highly intelligent and had already exercised power for two and a half decades since he took the reins of power in Scotland at the age of 11. But his inept judgement and shiftless personality let him down, and he made a shameful mess of his reign. His legacy stopped short of disaster only because he kept England at peace and bestowed on it one of the greatest treasures of English literature: the King James version of the Bible.

People had high hopes for their new king in March 1603, as he processed very grandly from Edinburgh to London doling out money and knighthoods. After centuries of crises over the royal succession, James's easy initial acceptance by the public was at least one great relief. He was generous – far too generous to his favourites – and bursting with ideas and outspoken writings. He was a fine horseman who put hunting far higher on his agenda than administering his kingdom. He and his wife, Anne of Denmark, soon emptied the royal coffers by spending lavishly on jewellery and clothes.

For the first nine years of his reign, James's government was in the experienced hands of Robert Cecil, who ended the war with Spain and tried unsuccessfully to educate the king about how best to work with Parliament. James's contempt for the steadying hand of the House of Commons was incorrigible: "I am surprised that my ancestors should ever have permitted such an institution to come into existence," he wrote. "I am a stranger, and found it here when I arrived … I am obliged to put up with what I cannot get rid of." He believed that only God had more authority than a king, and his insistence that the monarch had a divine right to rule was to drive his son Charles I to war with his own Parliament.

The major cause of conflict between James and Parliament was the refusal of the Commons to grant the king more spending money. The royal treasury had inherited a debt of £100,000 from Queen Elizabeth and by 1608, it had risen to £600,000 (£166 million today). James's failure to persuade Parliament to give him funds was a key reason he scrapped all sessions of the House of Commons for 19 of his 22 years on the throne. A friend in the Commons with the imperious name of Sir Julius Caesar gave James fulsome support, saying that if the king surrendered his prerogative to raise revenue it would mark "a ready passage to democracy which is the deadliest enemy of a monarchy".

Another early disappointment for James was his inability to implement what he believed his person embodied – the union of England and Scotland as Great Britain. Most Englishmen didn't want the "primitive" Scots diluting their sovereignty and the marriage of the two Parliaments had to wait another century.

The religious divide also proved too much for James. He hoped that his experience in Scotland of facing down some of the more extreme demands of the Presbyterian Church, while allowing Catholics to practise, would help him steer the judicious path Queen Elizabeth had successfully navigated between the extremes of ardent believers on both sides in England. As soon as he became king in 1603, he called a conference to create a religious consensus. It achieved little, apart from a bold decision to produce a new Bible in English, which proved a stunning success and endures as a beacon of English prose to the present day.

The depth of the religious divide was starkly illustrated in 1605 when a Catholic fanatic, Guy Fawkes, was discovered guarding no fewer than 36 barrels of gunpowder in the vault of the Houses of Parliament. If the planned explosion had destroyed the Palace of Westminster, the monarch and the entire political and legal establishment would have been blown to pieces. The conspirators who planned to replace James with his eldest daughter, nine-year-old Princess Elizabeth, were seized and put to death.

James's marriage to Anne of Denmark had begun in a flash of romance back in 1589, when he married the Danish princess by proxy. When North Sea storms forced her back to Scandinavia, her new husband braved the winter weather to sail across and escort her back to Scotland. It was the only foreign trip James undertook, and one wag in court remarked that it was the only romantic thing he ever did in his lifetime. The couple were close and had seven children, but James's ardour soon cooled. Anne was appalled by his heavy drinking and was furious when he denied her custody and the upbringing of their eldest son, Henry. The Prince of Wales, a very promising young man, died of typhoid in 1612 at the age of 18.

That same year, the king's veteran adviser Robert Cecil died, and his steadying hand was replaced by a man James now preferred to the company of his queen. Robert Carr, to whom Anne took an immediate dislike, was rapidly promoted to Viscount Rochester and then Earl of Somerset. Carr's relationship with James was already the subject of salacious court gossip. In 1613, it became triangular, to the apparent delight of James, when Carr married Frances Howard. She had already made an unsavoury name for herself at court when she claimed that her first husband, the third Earl of Essex, had been no good in bed. This cosy new three-way friendship was soon overtaken by scandal when it emerged that Carr and his wife poisoned a secretary who had called Frances a "base whore" and tried to prevent her marriage. James had no choice but to commit his two friends to the Tower, although he pardoned them after they were tried and found guilty.

Meanwhile, in 1614 the king had found himself another favourite, the young George Villiers, who was outstandingly handsome but had little else to recommend him. The king swiftly promoted him, just as he had Robert Carr, ennobling Villiers with the eminent title of Duke of Buckingham. Besotted, James called him "my sweet child and wife". The king largely ignored and lived separately from Queen Anne, who died in 1619.

Buckingham was a notorious spendthrift whose extravagance made him very unpopular, and as James's health began to deteriorate, the duke transferred his affections to the king's son and heir, Prince Charles. In an effort to keep England from going to war, James tried to secure a Spanish bride for Charles. Years of negotiation got nowhere, and in a bizarre escapade, Buckingham persuaded Charles to accompany him to Madrid incognito to win the hand of the Spanish king's sister. Off they went as brothers "Tom" and "Jack Smith", and their madcap adventure ended in humiliation. Charles snatched his first glimpse of the 16-year-old Infanta Maria Anna by climbing a garden wall. When he revealed his identity and met the Spanish King Philip IV face to face, he was given harsh terms for marrying her. Charles would have to spend a year on probation in Madrid and the English monarch would have to make concessions to English Catholics that he couldn't possibly accept. Charles and Buckingham returned to England with their mission in shreds. James had had good reason to prefer a bond with Spain. Back in 1613, he had married his daughter Elizabeth to Frederick, Elector of the Palatinate in Germany, one of Europe's leading Protestant rulers. In 1619, Frederick and Elizabeth were invited to be king and queen of Bohemia, only to be thrown out by the army of the Catholic Habsburg Emperor of Austria a year later. It was the start of the savagely destructive Thirty Years War in Europe, which James was desperate to avoid. James had hoped that a Spanish marriage for Charles would help persuade the Spanish to keep their hands off his daughter's and his son-in-law's Protestant possessions. His matchmaking failed, and when Frederick and Elizabeth fled Bohemia, they found the Spanish had seized their Palatinate. In the end, Charles turned to another country for a wife, marrying the French king's daughter Henrietta Maria less than two years later.

James was a very sick man by the early 1620s, and he watched in dismay as his son Charles and Buckingham stirred up enthusiasm for an alliance with France and war with Spain. A half-hearted military expedition into the Spanish provinces in the Netherlands in early 1625 achieved nothing, and in late March, with his remaining authority and influence effectively surrendered to Charles and Buckingham, King James died.

32

CHARLES I

1625-49

Charles I ruled over one of Britain's bloodiest upheavals and a constitutional convulsion unique in the country's history. The lesson of what happened to the first monarch to be publicly beheaded was never lost on his successors.

Charles was not a heartless autocrat who believed that he was empowered to crush all opposition. But, in his naïve arrogance, he believed that God had appointed him the benevolent father of the nation with the right to impose his stamp on society and its governance. The tragedy which unfolded was deepened by a group of passionately radical Parliamentarians. Their dispute with a king unwilling to compromise led to a vicious civil war, which split the country with a savagery that left people dumbfounded as families were divided and properties ravaged, often burned to the ground.

When young King Charles succeeded his indolent father in 1625, few could have guessed how dreadfully his reign would end. He was 24, short and shy with a stutter, but had a fine face with a neat, pointed beard. He was kind, courteous and had an insatiable taste for art. Charles and Henrietta Maria, the French princess he married five weeks after his coronation, amassed the most sumptuous collection of paintings the British royal court would ever see. Portraits of Charles and his wife by the Dutch artist Anthony van Dyck decorated palace walls. Like his father, Charles spent freely, and he soon ran into similar trouble with Parliament. Its members were ready to raise taxes for war with Spain, but not for the king's extravagance, and Charles soon found ways of bypassing Parliament. He financed much of his personal and national spending from customs dues and forced loans from men of property, and later from "ship money", cash he raised from local taxation to build ships for his fast-growing navy. Charles's enthusiasm for the navy was his most important contribution to national prestige.

Strength at sea was England's main asset in a Europe dominated by France and Spain. With a population of only four million, England was a minor European power. Foolishly, Charles, who had no standing army, scrapped his father's conciliatory attitude to England's two big rivals. The expeditions he sent to France and Spain, supervised by the flamboyant but militarily ineffective George Villiers, Duke of Buckingham, were a disaster. By the end of the 1620s, Charles's aggressive foreign policy was in shreds and Buckingham had been assassinated by a disgruntled army officer.

At home, Charles's habit of extracting taxes without approval made him unpopular with Parliament, most of whose members were men of property and complained that he was trampling on their rights. Parliament was also adamantly anti-Catholic and resented the undisguised Catholicism of Queen Henrietta Maria – and Charles's own inclination to resist Puritan demands to scrap ritual ceremony in the Church of England. In 1629, an exasperated Charles decided not to bother with Parliament anymore and dissolved it. He sent all its representatives home, saying he would not call any future Parliaments: "We shall account it presumption for any to prescribe unto us any time for parliaments." It was a declaration not far short of war, but Charles was wise enough to make peace with France and Spain, and for most of the 1630s, England was calm and prosperous.

During this relatively peaceful period, Charles enjoyed a happy personal life. He and his wife, Henrietta Maria, remained loyal to each other and had seven surviving children, including the future kings Charles II and his younger brother James II.

Parliament may have been powerless, but it was not inactive. The legislators' growing anger gave voice to campaigners like John Pym, one of the fathers of British democracy. He was a revolutionary whose moves to limit the king's power amounted to a call for the complete reversal of royal authority. With little scope for compromise, civil war became inevitable.

The storm broke in 1637 in Scotland. Charles and his assertive Archbishop of Canterbury, the conservative William Laud, were determined to keep extreme Puritanism at bay. They faced opposition enough in England, but when Charles tried to launch a more traditional prayer book in Scotland, all hell broke loose. It was too much for the radical Presbyterian kirk, which, like the Puritans, favoured religion without all the trappings. On 23 July, the introduction of a new prayer book in St Giles' Cathedral in Edinburgh prompted a group of infuriated Presbyterian women to pick up their prayer stools and hurl them down the aisle. Others tried to tear the surplices from preachers' backs. Riots followed, and the situation was soon out of control. The Scots wanted nothing to do with a return to what they saw as Popery.

Despite his Stuart family's Scottish roots, Charles was now seen as an absentee monarch living far away in London. He had disastrously underestimated Scottish revulsion at his determination to favour the traditional Church. Bishops, ceremonials, even church vestments ignited anger across Scotland. The meagre efforts at compromise Charles offered to calm fears did not go far enough. While he believed it was his God-given task to keep England and Scotland as close together as possible, Scots saw his efforts as denying their cherished independence.

By early 1638, this furious wave of opposition led to the mass signing of a National Covenant demanding religious freedom for Scotland. Charles reacted imperiously: "The question is whether we are their king or not ... so long as this covenant is in force, I have no more power in Scotland than as a duke of Venice." When he was told there were reports of Scots searching Europe for arms supplies, he concluded the Scots were in rebellion and that they had to be crushed. Desperate for an army which didn't exist, he called on the county Lord Lieutenants to summon recruits. But even as his orders rang out, the Scots assembled an impressive force of some 30,000. Initially, apart from a few skirmishes, both sides stopped short of war, but Charles pressed on with what he saw as his mission. To help him restore control, he called on the pugnacious Thomas Wentworth, who had earned the nickname "Black Tom Tyrant" for savagely imposing English Protestant rule on Ireland's rebellious Catholics. Wentworth, whom the king made Earl of Strafford, was soon immensely unpopular, and his heavy-handed advice to Charles to exert his authority over the Scots, coupled with the undisguised Catholicism of Queen Henrietta Maria, led to even more rumblings of discontent.

Many Parliamentarians, who had been dismissed for 11 years, sympathized with the Scots. When Charles recalled them in April 1640, it became known as the "Short Parliament" because he promptly shut them down when they refused him the cash to form an army.

Charles then made the mistake of proclaiming that he would fight the Scots without Parliament's consent. In August 1640, the Scots staged a forthright invasion and seized the city of Newcastle. It was deeply embarrassing for the king, and when he recalled Parliament again hoping for support, he was confronted by its Puritan majority, under the forceful leadership of John Pym. A series of punishing demands were made to curb the king's powers: an end to his right to dissolve Parliaments, no more royal taxes like ship money or customs duties, no more bishops and high church liturgy and an end to royal appointments to the Council. Parliament also insisted that Strafford and Laud should be jailed and condemned. The weakened king felt he had to agree to almost everything. He even signed the warrant that led to Strafford's execution in May 1641, an action that filled him with shame until his own execution eight years later.

That summer, a visit to Scotland where he was warmly welcomed encouraged Charles to agree to the Scots' religious reforms. He now felt able to take a stronger line in London. When Pym and his radical Puritans reasserted their calls for curbs on his powers, Charles made his biggest blunder yet: he literally invaded the House of Commons. Fired up by the threats to his remaining authority and encouraged by his queen, he marched into the Commons with an armed guard and demanded that the speaker hand over five MPs, including Pym, whom he accused of high treason. But the five had wisely quit the House in advance. Charles meekly admitted that "the birds have flown", and walked out of the chamber with what was left of his punctured dignity. Members, furious at the royal intrusion, asserted their independence by shouting "Privilege! Privilege!"

It was a humiliating fiasco for Charles and it united London against him as never before. A week later, he left the capital for York. He was not to return until six years later after he'd lost the civil war.

Charles spent the summer months of 1642 processing around the country – mainly the north and west – making speeches, proclaiming that he represented the popular will and asking for support for what he described as his crusade to protect the constitution and the freedom and religious rights of his subjects. Meanwhile, Parliament issued a list of demands that amounted to a call for the king's unconditional surrender and appealed to the country's militia for support. Charles raised his banner at Nottingham in August and his energy and regal aura inspired many to flock to his ranks. He soon raised an effective force of 20,000 men, with himself as commander-in-chief and generals, like his doughty nephew Prince Rupert, providing leadership with experience and flair. Parliament began the civil war with seasoned but uninspiring commanders, including the Earls of Essex and Manchester, who lacked the hard-nosed drive of later leaders, including Oliver Cromwell and Thomas Fairfax.

For people of all social classes, it was a moment of agonizing soul-searching. Some hoped they could stay neutral, but most could not avoid being swept up in the tussle for loyalty to one side or the other. Towns, villages, parishes and families were bitterly divided. Thousands found themselves sharing the pain of the Verney family, who lived at Claydon in Buckinghamshire. Sir Edmund, aged 51, was a member of Parliament, as was his son, Ralph. Edmund, a close friend of Charles, was torn between support for parliamentary reform and loyalty to the king. When Charles asked him to be his standard bearer, he told a friend, "I have eaten his bread and served him near thirty years and will not do so base a thing as to forsake him." His son Ralph sided with Parliament.

The first great battle of the English Civil War was fought at Edgehill in Warwickshire on 23 October 1642. Prince Rupert's cavalry scattered the parliamentary fighters, but pursued the enemy way beyond the battlefield, leaving the Royalist force suffering heavy casualties from Parliament's main force of infantry. Sir Edmund Verney fought gallantly, defiantly waving Charles's standard, but was cut down and killed. His body was lost and only his fist recovered, still gripping the banner. But it was the Parliamentarians who moved off the field, leaving the road to London open to Charles. His advance was half-hearted and the force he finally sent into the suburbs met too much resistance to press on into the city. Charles had blown his best chance of victory.

The Royalists, nicknamed "Cavaliers", had one or two early successes over the Parliamentarian "Roundheads", but from 1644, Charles suffered setback after setback. Rupert was severely beaten at the Battle of Marston Moor on 2 July. As the situation worsened, Queen Henrietta Maria departed for the Continent, never to return, though the king wrote her a letter a week for the rest of his life.

The winter of 1644 saw Parliament switch its leadership to the uncompromising commanders of the so-called "New Model Army". Generals like Manchester and Essex, who favoured peace with the Royalists, were fired and succeeded by Cromwell and Fairfax, who determined to fight to the finish. Together, they created an army of full-time professionals who spent months doing rigorous, tactical training. This new, disciplined force decisively crushed the Royalists at the Battle of Naseby on 14 June 1645. As the battle ended, a mortified Charles had to be forcibly restrained from charging into the fray by one of his aides, who seized his horse's bridle and dragged the king to safety.

After Naseby, Charles was doomed though he never gave up hope or indicated that he was ready to accept demands for a major forfeit of power. With no chance on the battlefield, he surrendered to the Scots in 1646, who handed him over to Parliament. Months of house arrest followed, with desultory attempts by some Parliamentarians to persuade him to agree terms. In June 1647, the army lost patience and a troop of horsemen was sent to capture him. He had no choice but to go with them. By the autumn, he was a prisoner at Hampton Court.

Charles believed he could win back enough support to regain power, and lax security at Hampton Court encouraged him to escape. With three attendants, he stole out through a cellar door, leaving two letters for his jailers. One thanked them for looking after him, the other asked them to care for two beloved dogs left behind. The four escapees rode south through the night and managed to find refuge at Carisbrooke Castle on the Isle of Wight. In one final act of cocky defiance, the king warned the Scots that Cromwell's army would crush their autonomy. This persuaded the Scots to change sides, support Charles and invade England, but Cromwell made short work of their incursion, routing them at the Battle of Preston in August 1648.

Some Parliamentarians still wished to compromise with Charles. Time and again, the king had the opportunity to make concessions which would have secured his throne and left him with much of the power of his predecessors. But Cromwell's authority was now overwhelming, and his patience had run out.

On his orders, Colonel Thomas Pride strode into the Commons with an armed guard and arrested those members who opposed a final showdown with Charles. The hawks who remained in what became known as the "Rump Parliament" voted to put Charles on trial. This effective army coup made Cromwell all-powerful.

Charles walked from Whitehall Palace to his trial in Westminster Hall in January 1649. He mocked the judges for daring to try their "rightful king", rejected the court's jurisdiction and refused to make any plea. He was found guilty, and after being condemned to death by beheading, was refused permission to say anything in reply.

Charles wrote an affectionate letter to his son Prince Charles, who was safely in exile on the Continent: "I know I shall go before you to a better kingdom … Farewell, till we meet, if not on earth, yet in heaven." The morning of 30 January was very cold, and Charles asked to wear an extra shirt to avoid a shiver which might be taken as a sign of fear. With the same quiet dignity he had shown at his trial, he was walked through the Banqueting House – under the magnificent ceiling he'd taken such pride in having painted by Rubens – and out onto the black-draped scaffold overlooking Whitehall. He was wearing his diamond-studded Order of the Garter. He told the executioner he would signal to him when to bring down the axe. Before he stooped and put his head down on the block, he said: "I go from a corruptible to an incorruptible crown, where no disturbance can be, no disturbance in the world." Then he thrust out his hands, and the axe fell.

Charles I was the first and last English king to be publicly beheaded. It was to take 10 years of army rule for the country to decide whether it wanted the monarchy back.

PART X

THE COMMONWEALTH

1649-1659

33

THE CROMWELLS

OLIVER CROMWELL

1649-58

Oliver Cromwell was a fine soldier, one of England's greatest, although he never fought abroad. But his military prowess was not matched by the political imagination needed to run the country as surely as he ran the army. He had an opportunity unparalleled in British history to create a republic out of the ashes of the discredited monarchy he destroyed. His botched attempts to construct an alternative to royal rule failed hopelessly. He ended a monarch himself, but without a crown or a credible successor. Cromwell had good qualities: little hunger for the supreme power that was finally thrust upon him, a measure of tolerance in intolerant times and a relatively humble background, which kept him focused on what ordinary people wanted. Sanctimonious but sincere, he was guided always by his Puritan belief that he was doing God's work.

Cromwell owed his surname to an ancestor who married the sister of Henry VIII's shrewd adviser Thomas Cromwell, whose name the family adopted. The only story told of Oliver Cromwell's early days is that when he and Prince Charles were little boys at a children's party half a century before he ordered the beheading of King Charles I, he is said to have punched the future king and given him a nosebleed.

Cromwell went on to enjoy a happy marriage to the wealthy Elizabeth Bourchier and they had nine children. He spent much of his life working as a farmer until he became MP for Cambridge in 1640 at the age of 41. He immediately shone as a fine speaker and a serious-minded, passionate Puritan. It was only in 1642 that, without any previous military experience, he threw himself into the task of helping raise an army to face Charles's Royalists. Cromwell recruited a company of cavalry, and his efficient, inspirational leadership so impressed army commanders that he played a major role at the Battle of Marston Moor in 1644. A year later, his cavalry "Ironsides" slashed their way through the Royalists at the decisive Battle of Naseby.

In 1649, he was the prime mover behind the trial that led to the king's execution and is said to have uttered the words "cruel necessity" upon seeing Charles's headless corpse on 30 January. In the political vacuum that followed, he was unchallenged leader of the army and Parliament, but made no move to seize supreme power. Instead, at the bidding of the Rump Parliament he inherited from Charles I's reign, he spent two years in Ireland and Scotland crushing all opposition. His suppression of Royalist and Catholic resistance in Drogheda and Wexford were shocking displays of brutality. The scars that Cromwell's atrocities left on Irish history fester to this day. In 1997, Irish Prime Minister Bertie Ahern refused to visit London's Foreign office until a picture of Cromwell was removed from the wall. Back on the mainland in September 1650, Cromwell destroyed the Scottish army at Dunbar. He pursued Charles's son, the future Charles II, to defeat at the Battle of Worcester in 1651.

With his wars over, the master of the battlefield acted with a measure of political restraint. England was now a republic run by the Rump Parliament of mainly traditionally minded MPs who had no appetite for democratic reform. The day-to-day administration of the country was managed by the Great Council. Cromwell, its president, was notably reluctant to exert dictatorial power. But there were limits to his progressive instincts. He had already seen off a campaign by the so-called "Levellers" to widen the vote and establish something like a full-blown democracy. Cromwell made it clear that their demands to extend the vote to more citizens would threaten his hold on the country and be a recipe for chaos.

He lacked the vision and intellectual imagination to fashion a lasting republican system, hoping that Parliamentarians would somehow do that job. But in the spring of 1653, exasperated by Parliament's fruitless dithering, Cromwell took his seat in the Commons and delivered a diatribe aimed at Parliament's lack of direction. With mounting anger, he declared, "You are no Parliament", and pointing to the mace, the symbol of MPs' independent authority, he shouted, "Take away this bauble!"

Cromwell then moved a step closer to autocracy without assuming all power for himself. He and his senior army officers replaced the Rump

Parliament with an assembly of 140 men who were tasked with deciding the shape of the future governance of the country. Their debate got nowhere, and Parliament was dissolved in December 1653. Three days later, Cromwell was proclaimed Lord Protector. It was a clear step toward dictatorship, a move he should have recognized would look like a reversion to the very monarchy he had condemned. From this moment on, Cromwell signed his name "Oliver P" for "Protector" and was addressed as "Your Highness".

Although he was clearly in charge, his exercise of power showed signs of moderation. Cromwell admitted Jews back into the city of London to trade after three and a half centuries of exile. He resisted calls for the complete abolition of Catholic worship. He pursued a foreign policy that would sow the seeds of empire. He opposed Dutch ambitions to dominate world trade by building up the navy, winning effective command of the English Channel. His top admiral, Robert Blake, won several victories over the Spanish and captured Jamaica.

At the beginning of 1655, Cromwell, in another fit of frustration about the shape of his so-called "Commonwealth", dissolved Parliament and launched his clumsiest reform yet. He appointed 11 of his major generals as governors of the country's regions. They soon aroused resentment by bombarding the public with a range of unpopular puritanical measures. There was a ban on alehouses, Sunday sports, dancing and parties, and an end to working on Sundays and to public gaiety such as dancing round the maypole. To put the cap on it, he imposed a tax of 10 per cent to finance the new regime.

By 1657, another Parliament was sitting, and most MPs reckoned Cromwell had so much power that he might as well be crowned king. Even some of his parliamentary critics took the view that it would be best to make the Lord Protector "King Oliver I", so that he would be subject to the long-held convention that the monarch could not spend money without their consent. There was a flurry of agonized negotiation as Cromwell's thoughts moved this way and that. He smoked obsessively and on 6 May, the day before he had to give his final decision, he told several acquaintances he would accept the crown. But hours later, as we are told by his spymaster John Thurloe, Cromwell took a walk in St James's Park and was met by three of his closest confidants, who warned him bluntly that they would not accept him as king. The following day, to general astonishment, he announced he could not "undertake his government with the title of a King". At the last moment, he stopped short of accepting a title which he'd fought a civil war to abolish.

But he did accept a move to entrench his supremacy with a lavish ceremony – a coronation without a crowning. On 26 June 1657, he was seated on the chair in Westminster Hall on which kings and queens had been crowned. Trumpets sounded and a great shout went up: "God save the Lord Protector!" His rule lasted only a year longer. On 3 September 1658 Oliver Cromwell fell ill and died after asking his advisers to appoint his son Richard as his successor.

RICHARD CROMWELL

1658-59

Even the most dedicated of Cromwell's republican followers quickly realized that his son was not up to the job. Richard had nowhere near Oliver Cromwell's intelligence, authority, or experience. The poor man was dubbed "Tumbledown Dick", and in April 1659, the army, which retained ultimate power, made him sign an act of resignation. England's one and only flirtation with republican rule was over. But the restoration of the monarchy would take another year.

PART XI

THE STUARTS RESTORED

1660-1714

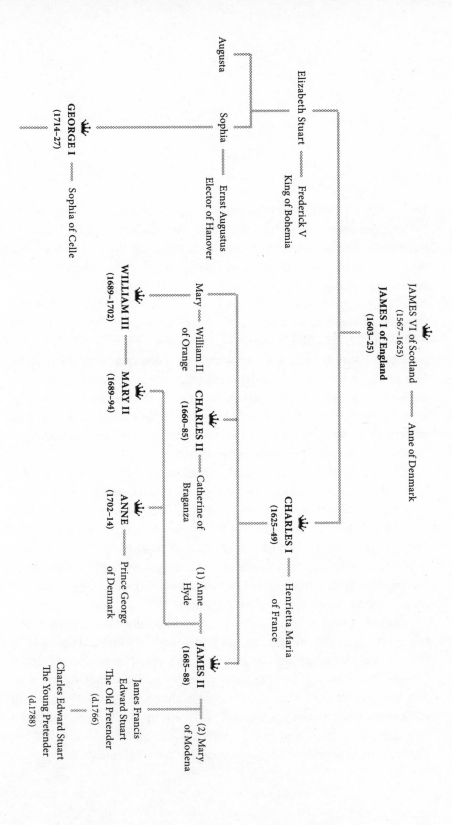

JAMES VI of Scotland
(1567–1625)
JAMES I of England
(1603–25)
⚜
⚜⚜⚜ Anne of Denmark

Elizabeth Stuart ⚜⚜⚜ Frederick V
King of Bohemia

Augusta

Sophia ⚜⚜⚜ Ernst Augustus
Elector of Hanover

GEORGE I
(1714–27) ⚜
⚜⚜⚜ Sophia of Celle

CHARLES I
(1625–49) ⚜
⚜⚜⚜ Henrietta Maria
of France

Mary ⚜⚜⚜ William II
of Orange

WILLIAM III
(1689–1702) ⚜
⚜⚜⚜ MARY II
(1689–94) ⚜

CHARLES II
(1660–85) ⚜
⚜⚜⚜ Catherine of
Braganza

ANNE
(1702–14) ⚜
⚜⚜⚜ Prince George
of Denmark

(1) Anne ⚜⚜⚜ JAMES II
Hyde   (1685–88) ⚜
⚜⚜⚜ (2) Mary
of Modena

James Francis
Edward Stuart
The Old Pretender
(d.1766)

Charles Edward Stuart
The Young Pretender
(d.1788)

34

CHARLES II
1660-85

Here was a king who set out to enjoy himself. And the behaviour of the "Merry Monarch", one of the laziest and most shameless of all England's kings, was no doubt a relief to people celebrating the end of the rigid austerity of the Cromwellian era. Under the reign of Charles II, the uncensored fun and creativity of the Restoration period bloomed. But he was a wayward captain of the ship of state, and his light hand on the tiller sent it weaving all over the place. Apart from his obsessive pursuit of women, Charles had few guiding principles. This allowed his ministers some latitude, and his reign saw the emergence of the country's first political parties. He wisely urged tolerance in the ongoing divisive battles over religion, and in his dealings with Parliament, although he often found himself at odds with MPs, his father's fate and the horrors of the recent civil war helped avoid open conflict. Charles was to enjoy a reign of 25 years without serious bloodshed.

The new king was tall and dark, a man of great charm and easy affability. He was crafty enough to have survived six weeks incognito after his defeat at the Battle of Worcester in 1651. His escape from Cromwell's army at the age of 21 sealed his reputation for cunning and courage. His disguise as a woodcutter was so effective that when a blacksmith told him that Charles I's son was still at large, the young fugitive replied, "If the rogue is taken, he deserves to be hanged." "Spoken like an honest man," replied the unsuspecting blacksmith.

Fugitive Charles managed to find a ship to take him to France. For nine years, he plotted his return, but it was only after Richard Cromwell's demise and the resulting anarchy that an opportunity opened up. A Cromwellian general, George Monck, respected for imposing order in Scotland, determined to restore stability in chaotic England. He marched to London, dismissed what was left of the Rump Parliament, ordered a new general election and opened secret communication with Charles, the only man he saw as capable of inspiring national unity.

RIGHT: Lady Jane Grey was queen for just nine days. One of history's victims, she was no match for a resolute Queen Mary.

BELOW: Queen Mary's marriage to Philip II of Spain was unpopular and failed to give her an heir.

Elizabeth I, one of the brightest stars in English history. Guided by an able team of advisers she ruled with a sure touch for more than four decades. She dressed flamboyantly as seen in this "Armada portrait" that celebrates her navy's victory over the Spanish fleet.

ABOVE LEFT: Mary Queen of Scots' claim to the throne made her a dangerous threat to her cousin Elizabeth, but her son was the first Stuart king.

ABOVE RIGHT: James I and his Stuart heirs were more famed for mistakes than successes. They misjudged the power of parliament.

BELOW: Charles I fell victim to his own conviction that he knew best and had a divine right to rule.

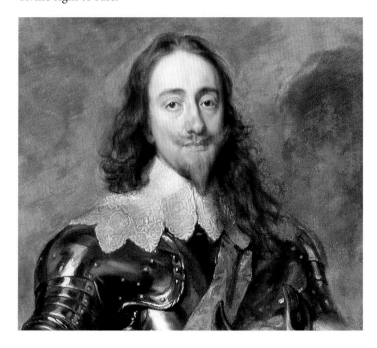

A large crowd watch as Charles I is beheaded outside London's Banqueting House. "Cruel necessity," observed Oliver Cromwell as he sent the king to his death.

LEFT: Oliver Cromwell was a brilliant general, but bungled his chance to make England a republic.

BELOW LEFT: Nell Gwyn, one of Charles II's many mistresses, was a spirited comedy actress.

BELOW: Charles II was one of the most fun-loving of England's kings and his restoration energized the arts and economy.

LEFT: James II's conversion to Catholicism prompted rebellion and a constitutional revolution.

BELOW: William III's crushing of James II's Catholic army on the River Boyne made him a Protestant hero.

LEFT: Anne's regal pose belies personal tragedy. She was pregnant at least 17 times but not one child lived beyond the age of 11.

RIGHT: George I, Elector of Hanover, did not speak English when he arrived in London to be crowned.

BELOW: George II, on his white horse, was the last British king to lead his troops into battle at Dettingen.

LEFT: George III is remembered as the mad king who lost America, but he was one of Britain's best loved and longest serving monarchs.

BELOW: British Redcoats killed five protesters at the Boston Massacre. This led to violent condemnation of King George III and his ministers, and to the American War of Independence.

RIGHT: Self-indulgent George IV was widely mocked. This Gilray cartoon shows his waistcoat bursting while he picks his teeth with a fork.

BELOW LEFT: Queen Caroline was despised by her husband George IV. He tried unsuccessfully to divorce her and banned her from attending his coronation.

BELOW RIGHT: William IV, "Sailor Bill", third son of George III, became king because neither of his older brothers had surviving children.

Victoria, the second-longest reigning British monarch, gave her name to an age of dynamic imperial expansion and economic growth. Pictured here with her beloved Albert and five of their nine children, she was devastated by his early death and withdrew from public life for many years.

ABOVE: Rumours swirled about Victoria and her Scottish servant John Brown. Royal staff called him "the queen's stallion". She was buried with a lock of his hair.

RIGHT: Victoria with three future kings. Her son (top right) became Edward VII; her grandson (left), George V; her great-grandson (bottom right), Edward VIII.

LEFT: Edward VII with his grandson (right), the future Edward VIII, and son (left), the future George V. George said when his father died, "I have lost my best friend."

RIGHT: George V with Queen Mary, recuperating from a chest infection. He changed his family name from Saxe-Coburg to Windsor during World War I.

ABOVE: Edward VIII broadcasting his abdication speech to the nation. He said he was not able to rule "without the help and support of the woman I love".

BELOW: Former King Edward VIII and his wife Wallis, now Duke and Duchess of Windsor, visit Hitler before World War II.

ABOVE: George VI and Queen Elizabeth celebrate the end of World War II with Winston Churchill, Princess Elizabeth (left) and Princess Margaret (right).

BELOW: George VI and Queen Elizabeth visit London's heavily bombed East End during World War II.

ABOVE LEFT: Princess Elizabeth married Prince Philip when she was 21. Their strong partnership lasted 73 years and she called him her "strength and stay".

ABOVE RIGHT: The queen, an accomplished horse rider, took pride most years in the Trooping the Colour ceremony on her official birthday.

BELOW: Elizabeth II has welcomed 112 world leaders on state visits to Britain, including Nelson Mandela.

A pared-down royal family appears on the Buckingham Palace balcony during the Queen's Platinum Jubilee celebrations in 2022. From left to right: the Duchess and Duke of Cornwall, Queen Elizabeth II, the Duke and Duchess of Cambridge and children George, Charlotte and Louis.

In exile in the Dutch city of Breda, Charles was naturally delighted and made (unusually for him) a well-judged move. He declared himself a champion of national reconciliation and religious tolerance and offered a pardon to all but those who had signed his father's death warrant. On 23 May 1660, he embarked from the Netherlands on the warship *Naseby*, whose name was rapidly repainted as *Royal Charles*. The diarist Samuel Pepys, on board with him, remembers being "ready to weep" at the harrowing stories Charles told of his escape from England nine years earlier. Another great Restoration diarist John Evelyn describes the ecstatic welcome Charles received in London, escorted "without one drop of blood shed" by the army that had executed his father.

In the early years of his reign, Charles enjoyed popular support and the country prospered. The new Parliament was soon labelled "Cavalier", as there was no surge of radical anti-Royalists. But there was a virulent wave of reaction against non-conformists, Puritans and others who threatened the Church of England. The House of Commons voted through a rigid new code which led to the eviction of some 2,000 preachers who refused to conform. Charles wanted to de-escalate religious division and tried unsuccessfully to reverse Parliament's most severe demands. He asked politicians for "indulgence", but they would have none of it.

The most notable feature of Charles's early reign was his display of unashamed depravity. As soon as he was comfortably installed in the giant master bedroom at Whitehall Palace, he invited one mistress after another to share it with him, or he visited them. The blatant licentiousness of Charles's court prompted John Evelyn to write, "He would doubtless have been an excellent prince had he been less addicted to women." His earliest conquest was the notorious Barbara Villiers, whose husband the king gratefully rewarded with the title Earl of Castlemaine. Barbara was stunningly beautiful, with a great mop of brunette hair, and Charles fathered at least five of her six children, all of whom received noble titles. His affair with Barbara did not stop the king from marrying the Portuguese princess Catherine of Braganza, a 23-year-old Roman Catholic imbued with the strict morality of her convent upbringing, in 1662. She had several clashes with his mistresses, whose influence and demands on her husband she deeply resented, but she remained faithful to Charles to the end.

Although Queen Catherine miscarried several times and failed to give Charles an heir, he fathered at least 12 illegitimate children with his procession of mistresses, including two with one of his favourites, the comedy actress Nell Gwyn. Pepys admired her as an enchanting performer and called her "pretty, witty Nell".

A more elevated arena in which Charles took great interest was foreign affairs. The two most powerful countries in Europe were Spain, only beginning to show signs of decline, and France, now hungry for expansion under its ambitious young king, Louis XIV. In their shadow were Britain and the Dutch Republic in the Netherlands, both constantly calculating which of the big two to cosy up to. Charles's family connections with France made him inclined to side with his first cousin Louis. England's Protestant sympathies should have made the Dutch Republic an ally, but Charles judged that Dutch naval and trading interests threatened England and in 1665, with enthusiastic parliamentary support, he went to war with the Dutch. English warships won the Battle of Lowestoft, but most of the rest of the war was a disaster, ending with the unforgettable embarrassment of Charles's proud Royal Navy being caught by a Dutch raid up the Medway, and the flagship *Royal Charles* being seized by the enemy. The combined shock of this and of Louis XIV's support for the Dutch proved too much, and Charles made peace in 1667.

Charles's reign had reached its nadir. England had just been wracked by the double catastrophe of the plague and the Great Fire of London. The bubonic plague of 1665 killed 70,000, the Great Fire of 1666 made at least 100,000 homeless. More than 13,000 houses were destroyed, along with 82 city churches and St Paul's Cathedral. Charles was wise enough to leave London during the plague but was courageously visible during the fire, which diarist Samuel Pepys describes so graphically:

"God grant my eyes may never behold the like, who now saw above 10,000 houses all in one flame: the noise, and cracking, and thunder of the impetuous flames, ye shrieking of women and children, the hurry of people, the fall of towers, houses, and churches, was like an hideous storme."

John Evelyn's diary reveals the king bustling about the streets – accompanied by his brother James, Duke of York – giving advice and encouragement. His presence was a powerful indicator of his humanity and wish to be identified with ordinary people.

Unfortunately, his popularity was dented by his energetic but misplaced interest in foreign policy. From 1668, his diplomatic judgement went from bad to worse, as he engaged in a most duplicitous piece of inter-state manipulation. By the end of the 1660s, Louis XIV's France appeared a dangerously threatening aggressor. Parliament and public opinion pressed Charles to support the Protestant Dutch against French Catholic expansion.

Charles had little time for this, as he still fumed about the Medway raid and saw Louis as a friend. He began to negotiate secretly with France using his sister Henriette, who was married to Louis's brother, the Duke of Orléans, as a valuable go-between. She was a wily negotiator, and in the secret Treaty of Dover, signed with France in 1670, Charles agreed to become a Catholic, to encourage Catholicism in England and to support Louis against the Dutch. In return, Louis undertook to pay Charles a generous annual cash grant. It was an astonishingly risky and ill-judged move on Charles's part. The cash may have proved useful but, as his French sympathies became apparent, he looked like an agent of the hated Catholic Church.

The religious divide in England was growing ever deeper, and in 1673, Parliament insisted – despite Charles's objections – on banning Catholics from public office. The so-called "Test Acts" remained in force until 1828, when the Duke of Wellington's government scrapped them. Charles's opposition to the Test Acts and his reluctance to stand up robustly for the Church of England took a severe knock when he added to his parade of mistresses Louise de Kérouaille, a Catholic close to the French court, and made her Duchess of Portsmouth. Riding in a coach one day, her rival Nell Gwyn was barracked by a crowd of fervent anti-Catholics who believed the vehicle was ferrying Louise to see the king. Nell stuck her head out of the window and exclaimed: "Pray, good people, be civil: I am the *Protestant* whore!"

Even more awkward for Charles was his commitment to help Louis fight the Dutch. A second Dutch war was no more successful than the first, and again Charles sued for peace after just two years.

By the mid-1670s, with shouts of "No popery!" growing louder, Charles reluctantly accepted that public and parliamentary opinion had swung strongly against France. William of Orange, his sister's son, had become stadtholder, the effective head of state, in Holland. In 1677, William married Charles's niece Mary. England and the Dutch Republic were now firmly linked. Louis of France, furious at what he saw as Charles's betrayal, stopped his payments. Although Charles had promised to become a Catholic in the Dover treaty, he had prudently never converted.

If Charles's foreign policy was largely a failure, he earned credit for his cultural achievements. Creative by nature, his amateur interest in science and astronomy inspired him to found the Royal Society and the Royal Observatory in Greenwich. His dismay at the destruction caused by the Great Fire made him an enthusiastic backer of the rebuilding of London, its churches and St Paul's Cathedral, with Christopher Wren as the chief architect.

But Charles couldn't escape the all-embracing toxicity of England's religious divide. The spectre of a Catholic coup exploded into a public scandal in August 1678 with the extraordinary claim by Titus Oates, a trained Jesuit with a dubious reputation, that a group of Catholic conspirators was planning to assassinate the king. The Oates "plot" was soon exposed as a fantasy, but it only heightened religious paranoia. The king's brother, James, a man of no great intellect or leadership potential, but a pious Catholic, was now seen as a dangerous threat who had to be excluded from the succession. The House of Commons, which had evolved into a lively debating chamber, featured two opposing parties, the Whigs and the Tories. The Tories were generally traditional royalists, the Whigs challengers, anxious for change. The Whig leader was the fiery Lord Shaftesbury, who led a powerful attack on James and proposed that the heir to the throne must be a Protestant. The most obvious candidate, the Whigs proclaimed, was Charles's first illegitimate child, James, Duke of Monmouth, a Protestant and proven military commander.

For three years, from 1678 to 1681, the king struggled with demands for his brother James's exclusion. Shaftesbury's Whigs made energetic efforts in Parliament to pass a bill that would rule out James's succession – and effectively allow MPs to choose Charles's successor. In response, Charles – remarkably, for a man whose judgement had been unsound for the first two decades of his reign – played a political blinder. He prorogued and dissolved Parliament to confuse and frustrate his opponents. And, most boldly, he proclaimed his own passionately held dictum that only the child of a genuine and legal royal marriage could succeed to the throne. He declared his brother James would succeed him and that, he insisted, was that. The bill to exclude James was passed by the Commons but defeated in the Lords. James tactfully stayed abroad for much of this time, and Charles encouraged the fear that if his brother did not succeed as king, the country might be plunged back into civil war.

Opinion slowly swung against the radical Whigs, and Shaftesbury went into political exile in 1682. In that same year, the Rye House Plot, a poorly conceived plan to assassinate both Charles and James, was exposed, and consolidated the king's hold on power. He faced no more threats until he died, aged 54, in early 1685 after apologizing to his wife, Catherine, for mistreating her. Legend has it that he also begged James (successfully, as it turned out) to give his beloved Nell Gwyn a pension, with the words "Don't let poor Nelly starve."

35

JAMES II

1685-88

The shortest reign of the ill-fated Stuart dynasty was also its most incompetent and foolish. James II had a particular stubbornness that eclipsed any of his predecessors. He was the last English king to wield the wide prerogative powers monarchs had enjoyed since Alfred, and his misuse of them led to his downfall. His greatest blunder was to tear apart the delicate compact his brother Charles II had achieved in smoothing the religious divide. His arrogant blindness to the fury his conduct caused prompted a foreign invasion arguably as transformative as the Norman Conquest 600 years earlier and propelled the country's monarchy into the modern age.

Young James was a poor student, and few saw him developing into a man of intelligence and good judgement. He showed most talent in the military field. When his father, Charles I, was defeated in the civil war of the 1640s, 15-year-old James was packed off in 1648 to exile on the Continent. There, in the 1650s, he fought with some courage on both sides in wars between France and its neighbours.

He was back in England on King Charles II's Restoration in 1660 and appointed Lord High Admiral, where his bravery rather than his leadership impressed. He notably maintained his composure at the Battle of Lowestoft in 1665, when an enemy Dutch marksman killed a senior ship's officer beside James, leaving James spattered in blood. He also became governor of, and the largest shareholder in, the Royal African Company, which managed the trade in slaves from Africa to the Caribbean. Although twice married, he was no less a lothario than his brother, Charles II. The diarist Samuel Pepys noted that James "did eye my wife mightily". Some, including Charles, questioned James's taste in mistresses and one of them, Catherine Smedley, admitted surprise at being chosen by James: "It cannot be my beauty, for he must see I have none. And it cannot be my wit, for he has not enough himself to know that I have any."

King Charles did not hold a very high opinion of his brother, either. He was appalled by James's conversion to Catholicism in 1672. As it became clear that Charles would have no legitimate children and that James would be his heir, England's Anglican ruling class pressured Charles to exclude James from the succession. Even though Charles doubted James's qualities, he loyally fought to secure his traditional right to pass on the crown to his brother as the next in line.

When Charles died in 1685, the dominant Tory elite, passionate devotees of the Protestant faith, reluctantly accepted his Catholic brother, James, as king. They calculated that, at 51 years old, he would not live long, and the crown would soon revert to the Protestant daughters he had with his first wife, Anne Hyde. The elder, Mary, soon to become queen, married William of Orange, the leader of the Dutch Republic. The younger, Anne, would later inherit the throne.

James's first months in office passed well. He had little trouble seeing off a rebellion by Charles II's illegitimate son, James, Duke of Monmouth, who landed with a pathetically small force at Lyme Regis in Dorset in June 1685. The new king's more professional army made short work of the invaders at the Battle of Sedgemoor on 6 July. Monmouth was caught hiding in a ditch, disguised as a shepherd, and was summarily condemned to the block, where it took several strokes to sever his head from his body. James then dispatched the infamous Judge Jeffreys to the West Country to root out and execute the surviving rebel leaders.

But James's strong start soon ground to a halt. He made it increasingly clear that his commitment to Roman Catholicism was not just a personal matter. He was out to convert the country, no matter how long it would take. As the contemporary historian Gilbert Burnet wrote: "He was resolved to bring [Catholicism] about or to die a martyr in endeavouring it." James began appointing Catholics to positions of authority, action categorically forbidden by the Test Acts passed under Charles II. In November 1685, when Parliament – which until now had been so obliging to James's rule – urged him to respect the Test Acts and stop promoting Catholics, James forcefully rejected their demands in a speech from the throne.

It was the first and most catastrophic of James's mistakes. When MPs resisted, he dismissed them, proroguing Parliament and saying that he, like monarchs before him, had a divine right to rule as he thought fit. Unlike many of his predecessors, he didn't know when to stop. Tories who had backed James as the legitimate heir and had been reassured by his promise to respect the Anglican Church now began to lose patience. Whigs had already given up in despair, and many of them had fled to the Protestant court of James's son-in-law William of Orange, in the Dutch Republic.

Blithely unaware of the outrage his actions were provoking, James issued his Declaration of Indulgence in April 1687, lifting restrictions on Catholic worship and allowing Catholics to be appointed to public office. He ordered Magdalen College, Oxford, to appoint a Catholic president. When rebellious fellows argued that the king's choice was not only the wrong religion but also a debauchee, James ordered the fellows to be thrown out of the college. No, retorted Magdalen, they were fellows with a freehold, an assured right of tenure. James, white with anger, burst into a fellows' meeting at the college and exclaimed: "Get you gone … I am your king … I command you to be gone." The expelled fellows became instant national heroes, and when James relented a year later and agreed to reappoint them, it was too late.

Next came a full-blown crisis: his second wife gave birth to a baby – a Catholic boy. After the death of his first wife, Anne Hyde, James had married Mary of Modena, a Catholic who appeared unable to have children. But in the spring of 1688, she gave birth to James Francis Edward Stuart. Even for loyalist Tories, a Catholic baby was too much. Rumours quickly spread that the queen had not been pregnant at all and that the baby was smuggled into the royal bed in a warming pan. Since the king's new son was heir to the throne, there was widespread despair that a Catholic succession seemed inescapable.

The unexpected birth came only a few weeks after James had reissued his unwelcome Declaration of Indulgence. His order that it be read from the country's pulpits was promptly rejected by six brave bishops and the Archbishop of Canterbury himself. They were summonsed to trial for treason. London then witnessed the astonishing sight of crowds clapping and cheering the bishops' boat as it glided down the Thames to the Tower of London. When they were tried in Westminster Hall, to James's fury, the bishops were acquitted.

The royal baby and the widespread clamour of public disaffection led to a decisive crunch. On 30 June, seven English leaders including the Bishop of London sent a letter to William of Orange, begging him to intervene. The Dutch leader responded enthusiastically, promising to help England secure its "freedom". It was the trigger for a revolution that would launch England, and soon Britain, on the path to greater democracy with a constitutional monarchy. William was motivated partly by support for his wife Mary's natural claim – through her father James II – to the English throne, but more importantly by the need to secure England as a powerful ally in his war with the aggressive French King Louis XIV.

It took William five months to prepare. By November, he was ready with a fleet and invasion force mightier than the Spanish Armada exactly 100 years earlier. He succeeded where Spain's Philip II had failed. His fleet was held up for a time by gales, but then the wind suddenly blew up from the east and bore him down the Channel, outwitting James's navy, which was trapped on anchor in the Thames by what was aptly dubbed the "Protestant Wind". William landed in Torbay and advanced slowly on London. James reacted timidly, and a spate of nosebleeds contributed to his mood of defeatism. Aware of his ebbing support, and finally deserted by key figures including a top general John Churchill, later Duke of Marlborough, and by his younger daughter, Anne, he finally accepted the game was up and fled across to France in December. It was left to William to seize the moment. Buoyed up by the vacancy left by James's departure, he demanded acceptance not just as the saviour of England's freedom but also as its new king. A new era was about to begin.

36

WILLIAM III AND MARY II

1689-1702

We owe a huge debt to King William III and his wife, Queen Mary II. Their reign marked a decisive acceleration in the drive toward the modern parliamentary democracy which set an example to much of the rest of the world.

When William of Orange invaded England and won the crown by deposing King James II, he found a Parliament hungry for more power. He was happy to concede authority in return for securing England as an ally of his Dutch homeland against French aggression. His obsession with Louis XIV endowed Britain with a constitutional revolution.

William and his wife Mary, who could claim to be heir to her father, James II, enhanced the image of the monarchy and did much to rescue the Stuarts from being remembered as the most unsavoury dynasty in British history. William married Mary in 1677. She was King Charles II's niece, an attractive and popular 15-year-old. Charles was anxious for peace with the Dutch Republic after two expensive wars and William, at 26, was the Captain General of the Dutch forces and the leading political figure in the Dutch Netherlands. He was not a striking person: short, unathletic and pasty-faced, with a hook nose, and he suffered from severe asthma. When Mary was told she was to marry him, she spent a whole day in tears. After their marriage, he was noticeably cool to his young bride. On their wedding night, William's sex-mad uncle, Charles II, poked his head through the curtains of the four poster and exclaimed "Now, nephew, to your work. Hey! Saint George for England."

Mary failed to bear William a child. She had two miscarriages in their first year together and he soon took up with one of her ladies-in-waiting, Elizabeth Villiers. Although Elizabeth was careful not to flaunt her dalliance with William, it was an open secret. However, Mary had come to adore her husband. She wrote in her journal when he sailed off to invade England in 1688: "It was as if my heart had been pierced through." When she joined him in London in the new year after his triumphant takeover, she declared that she would leave the exercise of all royal power to him. He grew very attached to her too, and when she died in 1694, he was said to have been almost suicidal and immediately dropped Villiers.

The highlight of the so-called "Glorious Revolution", which saw the non-violent removal of an unwanted king, was the Bill of Rights. Parliament presented it to the royal couple three months after William's invasion in November 1688. It promised MPs free speech, free elections and the exclusive right to create laws. The king could no longer raise taxes without parliamentary approval. The royal prerogative was severely cut back. From then on, Parliament met every year, not just at the will of the monarch.

This settlement was popular in England and William's moderation and tolerance of Catholics reduced religious rancour. But Ireland was a very different matter. Catholic firebrand Lord Tyrconnell, the Lord Deputy of Ireland, demanded that the Irish take an oath of loyalty to the exiled Catholic King James, who had decided to choose Ireland as his battleground to recover his throne. The struggle with James climaxed in the summer of 1690, when William landed at Carrickfergus in the north of Ireland on 14 June and marched south to confront James's army on the River Boyne. William was immensely brave, sometimes reckless. He was exposed to enemy fire on the north bank of the river on 30 June. A cannonball grazed his right shoulder, and when he led a cavalry charge across the Boyne the next day, his arm was so weak that he had to brandish his sword in his unaccustomed left hand. His horse got stuck in the mud, provoking a severe bout of asthma for the king, and he was lucky to be carried to the shore on the back of a beefy soldier. His gallant leadership – compared to the faint-hearted James, who fled with what was left of his army to Dublin – made "King Billy" a Protestant hero, and he remains the inspiration of Ulster unionists to this day. James withdrew to Paris and was for a time recognized by Louis XIV as England's rightful king, but died in 1701. His son and grandson led two failed Jacobite rebellions ending in final defeat at the Battle of Culloden 45 years later.

It was not until 1691 that William was free to return to the Netherlands and resume what he saw as his primary task – his campaign against Louis XIV of France. It was not an immediate success. The Royal Navy had been battered by the French at the Battle of Beachy Head a year earlier, and William suffered losses over the next two years in the Battles of Steenkerque and Landen. Things improved after that, and he was able to block any further French advances on the Netherlands and persuade Louis to agree to peace with the Treaty of Ryswick in 1697. France was compelled to accept that England was a major player in the Continental power struggle now that William was king.

William's zealous commitment to the war with France meant he was constantly asking Parliament for money. In the early 1690s, he had little trouble. MPs saw France as a threat and willingly stumped up the vast sums required. William remained true to his promise in the Bill of Rights to allow Parliament more freedom than ever before, a freedom that the new political parties, the Whigs and the Tories, made the most of. William largely ignored the mutual hostility between the parties and their factional infighting because he had no great interest in British politics. He may have felt more in sympathy with the traditionalist Tories, but he had regular business-like contact with both parties, and the new political compact worked well enough until the war with France was over. But after the peace of 1697, William faced strong parliamentary pressure to cut the army back in size. When MPs urged a reduction from around 30,000 to 7,000, the king was so appalled that he threatened to return to the Netherlands and leave England to defend itself. With similar strong-arm tactics, he managed to keep the army's size to at least 15,000 and many regiments were grateful to him when the next war with France, the War of the Spanish Succession, burst upon the country in 1701.

Another of William's goals was to soothe religious intolerance. He was a devout Calvinist but resisted the impulse of diehard Protestants to enforce discrimination. He tried, but failed, to restrain Irish Protestants from persecuting Catholics after his victory over James II. When MPs tried to keep Catholics from holding any offices, he again failed to resist their demands. He did succeed in actively supporting the founding of a Bank of England, an institution which transformed economic prospects by allowing the government to borrow in times of severe constraint.

William was never widely popular. A lonely figure, he found the trappings of kingship and the social whirl which had character-ized Charles II's court an embarrassment. He and Mary shunned the bustle of Whitehall Palace (which burned down in 1698) and enjoyed the more rural delights of Kensington Palace and Hampton Court where Christopher Wren designed and built an imposing new wing that dwarfed Cardinal Wolsey's original palace. Their private life was embittered by a personal feud between Mary and her sister Anne, whose friends John Churchill and his wife Sarah (later Duke and Duchess of Marlborough), the royal couple disliked.

After Mary's death from smallpox in 1694, the introverted William became even less visible. His small circle of close friends was dominated by Hans Willem Bentinck, a long-time companion whose skill had helped secure the Treaty of Ryswick with France, and a more recent devotee named Arnold van Keppel. Van Keppel was so handsome and charming that Bentinck became feverishly jealous. So close were these friendships that some suspected they were sexual.

William's reign was cut short when he was 51. He fell off his horse at Hampton Court and broke his collarbone. He appeared to recover, but then fell victim to pulmonary fever and died on 8 March 1702.

His reign was soon swept into relative obscurity by many historians who wrote more favourably of other English monarchs. But his "Glorious Revolution" remains a welcome milestone in British history, and to Protestant Ulster he is perhaps the greatest monarch of all.

37

ANNE

1702-14

Queen Anne is a much-maligned monarch. She has been portrayed as a dull, insecure, easily influenced woman with unhealthy attachments to female attendants, like the scheming Sarah, Duchess of Marlborough. In fact, Anne was a popular monarch who presided competently over England during an age of important political and cultural change.

Anne's upbringing did not prepare her for ruling a great power. Her father, James, was King Charles II's younger brother. It was thought highly unlikely that Anne would one day become queen, and an unhappy childhood left her lonely, unconfident, and shy. In 1668, aged three, she was sent to Paris to be treated for an eye disorder and lived with her grandmother, Henrietta Maria, the dowager queen. Within months of her return to England at the age of six, her mother died. She became estranged from her father, James, later King James II, after he converted to Catholicism. Her uncle King Charles II insisted that Lady Anne and her older sister, Lady Mary, be brought up as Protestants under the guidance of Henry Compton, Bishop of London. Like other aristocratic females at the time, they received little formal education. Knowing how to sew and sing were deemed more important than understanding the world around them.

On 28 July 1683, Anne married Prince George of Denmark, a quiet, retiring fellow summed up by King Charles II with the words "I have tried him drunk and tried him sober and there is nothing in him." However, Anne adored her husband and they offered each other great emotional support as they suffered the deaths of their children one after another. She was pregnant at least 17 times but only five babies survived childbirth. During one particularly devastating month, Anne suffered a miscarriage and two of her young daughters died of smallpox. A friend wrote that the queen and her husband took these deaths "very heavily … Sometimes they wept, sometimes they mourned in words; then sat silent, hand in hand; he sick in bed, [with smallpox] and she the carefullest nurse to him that can be imagined." Only one son, William, survived infancy. Tragically, he succumbed to smallpox at the age of 11.

By the time Anne became queen on 8 March 1702, ill health exacerbated by multiple pregnancies had left her an overweight invalid. Aged 37, she could hardly walk and had to be carried to her coronation in a sedan chair. She won widespread public support with her first speech to Parliament by promising to serve her subjects knowing her "own heart to be entirely English", a sly dig at her predecessor, William of Orange, whom she had disliked, privately referring to him to as "Mr Caliban" and "the Dutch monster". Anne was a staunch supporter of the Anglican Church of England and used her own money to help impoverished clergymen, further endearing her to the nation. Despite increasing infirmity, the queen took an active part in politics, working hard to keep a balance between the increasingly combative Tory and Whig parties. The conservative, upper-class Tories who supported the Church of England and the monarchy seemed obvious allies of the queen. But she refused to turn her back on the Whigs, who represented the merchant classes and were committed to limiting the power of the crown.

Anne attended debates in the House of Lords and presided over cabinet meetings, firmly insisting that she would not be "enslaved" by "the merciless men" of either party. She accepted that she was a constitutional monarch who could influence, but not overrule, Parliament – although she has gone down in history as the last monarch to wield the royal veto. In 1708, on the advice of her ministers, she refused to grant royal assent to a bill which would have allowed the Scottish militia to bear arms. They feared that Scots in the militia who supported the son of James II might turn their weapons against Anne.

The defining events of Queen Anne's reign were the Act of Union between England and Scotland and the War of the Spanish Succession. On 1 May 1707, England and Scotland officially became one country called the United Kingdom of Great Britain. After centuries of destabilizing disputes, they agreed to share a single Parliament. The queen eagerly followed the negotiations that led to union, even though she suffered terribly from gout. One witness unkindly reported: "Her face, which was red and spotted, was rendered something frightful by her negligent dress." He later wrote: "She appeared to me the most despicable mortal I had ever seen." Despite being unwell at the time, Anne later described the Act of Union as the "true happiness" of her reign.

The War of the Spanish Succession, which raged throughout her reign, propelled Great Britain to the status of a world power. On the death of Charles II of Spain in 1700, Austria laid claim to his empire. Charles had named a French Bourbon as his successor, but Austria's Habsburg ruler insisted he was the rightful heir. Great Britain and the Dutch Republic supported the Habsburgs and sided with Austria against France and Bourbon Spain. Queen Anne's close friend John Churchill, created an Earl of Marlborough by her predecessor William III and elevated to a dukedom by herself, became captain general of the Anglo-Dutch alliance. A military genius, he won a crushing victory at Blenheim on the Danube River in 1704, capturing the French army's commander and at least 13,000 of his men. Hailed as the greatest victory since Agincourt, Blenheim made Marlborough a national hero. Queen Anne gave him royal land at Woodstock, near Oxford, and Parliament approved money for the building of Marlborough's spectacular new home, Blenheim Palace.

More alliance victories followed, but the French and Spanish refused to give up. The allies won the Battle of Malplaquet in 1709 but lost 20,000 men, double the number of the French. This pyrrhic victory led Queen Anne to ask, "When will this bloodshed ever end?" Reflecting the public mood, she called for a stop to "this ruinous war". Final peace came in 1714, with treaties signed in the Dutch city of Utrecht, under which Britain emerged as the winner both commercially and territorially. Among the spoils of war were Gibraltar, Minorca, Newfoundland, and parts of Acadia (the eastern edge of modern Canada) and a monopoly of the slave trade between Africa and Spain's American colonies.

Anne's 12-year reign saw important cultural as well as political changes. Sir Christopher Wren completed St Paul's Cathedral, Sir Isaac Newton was elected president of the Royal Society, Alexander Pope and Jonathan Swift became household names, and "Queen Anne style" buildings set new standards of elegant architecture. Court composer George Frideric Handel was rewarded a lifelong pension by his grateful patron for his "Ode for the Birthday of Queen Anne".

No account of Queen Anne would be complete without mention of her love/hate relationship with Sarah, Duchess of Marlborough, wife of the famous general. They met as children and gradually, the attractive, lively Sarah came to dominate the future queen's life. The nicknames they used in letters to each other, show that they regarded themselves as equals. Anne's pen name was "Mrs Morley" and Sarah's "Mrs Freeman". When her sister Queen Mary tried unsuccessfully to force Anne to ban Sarah from her household in March 1692, Anne wrote: "My dear Mrs Freeman, never believe your faithful Mrs Morley will ever submit. She can wait with patience for a sunshine day."

Ten years later, when she became queen, one of Anne's first acts was to appoint Sarah Mistress of the Robes, Groom of the Stole and Keeper of the Privy Purse, roles which controlled access to the queen's private rooms, her clothing, jewels and money. For many years, the two were inseparable, but eventually the queen tired of Sarah's bullying behaviour and her overzealous support of the Whig political party. When Anne made Sarah's cousin Abigail Hill her favourite, a furious Sarah accused the queen of having "lesbian tendencies". Their final confrontation took place at a thanksgiving service in St Paul's Cathedral in 1708. The queen refused to wear heavy jewellery which Sarah, as Groom of the Stole, had placed out for her. This led to a heated argument on the drive to the cathedral and, as they stepped out of the carriage, Sarah was overheard telling the queen, "Be quiet!" Anne never forgave her. Sarah went on to describe the queen as "very ignorant, very fearful, with very little judgement". This and similarly nasty put-downs by Sarah did much to unfairly undermine Anne's legacy.

Queen Anne died aged 49 on 1 August 1714, after a stroke which left her speechless except for the words "yes" or "no". One of her doctors wrote: "I believe sleep was never more welcome to a weary traveller than death was to her." She was buried in Westminster Abbey beside her husband and their many children.

PART XII

THE HOUSE OF HANOVER

1714-1837

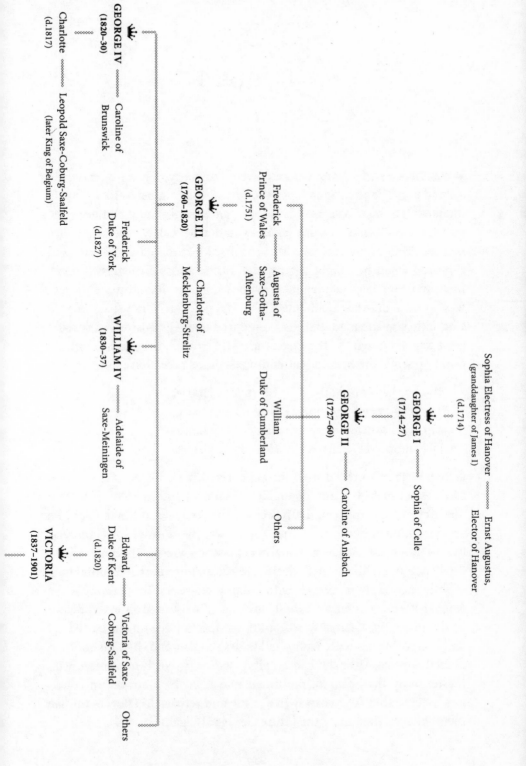

38

GEORGE I

1714-27

When Georg Ludwig von Braunschweig-Lüneburg, Elector of Hanover, arrived in England in September 1714, he seemed a most unlikely future monarch. He was 54 years old, did not speak English and had never set foot in Great Britain before. Satirists had a field day, especially since the new king brought along two servants, Mohammed and Mustapha, captured when he fought against the Turks, and his mistresses. One, Melusine von der Schulenburg, with whom he had three children, was so thin she was nicknamed "the Maypole". His half-sister Sophia Charlotte von Kielmansegg, also rumoured to be his mistress, was so fat she became known as "the Elephant". All featured in a cheeky contemporary poem "The Blessings attending George's accession":

"Hither he brought the dear Illustrious House;
That is, himself, his pipe, close stool and louse;
Two Turks, three whores and half a dozen nurses,
Five hundred Germans, all with empty purses."

George's claim to the British throne derived from his mother, Sophia, Electress of Hanover, granddaughter of James I and niece of Charles I. The Act of Settlement of 1701 decreed that only Protestants could be crowned king or queen, and since Sophia was the closest Protestant relation to the childless Queen Anne, her eldest son, George, became Anne's direct heir upon his mother's death. He was an unremarkable individual, slightly shorter than average, with bulging blue eyes. "In private life, he would have been called an honest blockhead," wrote one observer. Before he became king, George was best known for courage on the battlefield and hatred for his wife, who was his first cousin and, like his mother, named Sophia. After she had an affair with a Swedish nobleman, who mysteriously disappeared, presumed murdered by Hanoverian courtiers, George shut Sophia away in a castle and refused to allow her to see their children (including the future George II) again.

At first, the new king lived quietly in two sets of rooms at St James's Palace, avoiding royal appearances whenever possible. His speeches to Parliament consisted of one sentence spoken in broken English, with the rest read by his Lord Chancellor. Unlike Queen Anne, George was not in the habit of attending cabinet meetings, but he took a keen interest in politics, appointing ministers with whom he communicated in French. He favoured the Whig party, which had supported his succession, and mistrusted Tories, many of whom had plotted to replace him with James Stuart, son of the deposed Catholic King James II. In 1715, a year after George was crowned, there was a Jacobite uprising in Scotland. As many as 20,000 men took up arms and, just before Christmas, James Stuart arrived from France to lead them. The tall, taciturn 27-year-old known as the "Old Pretender" proved unequal to the task. Two months after he set foot in Scotland, news came that a government army was heading north. James abandoned the fight and fled back to France, never to return.

With James safely out of the way, George decided to spend 28 weeks in his beloved Hanover. Tradition dictated that his 33-year-old son, George, Prince of Wales, would govern Britain in the king's absence. But the two men despised each other, and the king refused to allow his son to make any important decisions. The humiliated Prince of Wales took revenge by making himself popular. He and his quick-witted wife, Princess Caroline of Ansbach, who both spoke English, gave large dinner parties at Hampton Court Palace and held lavish balls. They went to the theatre and sought the company of intellectuals like the writer Joseph Addison. When the king returned to Britain, he jealously followed his son's example and reluctantly started socializing.

Antipathy between the two Georges reached a crisis point in November 1717 at the christening of the Prince of Wales's infant son. The king insisted that his chancellor, the Duke of Newcastle, be named godfather. The prince despised Newcastle and, when he saw him at the ceremony, he muttered: "You are a rascal, but I shall find you out." The duke thought the prince said, "I will fight you", and complained to the king. George senior put his son and daughter-in-law under house arrest, then banished them from St James's Palace. He insisted their children stay with him, and then refused parental visits. The exiled royal couple set up an alternative court in their new Leicester Square home, which became the meeting point of up-and-coming Whig politicians like Robert Walpole, who later became Britain's first prime minister. Walpole spent hours with the astute Princess Caroline planning how to end the royal feud. In 1720, they managed to persuade Prince George to kneel before his father and ask for pardon. The king forgave him but uttered, "Votre conduite, votre conduite!" ("Your conduct, your conduct!") as he turned his back on his son and marched out of the room.

In one remarkably sensible move, the king made Walpole Paymaster General. It proved a very opportune appointment. Shortly after Walpole took office, there was a disastrous stock market crash known as the South Sea Bubble. The South Sea Company had been set up in 1711 to help finance the war against France. After the war, it made money for itself and the government by shipping slaves from Africa to Jamaica. In April 1720, Parliament passed a bill giving the company increased trading rights in the Americas in exchange for taking on a substantial chunk of the national debt. The company promised shareholders large returns, and businesses were set up to make items to sell in the new overseas markets.

Many of the new businesses were fraudulent. Among the scams were a company set up to produce guns that fired square bullets and another dedicated to the planting of 2,000 mulberry trees for breeding silkworms in Chelsea Park. As eager speculators piled in, South Sea share prices shot up by ten times in just six months. The new French word "millionaire" was coined, but when nervous shareholders started selling, panic ensued. Prices tumbled and fortunes were lost. King George was the governor of the South Sea Company, and his mistresses were active shareholders; their reputations were saved largely thanks to Walpole's loyal support and his adept management of Parliament. He came up with a rescue package which saved the company from bankruptcy and the grateful king made him first lord of the treasury (later known as prime minister) and chancellor of the exchequer, posts Walpole held from 1721 to 1742 in the longest administration in British history.

When George set out to visit Hanover for a sixth and final time in 1727, he left behind a nation that had enjoyed peace and prosperity during his reign and an administration run by expert politicians who had unprecedented freedom to govern. The king experienced stomach pains en route, but he blamed them on having eaten too many strawberries and oranges for supper. He insisted on continuing his journey, but had a stroke and died, aged 67, on 11 June. He was buried in Hanover in the family vault, next to his mother.

39

GEORGE II

1727-60

At the coronation of George II on 11 October 1727, the king's wife, Queen Caroline, wore a dress so encrusted with jewels that her skirt had to be lifted by a pulley when she knelt. Westminster Abbey resounded with music specially composed by royal favourite George Frideric Handel. His anthems included the rousing "Zadok the Priest", which has been played at every coronation since. It was a magnificent start to what turned out to be a less than glittering reign.

George II was the last British monarch born abroad. He moved to England from Hanover aged 30 when his father, George I, succeeded Queen Anne. He spoke English with a thick German accent, boasted that he had no time for books or letters and combined a lack of self-confidence with a vicious temper. Fortunately, he had a well-read, wise adviser in his wife Caroline, and an excellent Whig prime minister, Robert Walpole. The two would meet in secret to discuss the government's plans and Caroline would make sure that the king understood and agreed to them. Since Walpole needed the king's support to stay in power, he made sure that Parliament granted George more money than his father had received. The king rated Walpole so highly that he gave him a house – number 10 Downing Street – which the politician accepted on one condition: that it become the home of all future prime ministers.

Although George vowed to be a very different king from the father he hated, he behaved in a remarkably similar way: avoiding public appearances, running a dull court, and taking mistresses. The saying that Hanoverians "like pigs, trample their young" was borne out in the king's treatment of his eldest son, Prince Frederick. George treated his heir as abominably as his father had treated him. He called Frederick "a monster and the greatest villain that ever was born". In turn, Frederick labelled the king "an obstinate, self-indulgent, miserly martinet with an insatiable sexual appetite". Frederick and his wife lived separately from the king and queen (who themselves had lived separately from George

I) and their house in Leicester Square became a magnet for opposition Tory politicians and disenchanted Whigs like William Pitt the Elder, the brilliant orator and future prime minister. Frederick would not live to become king, dying unexpectedly in 1751. His 12-year-old son would later become King George III.

The early years of George II's reign went smoothly, as Walpole's Whig government pursued a policy of no wars, low taxes and increased trade. The spread of literacy allowed satire to flourish. Writers like John Gay took great delight in mocking the ruling elite. In his *Beggar's Opera*, politicians were portrayed as common criminals. Artist William Hogarth shed unpleasant but amusing light on decadent aristocrats in masterpieces like *A Rake's Progress*.

Ten years after George became king, Queen Caroline died. He may have been unfaithful and had once accused his wife of "being more of a schoolmistress than a queen", but the king loved her. He sat by her sickbed for days and, when Caroline urged George to remarry, he sobbed, "No, I will have mistresses."

In 1739, Walpole's attempts to keep Britain out of foreign conflict ended with the aptly named "War of Jenkins' Ear". Jenkins, a British sea captain, claimed sailors of the Spanish coast guard cut off his ear during a scuffle in the West Indies. Britain's declaration of war on Spain led to involvement in the War of the Austrian Succession, which pitted France and Prussia against Austria. King George, who was also Elector of Hanover, was anxious to safeguard his interests there, and keenly joined the fight on Austria's side. He took control of the British army and, at the age of 60, became the last British king to lead troops into battle. On 27 June 1743, he helped to win the Battle of Dettingen with sword in hand, shouting: "Now, boys, now for the honour of England; fire and behave bravely, and the French will soon run."

In July 1745, King George faced another foe. Twenty-four-year-old Charles Edward Stuart, "Bonnie Prince Charlie", landed in Scotland to claim the British throne. Grandson of King James II, who had been deposed in 1688, the "Young Pretender" and his supporters marched into England. They got as far as Derby, 124 miles from London, before retreating on news that the king's second son, the Duke of Cumberland, was preparing to fight them. The two sides met at Culloden, near Inverness, in April 1746. In the last pitched battle on British soil, Cumberland's heavily armed force crushed the rebel army in just one hour. Bonnie

Prince Charlie fled to France, ending once and for all the Jacobite threat to the British throne.

After Walpole's resignation in 1742, King George continued to favour the Whig party and exercised considerable power over the shape of Britain's government by choosing leaders he approved of. He tried his best to exclude William Pitt from high office after Pitt accused George of favouring Hanover at the expense of Britain. However, Pitt proved such an excellent statesman that the king eventually approved his appointment to the key role of secretary of state. The king could not have made a timelier decision, because Pitt effectively served as prime minister under Lord Newcastle during the Seven Years War, a conflict described by Winston Churchill as "the first world war".

Between 1756 and 1763, Britain, Prussia and other German states took on France, Austria, Sweden, and Russia. Pitt conducted the country's war effort, establishing Britain as a major imperial power by building up the navy. He concentrated on fighting in the colonies, while supporting Prussia's continental war effort with money rather than men. The king helped select military leaders and questioned some decisions but wisely let Pitt run the campaign. Pitt's name was immortalized in 1758 when Fort Duquesne, captured from the French, was later renamed Pittsburgh. British forces captured French forts in Africa, Guadeloupe was taken, and in September 1759, General James Wolfe won Quebec by leading his troops up a steep slope in the dead of night and surprising France's General Montcalm on the Plains of Abraham. The rest of Canada fell a few months later. British generals Robert Clive and Eyre Coote defeated the French in India, the French navy was destroyed in Quiberon Bay, and Havana and Manila were taken from the Spanish. The British Empire had been born.

George II died before the war ended, knowing that Britain ruled the waves and had colonies all over the world. He was blind in one eye and partially deaf, but at 76, he had lived longer than all previous monarchs. His end came suddenly and unromantically on the morning of 25 October 1760 when, after drinking his hot chocolate, he repaired to the lavatory. He had suffered from constipation for years and on this occasion, he had a fatal heart attack.

George was the last king to be buried in Westminster Abbey. He requested a sideless coffin so that his remains could mingle with those of his wife.

40

GEORGE III

1760-1820

King George III is best known as the mad king who lost America. In reality, he was one of Britain's hardest-working, longest-serving, and best-loved monarchs. George was 22 when he came to the throne in 1760, and he made it plain that he considered himself a true patriot king. "Born and educated in this country," he proclaimed, "I glory in the name of Britain". He may have inherited his ancestors' pale skin and bulging blue eyes, but he was the first Hanoverian who spoke English without a German accent. Unlike his predecessors, he was determined to take an active role in governing his country without favouring the Whig party, which had dominated politics for nearly half a century. He also broke the Hanoverian mould by not having any mistresses, fathering a record 15 children with his wife, Charlotte of Mecklenburg-Strelitz.

The first decade of George's reign was a political nightmare. Although determined to end the royal habit of favouring one political party over the other, he retained the right to appoint the prime minister. His insistence on giving the top job to people he judged would be best for the country, even if they did not have a majority in Parliament, led to political instability. First, the king selected Lord Bute, his old tutor, who was as inexperienced as George at managing the House of Commons. Bute resigned after one year, as did four successors chosen by the king.

This political chaos could not have come at a worse time. The Seven Years War (1756–63), which brought most of North America under British control, continued to prove punishingly expensive. By 1763, 10,000 soldiers and hundreds of officials were required to protect and run the new territories. British taxpayers footed most of the bill, many paying 26 shillings a year (£260 today), while those living in the colonies paid just 1 shilling (£10). In 1765, Parliament passed the Stamp Act, the first direct tax on the American colonies, which applied to all legal documents and printed material, including cards and dice. Stamps were placed on the items to prove that the purchaser had paid the required duty.

The tax, which was a common way of raising revenue in Britain, caused outrage among residents in the colonies who argued that only their elected assemblies could impose direct taxes. Protesters mobbed British tax collectors, and ships carrying the unwelcome stamps were turned away from American ports. Facing growing unrest, Parliament quickly repealed the act but reserved the right to impose taxes. In 1767, it passed the Townshend Acts, named after Britain's chancellor of the exchequer, which taxed goods ranging from dinner plates to paint and tea. Again, colonists rebelled, cried "no taxation without representation" and boycotted British goods. At first, King George, along with most of the British public, viewed the troublesome colonials as "rebellious children". Having at last found Lord North, a prime minister whose judgement he respected and who would stay in power for 12 years, George no longer felt that he had to play a major political role.

He turned his attention to serious family matters. One of his brothers, 22-year-old Henry, Duke of Cumberland, had secretly married a commoner widow and, in the king's view, "ruined himself". To prevent this happening again, George insisted that Parliament pass the Royal Marriages Act in 1772, which forbade members of the royal family under the age of 25 to marry without the monarch's permission – an act which survives today. Another brother, the Duke of Gloucester, then confessed that he had been secretly married for six years to the illegitimate daughter of a country gentleman. Neither wife was received in court.

Meanwhile, unrest across the Atlantic continued. On 5 March 1770, to reduce tension, Parliament repealed Townshend taxes on everything but tea. Three years later, angry patriots boarded three ships in Boston harbour and threw 342 chests of tea overboard. The British government, backed strongly by the king, reacted harshly to the Boston Tea Party, closing Boston's port and limiting the power of the Massachusetts assembly. In July 1776, 13 colonial states issued their famous Declaration of Independence, which called King George a tyrant "unfit to be the ruler of a free people" and listed 27 grievances against him and his government. The king soon had reason to regret his initial dismissal of his American colonists as an "unhappy, misled, deluded multitude". With the help of France and Spain, the Americans vanquished their British rulers. While George was not directly involved in the strategic mismanagement of the war, he promoted enlistment, reviewed troops and encouraged disheartened ministers. He talked Lord North out of resigning several times, even paying his debts to keep him on as prime minister.

The king nearly abdicated when it became clear America was winning the war. In 1782, he drafted a note saying that he no longer felt of use to Britain so would take "the painful step of quitting it forever" and move to Hanover. He was talked out of stepping down, and when Lord North finally did resign, the king reluctantly accepted a hostile coalition government. After angry exchanges with his new ministers, George updated his abdication letter. Covered in ink blots and scratched out words, it said he resolved "to resign my Crown and all the Dominions appertaining to it to the Prince of Wales, my eldest son and lawful successor". Once more, he decided not to send the letter. Instead, the king set about getting rid of his political opponents.

His opportunity came with the India Bill, designed to replace the East India Company with a board of commissioners to rule India. The bill received a majority vote in the Commons, but when it came to the House of Lords, the king made his opposition clear. He warned that he would regard those who voted for the bill as "not only as not my friends but as my absolute enemies". The Lords defeated the bill and George dismissed the prime minister and other top officials and, in 1783, brought in William Pitt the Younger. Son of the talented prime minister who had served both George and his father, Pitt was just 24, the youngest prime minister in British history. He remained in office, with the king's full support, for a total of 19 years.

With Pitt successfully running the country, the king chose to spend more time with his growing family and on hobbies. In London, he bought Buckingham House, now Buckingham Palace, and made it his family residence in the capital. For more rural surroundings, he chose Kew Palace with its marvellous gardens, now a public treasure, or stayed in Windsor Castle. The public admired the king and queen for their modest and deeply religious lifestyle and they became symbols of virtuous respectability and common sense. George studied botany and, under the pseudonym Ralph Robinson, wrote about agriculture, giving rise to his nickname "Farmer George".

He collected art and commissioned masters like Gainsborough to paint royal portraits. (Nearly half the artwork in today's Royal Collection was purchased by George III.) His reign coincided with the flowering of Georgian building, inspired by architects like the Adam brothers, Robert and James. The king hired Robert Adam to decorate the ceilings at Buckingham House and Benjamin West to restore St George's Chapel at Windsor. He helped found the Royal Academy and assembled a collection of 65,000 books, which his son later gave the nation. He also won plaudits for calmly surviving several attempts on his life. On one occasion, after being attacked by a woman armed with a dessert knife, he kindly remarked: "The poor creature is mad; do not hurt her, she has not hurt me."

The popularity of King George was in sharp contrast to that of his profligate eldest son. In 1779, in the middle of the American War of Independence, young George, just 17 years old, had an affair with an actress, Mary "Perdita" Robinson. When she threatened to publish his love letters, his embarrassed father loyally begged his ministers to grant £5,000 (nearly one million pounds today) to buy them. His son then fell for a twice-widowed Catholic, Maria Fitzherbert. After she resisted his advances, and threatened to leave the country, he stabbed himself in the chest. Maria relented and the couple were secretly married in 1785 by a priest who was let out of debtors' prison for the occasion. Not only did the prince go against two laws of the land (royals under the age of 25 could not marry without the monarch's permission, and it was forbidden to wed a Catholic) but he also ran up prodigious debts building a luxurious pavilion in Brighton and by making Carlton House, his home in London, the talk of the town. The Iranian ambassador who visited Carlton House wrote of "footmen in gold-trimmed livery bearing jewel-studded torches" and a garden "to compare with the Garden of Eden".

In the autumn of 1788, King George suffered the first of his notorious bouts of mental illness. Talking non-stop, his mouth foaming, he attacked and tried to strangle his son Prince George at Windsor Castle. He shouted insults at the queen and declared he was in love with one of her attendants. Moved to Kew, he was treated by a physician known as a "mad-doctor", who put the king in a straitjacket. At night, he was tied to his bed, by day he sat strapped in a contraption he pathetically called his "coronation chair". The king gradually recovered and in April 1789, joyous crowds gathered to watch him enter St Paul's Cathedral to attend a service of thanksgiving for his return to health.

Relief that he had regained his senses, combined with public horror at the increasingly bloody revolution going on in France, made the king more popular with each passing year. During a summer visit to Weymouth, onlookers cheered as he bathed in the sea, serenaded by a band that rushed into the water to play "God Save the King", which was fast replacing "Rule, Britannia!" as the national anthem. George's madness reoccurred in 1801 and 1804, by which time the queen, terrified by his violent behaviour, had locked her bedroom door to him. He went permanently insane in 1810. Just what caused his mental problems is debatable. It was thought that he had porphyria, a hereditary disease which affects the nervous system and can produce blue urine, but some modern experts believe that he suffered from severe bipolar disorder.

The final active years of George's life were overshadowed by his demanding sons. No sooner had he recovered from his first illness in 1789 than he received letters from Princes Frederick and William, begging for money. Another son, Prince Edward, whose daughter would later become Queen Victoria, received a stern lecture from his father about overspending. His favourite son, Frederick, Duke of York, was forced to resign as commander-in-chief of the British army after his mistress took money from officers to whom she promised promotion. The Duke of Wellington dismissed the royal princes as "the damnedest millstones about the neck of any Government that can be imagined". The heaviest burden – in every sense of the word – was the heir to the throne, Prince George, mockingly called "the Prince of Whales". By 1795, he was vastly overweight and so deeply in debt that no one would lend him money, so he agreed to marry his cousin Princess Caroline of Brunswick in the hope that Parliament would increase his allowance. The marriage was a disaster. Prince George marked their first meeting, just hours before the wedding, with the words: "I feel faint, a glass of brandy if you please." Caroline was equally disappointed and dismissed George as "very fat and he is nothing like as handsome as his portrait". The groom was drunk at the ceremony and complained that his new wife smelled. Within three days, he made a will leaving all his property to his mistress Maria Fitzherbert "my wife, the wife of my heart and soul". His real wife, Caroline, who later claimed her husband had only slept with her once, on their wedding night, gave birth to a daughter, Charlotte, exactly nine months after the marriage. George and Caroline separated shortly afterward.

While George III dealt with his errant sons, the new French Republic declared war on Britain in 1793 and the conflict intensified under Napoleon. The king remained fully informed but generally left matters to Prime Minister Pitt and his successors. When the French emperor threatened to invade Britain in 1803, the king made plans to defend his country. After reviewing 27,000 volunteers in London's Hyde Park, he wrote to a friend: "I shall certainly put myself at the head of mine [volunteers], and my other armed subjects, to repel them." In the event, there was nothing to repel because Napoleon didn't invade.

The king also kept a close eye on the turbulence in Ireland, which had been under English rule since 1650. To keep the Irish from siding with the French, the British government pressured the Irish Parliament to pass the Roman Catholic Relief Act in 1793, which allowed Catholics to vote and hold certain public offices in Ireland and attend Trinity College Dublin. George was reluctant to give Catholics power on the British mainland because he viewed as sacred his Coronation Oath to protect the Protestant Church of England. Although agreeing to limited Catholic emancipation in Ireland, he later threatened to use his royal veto if it was extended to the rest of Britain. After the British and Irish governments agreed on an Act of Union in 1800, George received a new title: king of the United Kingdom of Great Britain and Ireland. He rejected a suggestion that he be called "Emperor of the British Isles" and dropped the title "King of France", which British monarchs had used since the time of Edward III.

The British public largely supported the king's hard line on Catholic emancipation, but he was on the wrong side of the argument when it came to ending the slave trade. His support for the trade did not prevent the passing of a landmark bill that abolished the trading of slaves in the British Empire. It received large majorities in both houses of Parliament in 1807 and was signed into law by a king who recognized the monarchy's diminishing power.

King George's golden jubilee, celebrating his 50 years on the throne, took place on 25 October 1809. People danced in the streets and fireworks lit up the sky. A year later, George's insanity returned, this time for good. The king disappeared from public view and spent the final 10 years of his life wandering around Windsor Castle in a purple dressing gown with the Star of the Order of the Garter pinned to its front. Nearly deaf and blind, he talked to himself or to people long dead and banged the keys of a harpsichord which once belonged to Handel, saying: "This was a favourite piece of the king when he was alive." A sadly deranged George died on 29 January 1820, and was buried in St George's Chapel, Windsor, next to his wife and one of his daughters.

During his 60-year reign, in which the country was transformed by the Industrial Revolution, George III tried his best to preserve the rights of the crown. But the increasing complexity of governance, the rising power of political parties and the pressures of public opinion were making it harder for the monarch to exercise personal authority.

41

GEORGE IV
1820-30

No British monarch was as ridiculed as George IV and no artist made more fun of him than James Gillray, father of the political cartoon. His caricature *A Voluptuary under the Horrors of Digestion* portrays the heir to the throne as an overweight wastrel. George's gigantic stomach is covered by a bursting waistcoat as he picks the remains of dinner from his teeth with a fork. An overflowing chamber pot acts as a paperweight for unpaid bills, while bottles of medicine offering cures for venereal disease are stacked on a nearby table and empty wine decanters litter the floor (the prince was renowned for drinking up to three bottles of claret at one sitting). It is a merciless depiction of a self-indulgent prince who would become a third-rate king.

George was 57 when he came to the throne in January 1820. He had ruled as regent since 1811, after his father, King George III, became permanently deranged. During his regency, he showed little interest in politics, and while the government dealt with Napoleon and the American War of 1812, "Prinny" spent his time planning extravagant buildings, enjoying life with his mistresses, and amassing enormous debts. George IV may not have made his mark on British political history, but his passion for art left behind palaces full of treasures and transformed the look of London. He converted Buckingham House into the now famous palace, remodelled Windsor Castle and created the beautifully whimsical Royal Pavilion in Brighton, which one contemporary described as "a mixture of Moorish, Tartar, Gothic and Chinese".

He filled his buildings with elegant furniture and exquisite china. George bought paintings by Rembrandt and Rubens and supported British artists like Constable, Gainsborough, Reynolds, and Stubbs. He cultivated writers including Jane Austen, who dedicated her novel *Emma* (1815) to him. He commissioned John Nash to create elegant terraces that still surround the park named after him and curve down Regent Street to Pall Mall. George made the main streets of central London as grand as any in Europe. When Carlton House, his former London residence, was torn down to make way for a terrace overlooking St James's Park, its pillars were recycled as the portico of the new National Gallery in Trafalgar Square.

The prince regent, whose early good looks had run to fat, prided himself as a leader of fashion and, together with his dandy friend Beau Brummell, set the style of courtly dress. Although his father had not allowed him to have a military career – or any job for that matter – George loved designing uniforms. He was kind to children and to his sisters, most of whom remained unmarried under the strict eye of their mother. He was an excellent host, as long as he remained the centre of attention and such a good mimic that one admirer said that had he not been destined for higher things he could have been "the best comic actor in Europe".

George adored women – except for his wife. He had numerous affairs and an unlawful marriage to a Catholic widow Maria Fitzherbert. But he did his royal duty by marrying Princess Caroline of Brunswick in 1795. He found her unpleasant from the start, and the couple separated a year after the wedding. George returned to the arms of Mrs Fitzherbert, and Caroline was viewed as a wronged woman by those who took her side against the increasingly unpopular prince. When rumours circulated that Caroline had an affair and an illegitimate child, George insisted on a government inquiry in the hope of getting a divorce. His wife was cleared and became even more popular.

After Caroline moved to Europe in 1814, George urged foreign princes not to receive her and hired spies to send back reports on her activities. When their only child Charlotte, who would have succeeded George as monarch, died in London after giving birth to a stillborn son in 1817, George did not share the sad news with Caroline. He was dismayed when, upon becoming king, his wife returned to England as his queen. She received a rapturous welcome in London and received widespread sympathy when her husband accused her of committing adultery with the dashing Bartolomeo Pergami, a member of her household. The king forced the government to introduce a bill to end their marriage. When she attended her trial at the House of Lords, her supporters lined the streets, some carrying signs saying, "The Queen forever! The King in the River!" The bill was abandoned.

George's extravagance was astronomical. While his subjects went hungry after bad harvests, his dinner guests were offered choices of more than 100 dishes over nine courses, all accompanied by fine wines. As declining exports, and soldiers returning from wars in France and America led to soaring unemployment, demands for parliamentary reform grew, and on 16 August 1819, thousands of peaceful protesters crowded into St Peter's Field in Manchester. They were fired upon by government troops. Fifteen people died and hundreds were injured at what became known as the "Peterloo Massacre". The prince regent was booed by a large crowd that gathered outside his London house when it emerged that he had written a letter approving the use of force.

Public opinion is notoriously fickle, and two years after Peterloo, George was celebrated for staging the most magnificent coronation in British history. The king, looking like "a splendid bird of paradise", wore a velvet robe carried by half a dozen pages. His new crown contained over 12,000 diamonds. Eight professional boxers were hired to keep undesirables such as the queen from attending. Caroline tried getting into Westminster Abbey but was swiftly turned away. She died just three weeks later.

Buoyed by the success of his coronation, George embarked on a series of flamboyant royal visits. He travelled by steamboat to Ireland, the first king to visit that island since William of Orange fought James II for the English throne in 1690. He then headed to Hanover to be crowned elector. Stopping in Brussels en route, he was taken on a tour of the battlefield at Waterloo by the Duke of Wellington, who had defeated Napoleon there in 1815. Wellington reported that the king showed little interest until he was shown the spot where the amputated leg of brave Lord Anglesey was buried, at which point George burst into tears. A Scottish tour followed in August 1822, organized by the king's great friend, the writer Sir Walter Scott. Dressed in a kilt – an item of clothing his visit helped to revive – George processed through the streets of Edinburgh, attended a staged version of Scott's *Rob Roy* and generally wowed onlookers with his stylish demeanour. He became the first monarch to make ceremonial visits to far corners of the kingdom, a custom enthusiastically embraced by future rulers.

George's last few years were plagued by poor health. He was so over-weight that when his corset was removed, his stomach sagged to his knees. Badly swollen legs required he be carried up and down stairs, and cataracts left him nearly blind. Pain from gout, rheumatism and a bladder ailment were relieved by heavy doses of laudanum, a mixture containing opium. His behaviour was often so bizarre that some doubted his sanity. It was hard to tell if he was joking when he made wild claims about having fought at the Battle of Waterloo and riding the winner in a famous horserace.

The ailing king spent most of his time at Windsor, and it was from there that he summoned the Duke of Wellington, now the prime minister, and his cabinet to a meeting on 4 March 1829. A Catholic named Daniel O'Connor had been elected Member of Parliament in Ireland, but Catholics were not permitted to sit in the British House of Commons. To quell serious unrest in Ireland, government ministers had drawn up a bill allowing Catholics to sit in the House of Commons and to hold public office in Britain. George opposed the reforms and, at the 4 March meeting he railed against it, talking non-stop for more than five hours. When Wellington and his ministers refused to abandon the bill, the king demanded that they all resign, which they promptly did. The next day George changed his mind and wrote a contrite letter to Wellington saying: "As I find the country would be left without an administration, I have decided to yield my opinion to that which is considered by the Cabinet to be for the immediate interests of the country ... God knows what pain it cost me to write these words." Wellington and his ministers resumed their posts, and the king signed the Catholic Emancipation Act a month later.

George died at the age of 67 in the early hours of 26 June 1830. Beneath his nightclothes was a diamond locket containing a portrait of Mrs Fitzherbert which he had asked to be buried with him. The day after his funeral, the *Times* newspaper ran this pitiless editorial: "There never was an individual less regretted by his fellow creatures than the deceased king. What eye has wept for him? What heart has heaved one throb of unmercenary sorrow? If he ever had a friend — a devoted friend in any rank of life — we protest that the name of him or her never reached us."

42

WILLIAM IV

1830-37

No one expected William to become king. Born in 1765, the third son of King George III, he was a rambunctious, not particularly bright boy nicknamed "Silly Billy" by his sisters. His father thought a stint in the navy would calm William's fiery temperament, so sent him off to sea at the age of 11. For the next decade, William enjoyed a sailor's life, joining shipmates in brawls, tumbling from the rigging and seeing active service during the American War of Independence. While teen-aged William was stationed in New York, George Washington approved a plan to capture the British prince. It was abandoned when news of the plot leaked out. By the age of 21, William captained HMS *Pegasus* with a crew of 200, and counted the illustrious naval hero Horatio Nelson as a friend.

When William returned to life on land, he shocked his family by swearing, spitting, and drinking too much. He annoyed his politically conservative father, George III, by threatening to join the opposition Whig party as a member of Parliament. The king reluctantly gave him the title Duke of Clarence on the condition that he abandon any political ambitions.

William was as profligate as his brothers, spending extravagantly and keeping mistresses. In 1789, he fell for Dorothea Jordan, the most famous actress in London. They lived together for the next 20 years, mainly at Bushy House on the Hampton Court Estate, and had 10 children surnamed FitzClarence. Mrs Jordan generously helped pay the prince's bills, and when his love for her faded, William looked around for a rich heiress to marry. Several candidates turned him down and his search for a wife took on new urgency after the death in 1817 of his niece Princess Charlotte, who had been second in line to the throne. Her father, the prince regent and later George IV, was the only son of George III who had so far produced a legitimate heir. In fact, most of the king's many sons remained unmarried and, after Charlotte's death, they all raced to the altar. William found an ideal partner in the German Princess Adelaide of Saxe-Meiningen. When they married in 1818, she was 25, half William's age, but she transformed his life. She kept accounts, cut expenditure, stopped his drinking and made him take long walks. They had two daughters, both of whom died in infancy.

In 1827, William's elder brother, the Duke of York, died childless. As it was now clear that William would succeed his brother George IV as king, he was appointed Lord High Admiral to give him experience in public life. It was a disastrous mistake, as William refused to be a mere figurehead and, issued orders, argued with those in authority and resigned after just one year.

When, at the age of 64, William became king in 1830, he proved surprisingly sensible, down-to-earth and popular. Described as a "red-nosed, weather-beaten, jolly-looking person with an ungraceful air and carriage", he once walked up St James's Street and allowed passers-by to embrace and even kiss him. The expression "happy as a king" could have been invented for him, according to one diarist. His coronation in 1831 was so unassuming that it was dubbed the "Half-Crown-nation". He fired his late brother's French cooks and German musicians, cut the number of royal yachts from five to two, and treated 3,000 residents of Windsor to a roast beef dinner on his birthday. In London, the royal mews was demolished so the new square named after the Battle of Trafalgar could be enlarged. The king, affectionately known as "Sailor Bill", lived modestly in Clarence House and offered the much larger Buckingham Palace first to the army as a barracks, and then to politicians after fire destroyed the Houses of Parliament in 1834.

Revolution was in the air when William came to the throne. The French had thrown out Louis XVIII, the king who had been restored to the throne after Napoleon's fall. Belgians had revolted against the Dutch and there was widespread unrest in Britain. Agricultural workers in southern England rioted over the introduction of threshing machines, and workers in the north went on strike for better pay and working conditions. There were also growing demands to reform Britain's antiquated electoral system. During the Industrial Revolution, workers had poured into Birmingham, Leeds and Manchester, but none of these crowded centres had representation in Parliament. Tiny populations in so-called "rotten boroughs", on the other hand, could elect two Members of Parliament, who often bribed constituents to gain office.

Within months of William's accession, Tory prime minister the Duke of Wellington resigned, and the king asked Lord Grey (who gave his name to Earl Grey tea) to form the first Whig government for nearly 50 years. In March 1831, Grey introduced a reform bill that would reallocate parliamentary seats and allow more men to vote. The House of Commons narrowly passed the bill, but it was defeated in the House of Lords. When Grey sent a message urging the king to come and dissolve Parliament immediately, William's advisers informed him that it would take five hours to prepare the horses for the royal carriage to transport him there. Taking matters into his own hands, the king jumped into a hansom cab. In the ensuing election, the Whigs were re-elected and passed a second reform bill, but the lords again threw it out. This provoked the worst clashes in modern British history, with riots in London, Derby and Nottingham. Hundreds of people died in Bristol, where torched buildings burned for four days. Undeterred, the mainly Tory House of Lords defeated a third reform bill, which led the exasperated Grey to ask the king to appoint up to 50 new Whig peers who would support the bill and ensure its passage.

Traditionally, the king alone controlled the appointment of peers, so William refused, but after three weeks of rioting known as the "Days of May", he reconsidered. He informed Grey it was his duty to set his feelings aside and do what was best for the country. William became the first monarch to agree to appoint individuals to the House of Lords at the government's request – a surrender of royal power which marked a key moment in the development of Britain's modern constitutional monarchy. Ironically, the king did not have to appoint any lords in the end. He persuaded key Tories to abstain in the vote, and the Great Reform Act passed in June 1832. Fifty-six rotten boroughs were abolished, and new seats given to large towns. The number of male voters increased by one fifth and, although the new total represented just 18 per cent of adult men, smaller property holders were given the vote for the first time, opening the way to wider enfranchisement.

In 1833, William also gave royal assent to the Slavery Abolition Act, which freed more than 800,000 enslaved Africans throughout the British Empire. Before he became king, he had defended slavery, calling the great reformer William Wilberforce "a fanatic", but unlike his father and brother, who threatened to veto legislation they did not like, this king supported his government's policies whatever his own view.

William's final years were marked by a family dispute with the Duchess of Kent, widow of the king's younger brother and mother of young Princess Victoria. Even though Victoria was heir to the throne, the duchess prevented her from spending time at court in case she was tarnished by contact with William's illegitimate children. She further angered the king by taking Victoria on semi-royal tours, occupying rooms at Kensington Palace and using the royal yacht, all without his permission. He got his own back at his final birthday banquet in 1836. In front of 100 guests, he rose to his feet and announced he hoped to live until after Victoria turned 18 so that her "incompetent" mother and the duchess's "evil advisers" would not rule as regents. William died on 20 June 1837, one month after Victoria's eighteenth birthday. Mission accomplished.

PART XIII

THE HOUSE OF
SAXE-COBURG-GOTHA

1837-1910

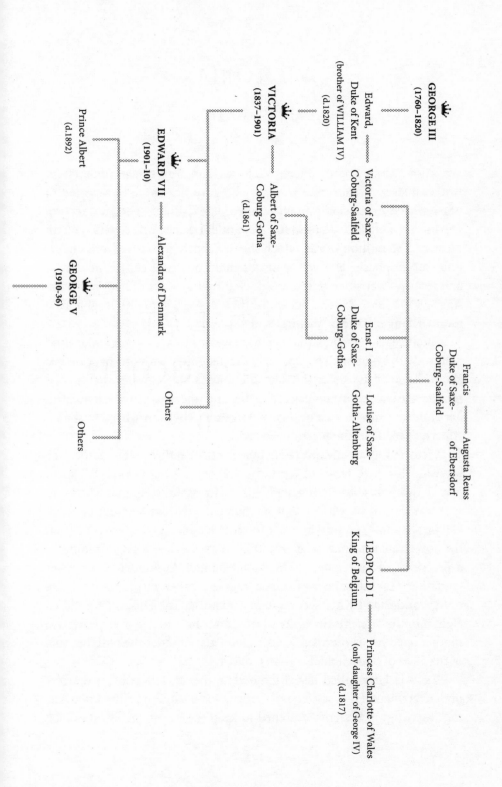

43

VICTORIA

1837-1901

We know more about Queen Victoria than any other monarch in British history because the woman who gave her name to a period of unparalleled expansion and enrichment left a unique personal record. During her long life, Victoria filled countless diaries and letters with an estimated 60 million words, which she frequently capitalized and underlined for emphasis. Her youngest daughter, Beatrice, edited the diaries and removed sensitive references, including those about her controversial servant John Brown, but more than enough remains to give us a mesmerizing picture of Victoria and her age.

She reveals herself as intelligently aware of what's going on around her, ready to argue with her ministers and identify with ordinary people about the great issues of the day. The diaries also expose what a poor mother she was, continuously criticizing and interfering in the lives of all her children, and how an obsessive devotion to her short-lived husband, Albert, shaped her often erratic behaviour.

Victoria was an unexpected heir to the British throne. Her father, the wayward Edward, Duke of Kent, fourth son of King George III, spent nearly three decades living with his mistress Julie de Saint-Laurent. It was not until he was 51 that he married Princess Victoria of Saxe-Coburg-Saalfeld, mainly in order to receive a marriage allowance from the government to pay off debts. Their only child was born "plump as a partridge" a year later, in 1819, and named Alexandrina, after her godfather Tsar Alexander of Russia. She was called Drina until the age of four and then by her second name, Victoria. The Duke of Kent died eight months after his daughter's birth, and she and her over-protective mother lived in his rooms at Kensington Palace, under the bullying rule of the head of household, Sir John Conroy.

Victoria later called her childhood "rather melancholy", a discreet understatement. Her mother and Conroy imposed strict rules known as the "Kensington System", designed to keep the young princess isolated and under their control. She rarely saw other children and she was kept away from royal uncles like William IV, whom her mother called "evil". She slept in the same bed as her mother until she was 18, was always watched over and could not even walk downstairs without someone holding her hand. Her main companion was her beloved governess, Baroness Lehzen, with whom she spent hours making and dressing her collection of 132 wooden dolls. The lively, intelligent, stubborn Victoria – who had a nasty temper – was well educated, spending several hours each day at her studies. It was during a history lesson, aged 10, that she discovered that, since all the other possible heirs in the family had died, she might become queen. "I will be good," she assured her governess.

Eighteen-year-old Victoria received news, while still in her dressing gown, that her uncle William IV had died early on 20 June 1837. As the new queen, who stood only 4 feet 11 inches tall, presided over her first Privy Council meeting, one witness was struck by her confidence, noting that it was "as if she had been doing it all her life". Another commented on her beautiful, clear voice and her eyes – "bright and calm, neither bold nor downcast".

One of Victoria's first acts was to distance herself from her mother. She demanded her own bedroom and dined alone. Within three weeks of her accession, the queen moved into the newly enlarged Buckingham Palace. Her mother was given a distant room and could see Victoria by invitation only. She banished the "arch-fiend" Sir John Conroy from her sight. The unworldly young woman found an understanding mentor in the handsome, helpful Prime Minister Lord Melbourne. A veteran Whig politician, he taught the new queen about politics, society, and the role of the monarch: "He has such stores of knowledge," she wrote emphatically.

At first, Victoria was warmly welcomed as queen. Her coronation on 28 June 1838 drew London's largest crowds ever, and she felt proud "to be the Queen of such a Nation". But a year later, two damaging events tarnished her reputation. The first involved Lady Flora Hastings, a lady-in-waiting to the queen's mother. Victoria regarded her as a spy and when she noticed that Lady Flora's stomach was swelling, the queen surmised that she was pregnant by none other than that "Monster and demon Incarnate" Sir John Conroy. To clear her name, poor Lady Flora subjected herself to a medical examination that proved she was a virgin. It turned out she had an incurable disease. Although Victoria apologized, newspapers were quick to take the victim's side and label the queen hard-hearted. Victoria was booed as she drove through London, and men refused to lift their hats to her.

On top of this, her friend Lord Melbourne's government was defeated. Sir Robert Peel, a Tory, tried to form a minority government and demanded that the queen get rid of any ladies-in-waiting who were married to opposition Whig politicians. In what became known as the "Bedchamber Crisis", Victoria refused to fire them. Peel, realizing that he lacked the queen's confidence, declined to form a new government, and Lord Melbourne and the Whigs returned to office. During the crisis, Victoria had taken the unconstitutional step of asking Melbourne for advice about how to deal with Peel's demands: "They wished to treat me like a girl," she wrote to Melbourne, "but I will show them that I am Queen of England". Victoria got her way and kept her ladies-in-waiting, but this was the last time a British monarch rejected a new government. She tried, without success, to stop Lord Palmerston from becoming prime minister in 1855.

It must have been a welcome distraction when Victoria's first cousin Albert of Saxe-Coburg-Gotha visited Windsor Castle in October 1839. She was immediately smitten: "It was with some emotion that I beheld Albert – who is <u>beautiful!</u>" Victoria proposed and the wedding took place four months later. Her description of their first night together leaves little to the imagination: "He clasped me in his arms, and we kissed each other again and again! ... bliss beyond belief!", noting, "we did not sleep much ... He does look so beautiful in his shirt only, with his beautiful throat seen". The next day, "My dearest Albert put on my stockings for me. I went in and saw him shave; a great delight for me." The devoted couple had nine children, although Victoria hated being pregnant, calling it "the <u>ONLY</u> thing I <u>dread</u>". She suffered from post-natal depression, which led to fears that she had inherited the madness of King George III. She complained that babies had "terrible frog-like" movements and made it clear that her offspring were a distracting worry.

Since the queen was busy giving birth to seven children in the first 10 years of her marriage, she increasingly relied on her husband to conduct business. Albert moved his desk beside hers and became a powerful, though unofficial, ruler. The queen spent hours each day reviewing official papers, but it was Albert who often met with ministers and dictated dispatches which Victoria copied, signed and sent. He had strong views about how a British monarch should rule and urged his wife to "watch and control the government", to be driven by a deep sense of duty and never to favour one political party over another.

Albert also took charge of the children and the royal household. He was so successful at cutting expenditure that the couple could afford to buy Osborne House on the Isle of Wight in 1845. Victoria wrote to her uncle Leopold, King of Belgium: "It sounds so snug and nice to have a place of one's own ... free from departments who really are the plague of one's life." Albert had the original Osborne House pulled down and helped design both the new house and Balmoral Castle in Scotland, which the couple bought seven years later. The prince consort believed that the royal family had "immense moral responsibility" and needed to set a good example, so royal residences became rather dull. Wine was rationed, gaming tables banished, and under strict new rules of etiquette, men had to stand in the queen's presence and back out of rooms so she did not have to look at their behinds.

Osborne House became a temporary refuge in April 1848 when violent uprisings all over Europe threatened to spread to Britain. When a mass march was planned in London by the Chartists, a movement demanding political reform, the queen and her family were evacuated to the Isle of Wight. Victoria, who had just given birth, was terrified: "I tremble at the thought of what may possibly await us". As it turned out, the march passed off peacefully.

The first day of May 1851 marked the opening of Albert's visionary triumph, London's Great Exhibition. It was, according to the queen, "the happiest, proudest day of my life". Housed in Joseph Paxton's Crystal Palace, the largest enclosed space in the world, the exhibition featured 100,000 objects from more than 40 countries. Pride of place went to items from Britain and its fast-growing empire. Six million people, one third of Britain's population, came to marvel at inventions ranging from a loco-motive engine, giant steam hammer and electric telegraph machine to an 80-blade knife, floating deck chair and buttonless shirt for bachelors. It ran for five and a half months and made enough money to help build the future Natural History, Science, and Victoria and Albert Museums as well as an arts centre, later called the Royal Albert Hall in the prince consort's memory.

Victoria herself enjoyed the fruits of scientific advance when, in 1853, she was given chloroform for the first time during labour with her eighth child, Leopold. She found it "soothing, quieting and delightful beyond measure". She demanded it again when she had her final baby, Beatrice, in 1857. When her doctor warned that any more children risked damaging the queen's health, she replied cheekily, "Can I have no more fun in bed?" Disastrously, Victoria passed the genetic disease haemophilia to some of her family. Leopold died of uncontrolled bleeding at the age of 30 and her daughters spread the disease when they married into royal European families. Her granddaughter Alexandra, wife of Tsar Nicholas II, gave birth to the haemophiliac Tsarevich Alexei.

Over the years, the queen, who believed that the monarch should preserve "the dignity, the power and the prestige" of Britain, developed a keen interest in foreign policy. During the Crimean War (1853–56), when Britain and France helped Turkey repel Russia, Victoria read military dispatches, studied maps, and bullied the government to build better military hospitals. In a letter to her daughter, she complained: "I regret exceedingly not to be a man and to be able to fight in the war." She and Albert invented and designed Victoria Crosses as special awards for bravery in battle and wrote letters to families of the dead. The queen and her daughters knitted socks, scarves and gloves for the soldiers, whom she called "my own children".

As much as Victoria adored Albert, their life together was not always harmonious. Her uncontrollable temper led to arguments, and her diaries are full of self-recrimination: "I have great difficulties in my own poor temper, violent feelings, disposition … I feel how sadly deficient I am." But nothing prepared the queen for "the utter desolation, darkness and loneliness" she suffered when the man she loved more than anything in the world unexpectedly died at the age of 42. In November 1861, Albert, suffering from a bad cold, had travelled to the University of Cambridge to scold their 19-year-old son, Bertie, who'd had an affair with an Irish courtesan, Nellie Clifden. Albert accused Bertie of sinking "into vice and debauchery" and called him "depraved". The two went for a long walk in the pouring rain, and Albert died three weeks later of what doctors said was typhoid.

Victoria, "shattered by grief and anxiety", was inconsolable. She slept clutching Albert's nightshirt, covered by his overcoat. She ordered the Windsor Castle room in which her prince had died to be preserved exactly as he left it – with fresh flowers, a jug of hot water and his clothes laid out each day. The queen, who wore black for the rest of her life, retreated into seclusion. She refused to receive government ministers and retreated to Osborne or Balmoral, where she had happy memories of Albert. Buckingham Palace remained empty for so long that some joker posted a sign saying, "These commanding premises to be let or sold in consequence of the late occupant's declining business."

After Victoria had remained hidden away for two and a half years, the *Times* newspaper ran an editorial saying it hoped to see the queen in public again. She replied in writing, insisting that public appearances would further damage her health. When Prime Minister Earl Russell asked her to open Parliament in 1865, four years after Albert's death, she said it was "totally out of the question" because her nerves were so shattered. The next year, she did open Parliament, but warned the prime minister that he would witness "the spectacle of a poor, broken-hearted widow, nervous and shrinking". Her children were so worried about their mother's condition that they asked her favourite Balmoral servant, John Brown, to travel to Osborne to keep the queen company. Their relationship remains the tantalizing mystery of Victoria's reign.

John Brown was uneducated, rudely outspoken, and sometimes drunk, but the queen became so dependent on him that he seldom left her side. He was protective of Victoria and limited access to her. He once chased a teenage boy who waved a gun at the royal carriage – one of eight assassination attempts on the queen's life, all by men, most of whom were mentally deranged. So close was the relationship between Victoria and her servant that her daughters, who despised the domineering Brown, called him "Mama's lover". Royal household staff dubbed him the "queen's stallion" and newspapers referred to the queen as "Mrs Brown". Rumours spread that they were having an affair, were secretly married or that the queen was in "an interesting condition". It's difficult to know exactly what went on between them because all references to Brown were removed from the queen's diaries by her daughter Beatrice, and 300 letters mentioning him were destroyed by Victoria's son Bertie (later Edward VII), but they were clearly very fond of each other. When Brown died in 1883, the queen wrote to her grandson: "I have lost my <u>dearest best</u> friend."

Salacious rumours about John Brown, combined with the queen's reluctance to appear in public for nearly a decade, fed a growing republican movement. The unpopular monarch was not helped by the behaviour of her eldest son and heir, Bertie. She blamed his sexual shenanigans for her husband's death, writing: "I never can, or shall, look at him without a shudder" and refused him any royal role. Yet it was Bertie who turned the republican tide. At the end of 1871, he was struck down by typhoid and nearly died. Liberal Prime Minister William Gladstone (who Victoria dismissed as a "ridiculous old man") persuaded the reluctant queen to attend a service of thanksgiving for her son's recovery at St Paul's Cathedral. The joyous response of the crowd when Victoria appeared with Bertie brought tears to her eyes and made the queen realize that her subjects loved and needed to see her.

It was Tory Prime Minister Benjamin Disraeli who ingeniously used his diplomatic skills to persuade Victoria to behave like a queen again. During a six-year term from 1874, he convinced her to open Parliament and do his bidding. "Everyone likes flattery; and when you come to Royalty you should lay it on with a trowel," he told a friend. He fawned upon her and called her the "Faery", yet complained that Victoria could be "very troublesome, very wilful and whimsical, like a spoilt child". Asked how he managed to control the queen he replied: "I never deny: I never contradict: I sometimes forget."

The queen did get her way in 1876, when she persuaded Disraeli to grant her the title Empress of India. With his encouragement, Victoria revived her interest in what was going on around her. When things were not going well in the Anglo-Zulu War of 1879, she urged the government "not to be downhearted for a moment but to show a bold front to the world". After a minister told the queen off for sending messages to generals in the field instead of through official government channels, Victoria briskly replied, "The Queen always has telegraphed direct to her Generals and always will do so." She was furious with the Prime Minister William Gladstone for failing to send an expeditionary force in time to rescue General Gordon in Khartoum. Her forthright manner and extreme self-confidence so impressed German Chancellor Otto von Bismarck that when they met in Berlin, Bismarck remarked, "Mein Gott! That was a woman. One could do business with her."

As the queen got older, she became more conservative. She was against home rule in Ireland and called the campaign for women's rights "a mad, wicked folly", dismissing it as "dangerous and unchristian and unnatural". She also had her doubts about the Representation of the People Act 1884, which gave more British men the vote, saying that she would "not be the Queen of a democratic monarchy". She warned those who demanded radical reforms that they "must look for another monarch" but doubted "they will find one".

Victoria's outspoken views reflected those of most of her subjects, and her popularity soared. Her Golden Jubilee in 1887, celebrating 50 years on the throne, reached a new pinnacle of pomp and pageantry and became a model for future monarchs. Victoria, now known as the "Grandmother of Europe", led a procession that included royalty from as far away as Japan and Hawaii – and 43 family members. Among the countries whose thrones her descendants went on to occupy are Russia, Germany, Sweden, Norway, Denmark, Spain, Greece and Romania.

Ten years later, Victoria's Diamond Jubilee had a quite different emphasis. This time, the vast British Empire was celebrated with a procession of troops from around the world, marching to an open-air service outside St Paul's Cathedral. The 78-year-old queen, who had trouble seeing and walking, sat in an open carriage.

Victoria's first entry in her diary for 1901 reads: "Another year begun – I am feeling so weak and unwell, that I enter upon it sadly." Two weeks later, she had a stroke. On 21 January, she called for the Prince of Wales, her successor, put out her arms to him and uttered her last word: "Bertie". She died the next day, with her doctor on one side and, on the other, her eldest grandson, Kaiser Wilhelm II of Germany, who would be at war with Britain 13 years later. The queen left a long list of items to be placed in her coffin. They included photos of all her family, along with rings from Albert and "a plain golden wedding ring" that had belonged to John Brown's mother. She also asked that a photograph of Brown and a lock of his hair be placed on her left hand.

Queen Victoria ruled for nearly 64 years, longer than any previous British monarch, and was a symbol of stability in a fast-changing world. She was the last monarch to try to overrule politicians she disagreed with and finally accepted the role of the monarch as ceremonial figure-head which became a lesson to her successors.

Victoria, more than any other queen or king, is remembered around the world in the names of cities, states and waterfalls. In Canada, the Monday on or before Queen Victoria's birthday on 24 May is a holiday still named in her honour.

44

EDWARD VII

1901-10

Neither Victoria nor her husband believed that their eldest son, Albert Edward, would make a good monarch. From an early age, the queen called him "sadly backward", while her husband Albert wrote him off as "a thorough and cunning lazybones". In later years, Victoria, despairing of her heir's dissolute lifestyle, declared that he was "totally unfit ... for ever becoming king". She would have been even more horrified had she known that when her son succeeded to the throne, he would not become King Albert, as agreed, but would choose to rule under his second name, Edward. Despite his parents' serious misgivings, King Edward VII became a widely admired monarch.

Albert Edward, known as Bertie, had a dismal childhood. From the age of six, his father imposed a strict academic programme which placed Bertie in the hands of a tutor for several hours each day, six days a week. His first governess reported he was "uncommonly averse to learning" and misbehaved by "getting under the table, upsetting the books". He spoke English, French and German, which so confused his accent that he stuttered and, although he took elocution lessons, he spoke with a slight German accent. His parents constantly compared Bertie unfavourably to his more intelligent older sister, Vicky, and it wasn't until he became the first Prince of Wales to visit Canada and the United States in 1860 that he realized he had something to offer.

The four-month tour of North America was a wild success, with excited crowds greeting the 18-year-old prince everywhere he went. He laid the cornerstone of Canada's new Parliament building in Ottawa, watched famous Charles Blondin cross Niagara Falls on a tightrope and stayed with US President James Buchanan in Washington. When he appeared in the ballroom of New York's Opera House, the floor partially collapsed under the weight of onlookers who'd crowded in to get a glimpse of Britain's future king. Bertie discovered that he had a talent for putting people at their ease, and loved being the centre of attention.

His relaxed manner served him well on future tours of the Middle East in 1862 and India in 1875. From India, the open-minded prince wrote home complaining about the way British officials treated the native population: "Because a man has a black face and a different religion from our own, there is no reason why he should be treated as a brute."

While Bertie toured the Middle East, Queen Victoria planned his wedding to Princess Alexandra of Denmark. They married in 1863 and moved into London's sumptuous Marlborough House, which Sir Christopher Wren had built for Queen Anne's nemesis, the Duchess of Marlborough. The couple became the centre of a glittering social set of aristocrats and rich businessmen, with nightly dinner parties, trips to the opera and weekends in stately homes. Princess "Alix" was tall, stately, and very beautiful, but not very bright. In fact, one acquaintance described her as "the stupidest woman in England".

She had six children in quick succession, and when doctors advised her to abstain from sex to avoid damaging her health, Bertie found no shortage of willing new partners. The playboy prince's long list of mistresses included actresses Lillie Langtry and Sarah Bernhardt, aristocrats Jennie Churchill (mother of Winston) and Daisy Greville, whom he addressed as his "adored little Daisywife". His favourite was Alice Keppel, who was very amusing and boasted "a deep throaty voice" – not unlike her great-great-granddaughter Camilla, who is now married to Prince Charles. Bertie tried to be discreet, although he once had to appear as a witness in a divorce case. His wife, who grew increasingly deaf and withdrawn, reluctantly accepted her husband's wanderings.

Queen Victoria's lack of confidence in Bertie meant that she refused to give him any proper jobs, so he successfully created his own role as a champion of public service. He campaigned for better housing for the poor, raised money for hospitals and opened bridges and schools. He helped plan the Royal Albert Hall and Royal College of Music and founded the Order of Merit, which recognized contributions to science, art, literature and the armed forces. By 1900, the prince was patron of 125 charities and 75 hospitals. Unlike his mother, Bertie understood the need for royalty to be highly visible and useful.

Bertie became Edward VII "King of the United Kingdom of Great Britain and Ireland", with the added title of "the British Dominions beyond the Seas and Emperor of India" on 22 January 1901. Three weeks later, he presided over the state opening of Parliament, planning every detail himself. For the first time in 40 years, the magnificent glass coach was used to carry the monarch to Westminster. He read the speech from the throne watched by female friends in the Ladies' Gallery. He would open Parliament every year of his reign, always emphasizing the pageantry which he knew his subjects loved.

Being king did not stop the aptly nicknamed "Edward the Caresser" from enjoying his mistresses or a privileged lifestyle. He bred racehorses, played bridge, gambled at cards, loved shooting and sailing, holidayed in Europe (often with Alice Keppel by his side), delighted in travelling fast in newly invented motor cars, ate multi-course meals which expanded his waist to 48 inches and smoked 12 cigars a day supplemented by 20 cigarettes. He complained that Buckingham Palace and Windsor Castle looked like "Scottish funeral parlours", so he cleared them out. A theatre designer was hired to make Buckingham Palace a showcase in white, gold and scarlet. The Mall was widened, Admiralty Arch built, and the now famous public space was created outside the palace. He gave Osborne House to the nation and spent time at his new purchase, the Sandringham Estate in Norfolk, where clocks were set half an hour ahead to allow more daylight for shooting parties.

Although he was far less interested in government than his mother, the new king read official papers and discussed issues with ministers, but mostly left them to get on with it. He took his role as head of the armed forces seriously, supporting the building of new dreadnaught battleships and indulging his love of uniforms. Celebrated wherever he went, Edward developed excellent diplomatic skills. His attempts to quell growing conflict in Europe earned him another nickname: "Edward the Peacemaker". In 1903, on his own initiative, he visited Paris and charmed the French by heaping praise on their country. When Britain and France signed the Entente Cordiale a year later, ending centuries of Anglo-French conflict, King Edward won much credit. Being related to most European royals proved a huge advantage, and in 1908, he became the first British monarch to visit Russia for a friendly meeting with his nephew Tsar Nicholas II. Another nephew, the unstable Kaiser Wilhelm II, proved less agreeable. The two men did not get on, with the Kaiser accusing Edward of treating him like a child rather than an emperor, while the British king complained that volatile Wilhelm needed to learn that he was "living at the end of the nineteenth century and not in the Middle Ages". Domestic politics dominated the final year of Edward's reign. In April 1909, Liberal Chancellor David Lloyd George introduced a "People's Budget" which, among other things, increased old age pensions by raising taxes on the rich. The House of Commons passed the bill, but it was defeated in the House of Lords. The king, who had privately urged key lords to support the bill, was asked by Prime Minister Asquith to appoint 300 new Liberal members to the House of Lords. He refused to do so until after an election. When Asquith was re-elected, the lords relented and approved the bill, so the king – to his great relief – was not required to act.

On 6 May 1910, just seven days after the crucial budget vote, Edward suffered a massive heart attack. Shortly before he died, his second son, the future King George V, told him that one of his horses had won a race. "I am very glad" were the king's final words.

King Edward VII opted for pomp and spectacle even in death. His coffin travelled from Buckingham Palace to Westminster Hall on a gun carriage drawn by black horses and was placed on public display. A quarter of a million people filed past it before the royal coffin was paraded through packed streets to Paddington Station, followed on horseback by 10 monarchs, including Kaiser Wilhelm, along with Edward's favourite horse and dog. He was buried in Windsor's Royal Vault.

The man many expected would be a footnote to royal history succeeded in creating a new, glamourous, and very public role for the monarchy. As the king's *Times* obituary recorded, his influence was "not the same as that exercised by Queen Victoria but in some respects, it was almost the stronger of the two".

PART XIV

THE HOUSE OF WINDSOR

1910-Present

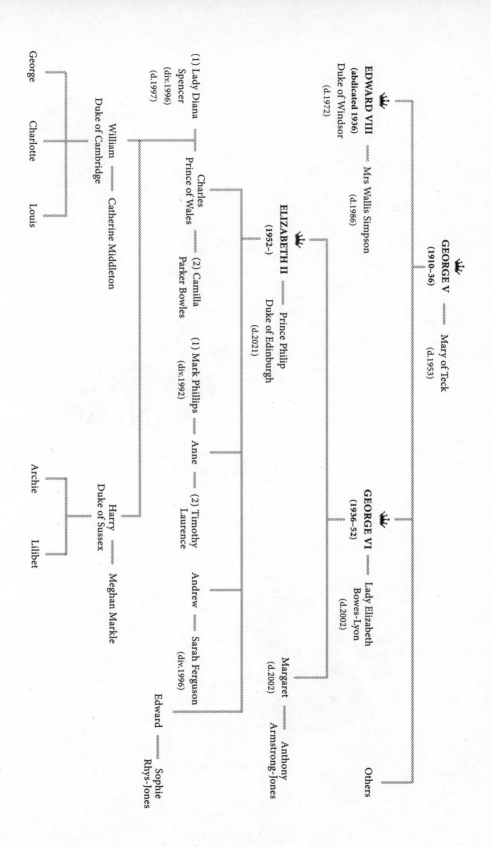

GEORGE V
(1910–36)

Mary of Teck
(d.1953)

EDWARD VIII
(abdicated 1936)
Duke of Windsor
(d.1972)

Mrs Wallis Simpson
(d.1986)

GEORGE VI
(1936–52)

Lady Elizabeth
Bowes-Lyon
(d.2002)

ELIZABETH II
(1952–)

Prince Philip
Duke of Edinburgh
(d.2021)

Margaret
(d.2002)

Anthony
Armstrong-Jones

Others

(1) Lady Diana
Spencer
(div.1996)
(d.1997)

Charles
Prince of Wales

(2) Camilla
Parker Bowles

(1) Mark Phillips
(div.1992)

Anne

(2) Timothy
Laurence

Andrew

Sarah Ferguson
(div.1996)

Edward

Sophie
Rhys-Jones

William
Duke of Cambridge

Catherine Middleton

Harry
Duke of Sussex

Meghan Markle

George

Charlotte

Louis

Archie

Lilibet

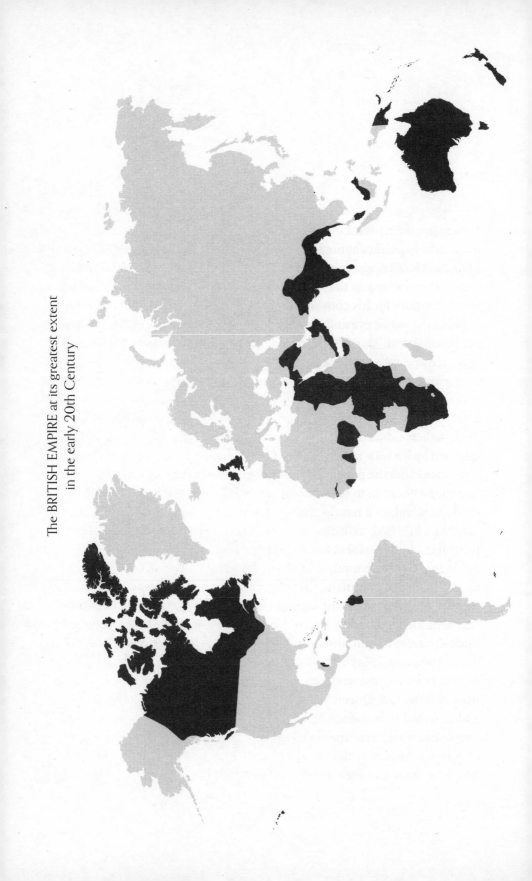

The BRITISH EMPIRE at its greatest extent
in the early 20th Century

45

GEORGE V

1910-36

He was not born to be king, but George V reigned doggedly and skilfully over turbulent times at home and abroad. He came to the throne during a constitutional crisis, raised morale during the First World War, sympathized with victims of the Great Depression and steadfastly did what he saw as his duty for his country and the British Empire. He did not enjoy being in the public eye and described state occasions such as the opening of Parliament as "the most terrible ordeal", but he understood what was expected and rose to the occasion.

George was born 17 months after his older brother, Prince Albert Victor, known as Eddy, and they grew up together. Eddy was to turn out as empty-headed and irresponsible as George was conscientious and dutiful. Their father, Edward VII, traumatized by the grim educational regime imposed by his own father, Prince Albert, insisted on minimal schooling. Convinced that the navy was the "best possible training for any boy", he sent the brothers off to sea when George was 12. For three years, they travelled the world on a naval training ship, where George worked hard and excelled while Eddy failed to master even the most basic tasks. As heir to the throne, Eddy was sent to the University of Cambridge in 1883.

While George happily continued his naval career, working his way up the ladder of command, his older brother had affairs with married women, received treatment for gonorrhoea and allegedly visited a homosexual brothel in London. Queen Victoria was not pleased, and she urged Eddy's parents to find him a wife. They chose Princess Victoria Mary of Teck, known as "May", the daughter of the queen's impoverished first cousin; however, just weeks after their December 1891 engagement, Eddy died of influenza. Queen Victoria pressured George, now Duke of York and destined to become king, to marry his dead brother's fiancée. The couple had little in common except mutual shyness and identical heights of 5 feet 6 inches. Unlike her husband, May had been well educated, spoke German and French, and was interested in the arts, but it proved a loving and successful partnership, with May offering her husband much-needed reassurance and excellent advice.

Fifteen years in the navy had a profound effect on George's character. His loud voice and bluff manner were accompanied by a compulsion for discipline, punctuality and routine. He tapped his barometer first thing each morning and last thing at night and preferred a quiet country life to the social whirl and many mistresses his father relished. Whenever possible, George, his wife and their six children retreated to York Cottage, a drab house on the Sandringham Estate that he had personally decorated with furniture from a London shop and reproductions of Royal Academy paintings. There, the future king indulged in his passion for shooting birds and building the world's most lavish stamp collection. When a royal courtier exclaimed, "Did you hear that some damned fool has just paid £1,450 (nearly £200,000 today) for a single stamp?" George replied, "I was the damned fool." His 250,000 stamps filled 325 albums.

When George's father became Edward VII in 1901, he did something Queen Victoria had refused to do: he prepared his son for the throne. He moved George's desk next to his in Buckingham Palace, showed him government papers and urged him to discuss political issues with officials. He sent George and his wife on a 231-day tour of the British Empire in 1901 and to India and Burma in 1905, where George wisely recommended that "the natives" should be handled more politely and given more power. He was devoted to his father, and when Edward VII died in 1910, the new king lamented, "I have lost my best friend and the best of fathers."

King George V inherited a domestic crisis along with his throne. The Liberal government, led by Herbert Asquith, had tried unsuccessfully to enact a Parliament bill to curb the power of the conservative House of Lords. The new monarch secretly agreed that if the Liberals won the upcoming election, he would appoint enough new Liberal peers to ensure the bill passed the recalcitrant House of Lords. The Liberals won the election and the bill's supporters strategically revealed the king's secret deal, inducing 300 Conservative lords to abstain rather than face an influx of opposing peers. The bill, which prevented the lords from rejecting budgets and limited the amount of time they could delay other Commons bills, passed by 17 votes. Although King George later described the revelation of his secret deal as a "dirty, low-down trick", he accepted the outcome and signed the bill into law.

In November 1911, George and his wife, now known as Queen Mary, travelled to Delhi to be celebrated as Emperor and Empress of India in a spectacular great durbar. It was followed by a shooting trip organized by the Maharajah of Nepal, during which the king killed 21 tigers, 8 rhinos and a bear. The couple returned home to a nation beset by problems. The growing power of unions led to strikes by dissatisfied miners, dockers and railway workers. Women demanding the vote were becoming more militant, and in 1913, a suffragette named Emily Davison died after throwing herself in front of the king's horse during a race. There was unrest in Ireland, but overshadowing everything was conflict in Europe, which led to the First World War.

On 4 August 1914, the British government declared war on Germany for invading neutral Belgium, a decision endorsed by the Privy Council. The king noted this landmark event rather casually in his diary as: "Warm, showers and windy ... I held a Council at 10.45 to declare war with Germany, it is a terrible catastrophe but it is not our fault." Most of the country rallied behind Britain's war effort, and the king and his family worked tirelessly to boost morale. They made hundreds of trips to hospitals, shipyards, and factories, and visited troops at home and on the Western Front. In October 1915, members of the Royal Flying Corps greeted George with such loud cheers that his startled horse reared, leaving the king on the ground with a fractured pelvis.

In the middle of the war, when lacklustre Prime Minister Asquith resigned, George emerged as an effective conciliator. After deadlock over who should succeed Asquith, he invited politicians from different parties to a meeting in Buckingham Palace, which resulted in a coalition government led by Liberal David Lloyd George. The king had no choice but to appoint Lloyd George, but he did so reluctantly. In the past, he had called the fiery Welshman a "damned fellow" because he had little time for rich aristocrats. During the war, the king introduced changes designed to bring the monarchy closer to the people. Aware that the honours system favoured the upper classes, George created the Order of the British Empire, whose recipients included labour leaders who were being honoured for their contributions for the first time. Sensitive to anti-German feeling in Britain and the Empire, he changed his family name from Saxe-Coburg-Gotha to Windsor, and decreed that members of the royal family no longer had to marry European nobles. When the British government offered to give the Russian royal family refuge after Tsar Nicholas II was deposed during the Bolshevik revolution in 1917, George successfully advised against the plan. The tsar was his cousin, but the king feared that bringing him to Britain would stir up socialist and republican discontent, so the Romanovs were left to their grisly fate.

The king and his family appeared on the balcony of Buckingham Palace to celebrate the end of the war on 11 November 1918, and crowds cheered so loudly that George was unable to make his planned speech. But he was soon enmeshed in another crisis: conflict over Ireland. The 1918 election returned an overwhelming majority for Lloyd George's coalition government, but 73 of 105 Irish seats at Westminster were won by Eamon de Valera's Sinn Féin party. The new Irish MPs refused to take their seats in the Commons and declared Ireland an independent country. After violent clashes between Irish patriots and British troops, the British government passed legislation in 1920 giving Catholic southern Ireland and the Protestant north separate Parliaments with limited powers. Again, the king acted as a conciliator, urging Lloyd George not to be too tough on rebels in the south. In 1922, George V approved a treaty which established the Irish Free State as a separate dominion within the British Empire.

In the post-war years, as soldiers returned home and unemployment soared, the king and queen visited impoverished communities across the land. When he heard striking workers being called "revolutionaries", George admonished: "Try living on their wages before you judge them." In 1924, he appointed Britain's first Labour prime minister, Ramsay MacDonald, writing in his diary that he wondered what his grandmother Queen Victoria "would have thought...". When MacDonald threatened to resign in 1931, the king persuaded him to stay, called a conference of party leaders and helped negotiate a coalition National Government. One of the new government's first acts was the Statute of Westminster, which gave the dominions of Canada, Australia, New Zealand, South Africa, the Irish Free State and Newfoundland the right to control their own domestic and foreign affairs. George disliked the bill because he believed that it weakened his beloved Empire which he saw as a major force for world peace and progress. But, while his royal grandmother had interfered in politics and his father tried to influence foreign policy, King George accepted his governments' decisions even if he disagreed with them.

Throughout his reign, George took time to race his royal yacht *Britannia* and improve Sandringham's stud farm. He also established the royal tradition of attending horse races at Ascot, finals of tennis at Wimbledon, rugby at Twickenham, football at Wembley and cricket at Lords. And he emerged as the first royal radio star after the newly formed BBC started broadcasting his speeches. The broadcasts proved so popular that the BBC asked him to record a Christmas message. The king, naturally a shy man, refused at first, but finally agreed in 1932. Writer and poet Rudyard Kipling wrote the first two-and-a-half-minute message, which began, "I speak now from my home and from my heart to you all."

Surprisingly, for a man who was thoughtful and kind, George was a major failure as a father. He bullied and criticized his children, which made his heir, Edward, deeply resentful. The king complained that his son spent too much time enjoying himself and had "not a single friend who is a gentleman". When, in the early 1930s, Edward fell in love with Wallis Simpson, a married American divorcee, George was furious and banned her from the palace. He told a friend: "I pray to God that my eldest son will never marry and have children and that nothing will come between Bertie and Lilibet and the throne." Bertie was the king's second son, later King George VI, and Lilibet became the future Queen Elizabeth II. George V nicknamed his granddaughter Lilibet when, as a toddler, she was unable to pronounce Elizabeth. She called him Grandpa England.

May 1935 marked King George's silver jubilee. Typically, he did not want an expensive fuss, but the National Government, worried about unrest at home and rising fascism in Germany and Italy, wanted a celebration which would bring the nation together. Over successive weeks, the king attended a service of thanksgiving at St Paul's Cathedral, appeared on the Buckingham Palace balcony, met prime ministers of the British Dominions, presided over a state opening of Parliament and reviewed 160 warships – so many events that one observer later claimed that the silver jubilee killed the king. He had long suffered from bronchial problems due to heavy smoking, and within months of the jubilee, George lay dying at Sandringham. There are two accounts of his final words. The most famous is "Bugger Bognor", the two-word reply he gave to a cheerful doctor who suggested that he recuperate in the seaside town of Bognor Regis when he felt better. Another witness claimed George asked, "How is the Empire?" before slipping away. His obvious sense of duty and down-to-earth manner had made him a popular ruler and provided a much-needed continuity through 25 tumultuous years.

The king's body was taken by gun carriage to lie in Westminster Hall, his four sons following on foot. When the Imperial State Crown arrived at Westminster perilously balanced on the coffin, the jewelled Maltese cross atop the Crown fell off. It was, wrote biographer Harold Nicholson, "a most terrible omen of what might soon be to come".

46

EDWARD VIII

20 January-11 December 1936

A year before he died, King George V made a dire prediction: "After I am dead, the boy [his heir, Edward] will ruin himself in twelve months." He was out by a month. Edward VIII reigned for just 325 days before becoming the first British monarch to abdicate by choice. For all the world, he seemed the perfect Prince Charming – handsome, charismatic and great fun. But behind this façade lurked a vain, carping, royal misfit unwilling to put duty before pleasure. He chose to marry Wallis Simpson, a twice-divorced American, rather than rule over Great Britain and the Empire. "All that matters is our happiness," he informed his mother, Queen Mary, when she begged him not to marry Mrs Simpson.

Prince Edward (known as David) was born during Queen Victoria's reign in 1894. He was a handsome boy with fine features, blond hair, and bright blue eyes, and when he was sent off to the Royal Naval College at the age of 13, he made friends easily. They nicknamed him "Sardine" because of his slight build and as a play on his future title of Prince of Wales. In 1912, the heir to the throne attended the University of Oxford, where he played polo, football, cricket and squash, but emerged without a degree. "Bookish he will never be," judged his tutor. He joined the Grenadier Guards in 1914 and was keen to fight in the First World War, but Secretary of State for War Lord Kitchener insisted that he remain well behind the front lines to avoid being killed or taken prisoner. In 1916, two equerries took the 22-year-old virgin prince to visit a French prostitute called Paulette, and he found his calling. "I don't think of anything but women now," he wrote.

His tireless pursuit of women, combined with his growing criticism of court life, led to conflict with his father. "What rot and a waste of time, money, and energy all these State visits are," the young prince complained in a letter. The king was furious when David called royal ceremony "stunting" and "good propaganda", but the prince did not disguise the fact that he found being heir to the throne a torment. "I should shoot or drown myself, to escape from this life which has become so so foul and sad and depressing and miserable for me!!" he wrote to his married mistress, Freda Dudley Ward, in 1919.

Yet that same year, he emerged as an international superstar on a trip to Canada and the United States. British Prime Minister David Lloyd George came up with the idea of sending the Prince of Wales on tours of the Empire to thank governments for support in the First World War. David's good looks and friendly, relaxed style made him a hit wherever he went. He became the first royal to shake hands with everyone he met. When his right hand got bruised, he shook with his left. Between 1919 and 1925, the prince visited 45 countries, and, although he was treated like a movie star, the adulation was not enough. He told his cousin Louis "Dickie" Mountbatten that he would give anything to change places with him. "Christ how I hate my job," he complained to his private secretary Godfrey Thomas.

He showed shameless contempt for the people he met. From Australia, he wrote that Aboriginals were "the most revolting form of living creatures I've ever seen". At a ball in India, he was overheard saying "I will not dance with a black woman" after refusing to waltz with a maharajah's wife. But the world's most eligible bachelor could do no wrong in the eyes of his fans or the media. "The average young man in America is more interested in the clothes of the Prince of Wales than in the clothes of any other individual on earth," reported *Men's Wear* magazine in 1924. "I've danced with a man, who's danced with a girl, who's danced with the Prince of Wales" became a hit song in 1927.

When in England, the prince reluctantly carried out royal duties, but much preferred going to parties and nightclubs. He entertained friends at Fort Belvedere in Windsor Great Park, playing the ukulele and bagpipes after dinner. In 1931, another married mistress, Thelma Furness introduced him to a friend who would upend royal history: Wallis Simpson, elegant, witty but brittle and a shameless social climber. An American, she had divorced her first husband and settled in London with her second. She soon became a regular visitor to Fort Belvedere, and when Thelma took a trip to New York, she asked Wallis to "look after him [the prince] while I am away". Wallis did more than that. She made herself so indispensable to the future king that one equerry noted "he follows W around like a dog". By 1934, the two of them were inseparable, much to the horror of the royal family.

David was 41 when he succeeded his father in January 1936, as King Edward VIII. He saw himself, in his own words, "as an innovator" who would push the monarchy into the twentieth century. He cut staff at royal residences, resisted moving into Buckingham Palace, which he found "gloomy", and insisted on walking freely in the streets. In a move of undisguised vanity, he ignored the convention that the monarch's profile on coins and stamps was changed from one side to the other with each successive ruler. Instead of switching to the right, he broke the rule and looked left like his father because he believed that was his best side. He also ended the tradition embraced by George V of running clocks at the Sandringham Estate half an hour ahead to ensure extra daylight for shooting. This was viewed by novelist Virginia Woolf as a sign that Edward rejected his father's traditions and most other things that he stood for. She wrote that Edward had been "daily so insulted by the King that he was determined immediately to expunge his memory".

At first, the new king worked diligently, read official papers and consulted politicians, but soon the papers were returned more slowly, often stained by wine-glass marks. Not only was Edward bored with official work, but he also showed Wallis and other acquaintances confidential documents. In August 1936, while seven million souvenir mugs were being manufactured for his coronation that would never take place, the king went on a cruise with Wallis. When they returned to London, she started divorce proceedings against her husband, Ernest.

The king asked his friend, British press baron Lord Beaverbrook, not to report the news because Mrs Simpson was "distressed by the thought of notoriety". Beaverbrook, delighted to oblige, got fellow press owners to agree to embargo news about the king and Wallis. European and American papers carried salacious stories about the affair, but British newsagents cut out all reports from imported publications, leaving their readers in the dark. On 16 November, when warned that the British papers planned to end their embargo, the king told Prime Minister Stanley Baldwin that he was determined to marry Wallis and would renounce the throne if necessary. He suggested a morganatic marriage, making Wallis his consort, not his queen, and barring their children from inheriting the throne. The British cabinet and leaders of the Dominions rejected this proposal.

Just one week before Edward abdicated, the British press ended its self-imposed silence and, on 2 December, a shocked nation woke to the news that their king, head of the Church of England, planned to marry a twice-divorced woman. There was explosive controversy, pitting an outraged older generation against a more sympathetic younger one. After Wallis received threatening letters and a stone was thrown through her window, she moved into Fort Belvedere with her Aunt Bessie as chaperone. On 3 December, she sought refuge in France. Edward's parting words were: "I shall never give you up." When the king's family begged him not to abdicate, he told his brother the Duke of Kent that he could not "stick" being king and "could never tolerate the restrictions, the etiquette, the loneliness".

On 10 December, Edward signed an "Instrument of Abdication" in front of his three brothers, the eldest of whom, Albert (known as Bertie), became King George VI. The next evening, he sat down to broadcast a speech he wrote with the help of his friend Winston Churchill. It included the famous line, "I have found it impossible to carry the heavy burden of responsibility and to discharge my duties as King as I would wish to do without the help and support of the woman I love."

While Wallis waited in France for her divorce to come through, the newly titled Duke of Windsor stayed as a guest of Baroness Rothschild in Austria. Just one friend, Captain Edward "Fruity" Metcalfe accompanied him – the rest of his staff refused. He was reunited with Wallis on 4 May 1937, the day after her divorce. When they married a month later, no family members and very few friends attended. Fruity acted as best man.

Five months after their wedding, the couple hit the headlines for visiting Hitler's Germany, ostensibly to study housing and working conditions. They travelled in the Führer's train, had tea with Hitler and gave Nazi salutes. The duke had frequently praised Hitler in the past, and the German leader hoped the former king would persuade Britain not to enter the impending war.

The Windsors settled in France, and the duke constantly badgered his family to allow Wallis to add HRH (Her Royal Highness) to her title, Duchess of Windsor. Every request was refused, a slight the duke and his wife never forgave. When the Second World War started in 1939, the duke begged for a job and was assigned to the British Military Mission in Paris to liaise with the French High Command. He did not cover himself in glory when the Germans advanced into France in 1940. Without telling his senior staff, he filled his car with valuables and drove to Biarritz, where Wallis was staying. They escaped to Madrid, racing through roadblocks with the duke shouting (in French), "I am the Prince of Wales. Let me pass, please!" There was a German plot to kidnap the duke in order to pressure Britain to withdraw from the war, but it failed and the Windsors ended up in Portugal. From there, during the darkest days of the war, the duke pestered British Prime Minister Churchill to find him another job. He was appointed Governor of the Bahamas, but when he demanded that some of his former servants be released from active service to accompany him, Churchill said no.

After five years in the Bahamas, the couple returned to Paris, where city officials provided a house in the Bois de Boulogne for very low rent. The Windsors walked their beloved pugs, played golf, did jigsaws and entertained very grandly. One visitor recalled dining at their house was "like stepping into a fairyland of fantastic luxury. Everything seemed to be made of gold or crystal." To help support their sumptuous lifestyle, the couple wrote bestselling books. The first of the duke's three works, *A King's Story*, was published in 1951, followed by Wallis's *The Heart Has Its Reasons* five years later. They travelled to England occasionally, where the duke saw his mother, but she resolutely refused to meet "that woman". Wallis did not accompany him to the funeral of King George VI in 1952. After his mother, Queen Mary, died in 1953, the duke wrote to Wallis: "What a smug stinking lot my relations are", and accused the late queen of being unloving and cruel: "the fluids in her veins have always been as icy cold as they now are in death".

In 1971, the duke, a heavy smoker, was diagnosed with terminal throat cancer, and Queen Elizabeth II visited him for the first time. He insisted on leaving his sickbed and bowing to his niece even though he was attached to a drip. When he died in May 1972, his body lay in state in St George's Chapel at Windsor Castle before being buried in the royal necropolis at Frogmore. The duchess, who drifted into senility, died in 1986 and is buried with her husband of 35 years. There are those who believe that King Edward VIII should have been allowed to remain on the throne after marrying Wallis, but we share the view of the great Noël Coward that "a statue to Mrs Simpson should be erected on every village green", because she saved Britain from a disastrous monarch.

47

GEORGE VI

1936-52

"I feel like the proverbial sheep being led to the slaughter," wrote Prince Albert in 1936, just days before his elder brother, Edward VIII, abdicated to marry American divorcee Wallis Simpson. He had every reason to fear the worst. Shy and insecure, with a debilitating stutter, he had grown up in the shadow of his charismatic elder brother; however, unlike the absconding king, he had a strong sense of duty and more than lived up to his stated promise: "to make amends for what has happened". His straightforward decency and obvious concern for his subjects left his daughter Queen Elizabeth II one of the most stable thrones in British history.

The future king was not initially welcomed by his great-grandmother Queen Victoria in 1895 because he was born on a dark anniversary, 14 December, the very date that her beloved husband, Albert, had died in 1861. The young prince was called Albert to win the old queen over, and it worked. She gave him a muted welcome and agreed to become his godmother. He had a difficult childhood, suffering from knock knees, which required wearing painful splints day and night, and had a terrible stutter, possibly caused by being forced to write with his right hand when he was naturally left-handed. His father, the future King George V, did not help by shouting "Get it out, boy!" when Bertie, as he was called, stumbled over his words.

Like his elder brother Edward, Bertie was sent to the Royal Naval College on the Isle of Wight at the age of 14. Learning was not his strong point – he came 68th out of 68 in his final exams – but he was an excellent and popular sportsman. (He played in the Wimbledon men's doubles in 1926 but was eliminated in the first round.) After training as a naval officer in Dartmouth, Bertie went to sea as a midshipman in 1913. As second son of George V, he assumed his career would be in the navy. Gastric problems, including appendicitis and an ulcer, kept him on land for much of the First World War, but he was on board HMS *Collingwood* for the Battle of Jutland, the only major naval confrontation of the First World War.

The British navy had successfully kept Germany's fleet from leaving port and entering the North Sea, but at the end of May 1915, German ships tried to break out. HMS *Collingwood* sank two enemy cruisers, but when it was fired upon, Bertie wrote: "I was distinctly startled and jumped down the hole in the top of the turret like a shot rabbit!!" The German fleet returned to port for the rest of the war, and Bertie moved on to the newly formed Royal Naval Air Service. When the Royal Air Force was founded in April 1918, Flight Lieutenant Prince Albert, who had gained his pilot's licence, was one of its first officers.

Bertie would have happily stayed in the navy, but his domineering father had other plans. To prepare him for taking on more royal responsibilities, he was sent to the University of Cambridge. While studying history and economics, he became so interested in industrial relations that his family called him "the Foreman". He gained valuable experience touring Britain as President of the Industrial Welfare Society, meeting trade union leaders and visiting factories. One manager remarked he had never met a visitor "who asked more sensible questions or showed greater understanding of our fundamental problems". In 1920, he was created Duke of York, and came up with the progressive idea of holding summer camps where working-class boys and more privileged teenagers would mix to play games and have singsongs. The duke himself attended the camps as "Great Chief".

Bertie fell in love with the woman who was to become his devoted wife and lifelong anchor at a dance in 1920. Lady Elizabeth Bowes-Lyon, daughter of the Scottish Earl of Strathmore, combined "radiant vitality and a blending of gaiety, kindness and sincerity [which] made her irresistible to men", according to one courtier. Bertie asked her to marry him, but Elizabeth worried about the restrictions royal life would bring, and the duke had to propose three times before she finally accepted. When they married in 1923, Westminster Abbey's congregation included 52 boys from London's impoverished East End, personal guests of Bertie.

Elizabeth's common sense and constant encouragement gave her husband a new lease of life. To help him overcome his stutter, she accompanied him to appointments with the Australian speech therapist Lionel Logue, helped write and rehearse speeches and thoughtfully removed words that Bertie struggled to pronounce. Their marriage was blessed by the arrival of two daughters, Elizabeth in 1926 and Margaret in 1930, but any hopes of a happy family life away from the main spotlight were shattered on 11 December 1936 when Edward VIII became the first king to agree to abdicate. Bertie called it "that dreadful day" and confessed to his cousin Lord Mountbatten that he felt inadequate, because his only experience was as a naval officer, whereas his brother, who had been 41 years old when he became king, had plenty of time to prepare for the role. Neither Bertie's wife nor his mother, Queen Mary, ever forgave the departing king for forcing the crown on Bertie's unready head.

The new king was terrified that the monarchy would "crumble" under what he called "the shock and strain" of the abdication. He chose the title "King George" as a tribute to his father and a mark of stable continuity. The coronation planned for Edward VIII went ahead, but it was George VI who was crowned on 12 May 1937, with Queen Elizabeth at his side and their daughters, Princesses Elizabeth and Margaret, looking on. The king insisted that the coronation service be broadcast live on radio for the first time and that newsreel cameras be allowed into Westminster Abbey, a canny move to share the event with as many of his subjects as possible.

In addition to dealing with his new job, the king had to put up with endless complaints from his brother, now known as the Duke of Windsor, who was living in Austria awaiting Wallis Simpson's divorce. He demanded that his future wife be called Her Royal Highness and that she be accepted in royal circles. The duke also haggled over details of a promised annual allowance, even though he had a private fortune of a million pounds (£70 million today). The king finally stopped taking his telephone calls.

Unlike his brother, the new monarch worked tirelessly, reading official papers, meeting government ministers and carrying out official duties. As the threat of conflict with Germany grew, George VI sided with Conservative Prime Minister Neville Chamberlain who called for appeasement, not hostility. The king offered to contact Hitler to urge him to stop his aggressive actions but accepted ministerial advice not to get involved. He travelled to France to show solidarity, and publicly welcomed Chamberlain's words – "peace for our time" – when the prime minister returned from Germany in September 1938, carrying the Munich Agreement, in which Hitler falsely promised not to invade Czechoslovakia. The king invited Chamberlain to join him on the balcony of Buckingham Palace to celebrate the agreement, which prompted some to complain that it was unconstitutional for a monarch to support a politician so openly.

In May 1939, King George and Queen Elizabeth travelled to Canada and the United States ostensibly on state visits but hoping to drum up support for what looked like another world war. It was the first time a British king and queen visited North America, and they received a rapturous reception. Canada's Governor General at the time was the author John Buchan, Lord Tweedsmuir, who described the king as a wonderful mixture "of shrewdness, kindliness and humour" and wrote that the queen "has a perfect genius for the right kind of publicity". The royal couple stayed with President Franklin D Roosevelt at the White House and at his private residence in New York State. The king impressed the American leader with his knowledge of US government policy, and the two spent hours chatting. The king enjoyed their talks so much that at 1:30 one morning, the president had to say: "Young man, it's time to go to bed." George carried his notes of their conversations in his briefcase throughout the Second World War.

After Britain declared war on Germany on 3 September 1939, King George, as commander-in-chief of Britain's armed forces, was kept fully informed. He was one of a handful of people aware of the secrets revealed by Ultra, the intelligence operation focused on the cracking of German ciphers, based at Bletchley Park. The king also helped with the D-Day deception by visiting areas in Kent in advance of the invasion, to make it look as if the Allies were planning to land in Calais, not on the Normandy beaches. He lunched privately with wartime Prime Minister Winston Churchill every week, and although their relationship was uncomfortable at first – not least because Churchill had been an ardent supporter of Edward VIII during the abdication crisis – they soon became firm allies.

The king's main task was to boost morale by visiting troops, handing out medals and, most importantly, setting a good example. He and the queen remained in London throughout the war and installed a shooting range at Buckingham Palace so they could practise in case the Germans invaded. They turned down a suggestion by members of the cabinet that their daughters be sent to Canada for safety, and they endured rationing like everyone else. When the government encouraged people to use less hot water in order to conserve precious fuel supplies, the king arranged for lines to be drawn around royal bathtubs which limited the depth of water to five inches. During the Blitz in 1940, when German planes bombed industrial centres all over Britain, the king and queen visited stricken cities and commiserated with survivors. Photos of them walking through the wreckage of the East End of London set a new standard for caring monarchs. Buckingham Palace was hit nine times altogether, with one bomb landing just below the king's study. The royal couple spent nights at Windsor Castle but returned to London each day, and the queen announced: "I'm glad we've been bombed. It makes me feel I can look the East End in the face."

The king was so moved by the bravery he witnessed after air raids that he created and designed the George Cross for civilians, equivalent to the Victoria Cross for gallant members of the military. He suffered his own personal tragedy, losing his brother Prince George in a military plane crash, and made inspired broadcasts urging his subjects to put their trust in "the unconquerable spirit of our peoples". On Victory in Europe (VE) Day, 8 May 1945, thousands of people gathered outside Buckingham Palace, shouting, "We want the king!" He and the queen invited Winston Churchill to join them on the famous balcony, and the enthusiastic crowd made them reappear seven times.

The years following the war were tough for Britain and for the king. Winston Churchill's Conservative party was unexpectedly defeated in the July 1945 election and Labour leader Clement Attlee became prime minister. Post-war debt, unemployment, continued rationing and a record cold winter in 1947 made life miserable. When the Labour government embarked on a programme of nationalization, and created a welfare state, King George was privately dismayed, but he supported the government publicly and did not interfere. He also watched helplessly as the British Empire continued to disintegrate. India won its independence in 1947, splitting into the Dominions of India and Pakistan. When India became a Republic in 1950, the king lost the title "Emperor of India" but was promised a new honour: "Head of the Commonwealth".

"I feel burned out," the king often complained in his last years. Like many of his predecessors, he was a heavy smoker, a habit that led to arteriosclerosis, a thickening of his blood vessels. After undergoing a successful operation in 1949, he appeared for a final examination and surprised his surgeon by saying: "You used a knife on me, now I'm going to use one on you." He produced a sword and knighted the doctor. In September 1951, he had a far more serious operation: his left lung was removed. He was never told that it was cancerous.

On 31 January 1952, the king appeared in public for the last time. Ignoring doctors' advice, he went to London Airport to wave off Princess Elizabeth and her husband, Prince Philip, on a tour to Australia via Kenya. Six days later, at the age of 56, George VI died in his sleep of a heart attack.

48

ELIZABETH II
1952-Present

It seems fitting to end this book with the longest-serving female monarch in world history. Few of us can remember a time without the familiar face of Queen Elizabeth II looking out from newspapers, television screens, coins and stamps. During the seven decades that she has reigned over the United Kingdom and many other Commonwealth countries, the world has changed unimaginably but, as the queen's son and heir, Prince Charles, observed during her golden jubilee celebrations in 2002, Elizabeth remains "a beacon of tradition and stability in the midst of profound, sometimes perilous change".

Like many of her ancestors, she was not born to rule. Her father's elder brother, destined to become King Edward VIII, was expected to marry, and have children who would push Elizabeth down the line of succession. Her parents adored "Lilibet" and her younger sister, Margaret, and gave them a happy, secure childhood. They were educated at home under the loving care of Marion "Crawfie" Crawford, their governess for 17 years. In her book, *The Little Princesses*, she describes Elizabeth as a very obedient, well-organized child who loved dogs and horses. (She wrote the book after retiring and without the royal family's approval. They were outraged and never spoke to Crawfie again.) The cosy family life changed abruptly in 1936 when Edward VIII abdicated to marry twice-divorced American Wallis Simpson, leaving Elizabeth's father to become King George VI. "Does this mean you will have to be the next queen?" Princess Margaret asked her sister. "Yes, someday," replied Elizabeth. "Poor you," commiserated Margaret.

In 1939, the 13-year-old heir to the throne became a private pupil of Sir Henry Marten, vice provost of the exclusive boy's school Eton College. Books with words underlined by the future queen can still be seen in Eton's library. She showed particular interest in Sir William Anson's *The Law and Custom of the Constitution*, and later impressed prime ministers with her deep understanding of the British state.

During the Second World War, Elizabeth and Margaret lived in royal homes outside London while their parents worked from Buckingham Palace. In 1940, the future queen made her debut as a working member of what her father labelled "the family firm". In her first radio broadcast, she sympathized with evacuee children, saying, "My sister Margaret Rose and I feel so much for you as we know from experience what it means to be away from those we love most of all." She posed for photos in her Windsor Castle allotment, promoting the government's "Dig for Victory" campaign, which encouraged people to combat food shortages by growing their own. As a proud member of the Auxiliary Territorial Service (ATS), the women's branch of the British army, she learned how to drive a 3-ton truck, change tyres and strip down engines. On 8 May 1945, to celebrate VE Day, 19-year-old Elizabeth donned her ATS uniform and, incognito, joined the cheering crowds outside Buckingham Palace. She remembered linking arms with strangers and being "swept along on a tide of happiness and relief".

Throughout the war, Elizabeth exchanged letters with Prince Philip of Greece, a dashingly handsome officer in the British navy who would become the love of her life. She had fallen for him years earlier when Philip, her third cousin, guided the family around the Royal Naval College. Governess Crawfie noticed that the princess, just 13, "never took her eyes off him". Philip, on the other hand, who was five years older, "didn't pay her any special attention". When he did finally take notice, Elizabeth's parents feared that the impoverished Greek exile would not make a good husband. One courtier dismissed him as a "rough, ill-mannered, uneducated [man] who would probably not be faithful". When Philip asked for Elizabeth's hand in 1946, King George, knowing that his daughter was deeply in love, accepted on the condition that the engagement was kept secret until Elizabeth turned 21 a year later.

In February 1947, the royal family headed off for a three-month tour of South Africa and Rhodesia (now Zimbabwe). It was the first time the princesses had travelled abroad, and from Cape Town, Elizabeth made a momentous vow. On 21 April, the day of her twenty-first birthday, she broadcast a message dedicated "to all peoples of the British Commonwealth and Empire", saying, "my whole life whether it be long or short shall be devoted to your service and the service of all our great imperial family to which we all belong" (a vow which she repeated during her platinum jubilee in 2022 when she was 96 years old). She has kept that promise, putting Great Britain and the Commonwealth at the centre of her life, and ruling out abdication.

On 20 November 1947, Elizabeth married her Prince Charming, who was given the title Duke of Edinburgh, and gave birth to their first son, Prince Charles, a year later. Philip continued his naval career and when he was posted to Malta, his wife went with him, leaving one-year-old Charles with her parents. She frequently returned to Britain to see him, but relished her time in Malta, later saying that living as an almost normal "sailor's wife" was one of the happiest periods of her life. By the time Princess Anne was born in 1950, King George's health was failing, Elizabeth had to take on more royal duties, and Prince Philip reluctantly gave up his naval career to support her. "That's life. I accepted it. I tried to make the best of it," was his stoical comment.

In February 1952, Elizabeth and Philip were at Treetops Hotel in Kenya when news reached them that 56-year-old King George had died. Her travel companions knew that the new queen was devastated by the loss of her beloved father, but she remained remarkably composed. On the plane back to London, she apologized for "upsetting everyone's plans".

The 25-year-old queen settled smoothly into her new role, following her father's and grandfather's examples of putting duty and service first. She diligently went through red boxes full of government papers and held weekly meetings with the prime minister, forming a strong bond with her first, Winston Churchill, who found her "confident, well informed and ready to take advice". When the queen deliberated over her family name – Philip wanted "Mountbatten" while the Queen Mother and Churchill favoured "Windsor" – Elizabeth sided with her mother and Churchill. Philip moaned to friends that he was "an amoeba ... the only man in the country not allowed to give his name to his children", but his wife made him head of the household, in charge of their children. He also became her loyal and astute adviser. (In 1960, the queen reopened the question of her family surname with Prime Minister Harold Macmillan. They agreed that any descendants not in direct line to the throne could use the name "Mountbatten-Windsor".)

The queen's coronation on 2 June 1953 was a breakthrough in ways both royal and technological. For the first time, people gathered around newly invented television sets to watch a monarch being crowned. Elizabeth had her doubts about televising the sacred ceremony, but Philip and other advisers convinced her to move with the times. The spectacle of the crown of Saint Edward, covered with hundreds of sparkling semi-precious stones, being placed on Elizabeth II's head in Westminster Abbey was an unforgettable sight for those who watched.

Her early reign was marked by the first of many family dramas. Shortly before the coronation, Princess Margaret informed the queen that she wanted to marry Peter Townsend, a divorcee with two children. The Church of England did not permit remarriage after divorce. Even though the queen was Head of the Church, she wanted Margaret to be happy, so she left her sister to decide her own future. It was Prime Minister Churchill and his successor, Anthony Eden, who eventually ruled that if Margaret married Townsend, she would have to renounce her right to the throne and her royal allowance. She ended the relationship, and went on to wed Antony Armstrong-Jones, a photographer whom she later divorced.

In her first years as queen, Elizabeth faced criticism for looking grim and sounding old-fashioned. One detractor complained that the "tweedy" aristocrats who wrote her speeches made her come across as a "priggish schoolgirl". Prince Philip drafted in the BBC's David Attenborough, who encouraged the queen to lower her voice and sound less posh. In 1957, Philip convinced his wife to reach a wider audience by moving her Christmas message from radio to television. They wrote the words together over several months and the queen read them (as she does all her speeches) sitting at a desk in the Long Library at Sandringham, surrounded by family photos and Christmas cards. "I cannot lead you into battle," she said. "But I can do something else. I can give you my heart and my devotion to these old islands and to all the peoples of our brotherhood of nations."

As the years passed, Prince Philip helped the queen appear more relaxed. He told her to smile (she agrees with her family that her face in repose looks like Miss Piggy, from *The Muppets*) and to stay in touch with what was going on by inviting leaders of the arts, science, and business communities to informal lunches. He encouraged her to appear in a documentary – *Royal Family*, broadcast in 1969, designed to make the monarch seem more relevant and down-to-earth. Covering a year in the queen's life, it shows her working at her desk in Buckingham Palace, greeting new ambassadors, hosting a garden party and on a royal tour. We also see her as a mother, at a family barbecue with her grown-up children, Charles and Anne, and "second family" Andrew (born 1960) and Edward (born 1964). Millions of people around the world watched the documentary and most loved seeing the queen in action, but critics complained that it damaged royal mystique and created an insatiable appetite for stories about her and her family.

The so-called royal soap opera went into overdrive when Prince Charles became engaged to Lady Diana Spencer in February 1981. He was 32, his name had been linked to various women (including Diana's sister) and his parents believed it was time he settled down. Nineteen-year-old Diana seemed the ideal partner. She came from an aristocratic family, had a spotless past and was in love with Charles. At their July wedding, the Archbishop of Canterbury proclaimed: "Here is the stuff of which fairy tales are made." He could not have been more mistaken. On their honeymoon, Diana struggled with the eating disorder bulimia and was devastated to discover that Charles was in touch with his former girlfriend Camilla Parker Bowles.

When the couple returned to London, there was so much media interest that Diana feared leaving home. The queen took the unprecedented step of summoning 21 newspaper editors to Buckingham Palace to ask them to leave Diana alone. Despite Diana's erratic behaviour and Charles's continued contact with Camilla, the couple presented a united front with their sons William (born 1982) and Harry (born 1984). But behind the scenes, the partnership was falling apart – as would the marriages of three of the queen's four children.

The queen has always done her best not to allow family problems interfere with her job, nor has she shown signs of distress in unnerving situations. In June 1981, shortly before Charles and Diana's wedding, Elizabeth was riding her horse Burmese in London's annual Trooping the Colour parade when six shots rang out. A 17-year-old man in the crowd was aiming a gun directly at the queen. Elizabeth serenely controlled her startled horse and rode on. It was only later that she learned the bullets were blanks. In 1983, an intruder turned up in the queen's bedroom. Michael Fagan had climbed over a Buckingham Palace wall and entered through a window. Elizabeth tried calling for help, but when no one answered, she settled down in bed and asked Fagan about himself. They chatted for a few minutes and when he asked for a cigarette, the queen accompanied him to another room. A passing chambermaid couldn't believe her eyes: "Bloody hell, ma'am! What's he doing here?" Fagan was arrested and spent time in a psychiatric hospital. When an acquaintance congratulated the queen on her sangfroid, she replied: "You seem to forget that I spend most of my time conversing with complete strangers."

One of the few times that the queen has publicly revealed her feelings was at a luncheon to celebrate her fortieth year on the throne. It was November 1992, just four days after a fierce blaze seriously damaged Windsor Castle. She admitted: "1992 is not a year on which I shall look back with undiluted pleasure." It had been, she added, an "annus horribilis". Earlier that year, Princess Anne's marriage ended in divorce, Diana collaborated on a book which chronicled her unhappy marriage in gruesome detail and Prince Andrew left his wife, Sarah, after the publication of pictures showing her kissing another man's feet. And there was worse to come. Taxpayers objected to footing the bill for Windsor Castle repairs, so the queen had to meet the costs herself by opening Buckingham Palace state rooms to the public. She also agreed to pay income tax for the first time and to reduced government payments to members of her family.

In June 1994, Prince Charles laid bare his troubled relationship with Diana. In a television documentary, the heir to the throne admitted that their marriage had broken down and that he had subsequently been unfaithful to his wife. A biography linked to the documentary portrayed Charles as the victim of an unhappy childhood, ignored by an uncaring mother and bullied by an overbearing father. The following year, Diana dished the dirt in an explosive television interview. She suggested that her husband was unfit to be king, and famously lamented Charles's affair with Camilla: "There were three of us in this marriage, so it was a bit crowded." Within days of Diana's interview, the queen informed Prime Minister John Major that she had written to both her son and daughter-in-law demanding that they get "an early divorce ... in the best interests of the country".

The tragic death of Diana in a car crash in Paris on 31 August 1997 was a defining moment in the reign of Elizabeth II. The queen was on her usual summer break at Balmoral Castle in the company of Prince Charles and his sons, William and Harry. As flowers and tributes to "the People's Princess" piled up outside palaces in London, the royal family remained firmly in Scotland, the queen convinced that she was protecting her young grandsons by letting them grieve privately. She refused to bow to demands that a flag be flown at half-mast over Buckingham Palace on the grounds that it was against royal tradition. She also ignored pleas to return to London. But as the days passed and she sensed the rising tide of public feeling, the queen changed her mind. Five days after

Diana's death, she and Prince Philip flew to London and stood outside the gates of Buckingham Palace, inspecting the wall of flowers. Even after the royal couple's appearance, those of us in the crowd continued to hear angry mumblings, but the mood changed dramatically when the back of the queen's head appeared in a palace window as she made a live broadcast honouring Diana. "We have all been trying in our different ways to cope," she said. She called Diana "an exceptional and gifted human being" whom she "admired and respected". The speech, which lasted just three minutes and nine seconds, defused a potentially explosive situation. It had been a dangerous moment – one of Elizabeth's very few misjudgements. On the day of Diana's funeral, the Union Jack flag flew at half-mast for the first time over Buckingham Palace.

As the decades passed, the queen celebrated her golden jubilee in 2002, which featured concerts in the garden of Buckingham Palace. The sight of Brian May, guitarist from the band Queen, playing the national anthem on the palace roof emphasized just how much things had changed. A diamond jubilee in 2012 was followed by an unprecedented platinum jubilee in 2022. For the first time, the queen was not accompanied by her husband, Prince Philip, who died aged 99 in 2021. They spent his last months happily together, sheltering from Covid-19 in Windsor Castle, and the queen told friends how wonderful it was to have lunch with Philip every day. In a heartfelt message to the nation marking her 70 years on the throne she paid tribute to her late husband as "a partner willing to carry out the role of consort and unselfishly make the sacrifices that go with it". She went on to say that it was her "sincere wish" that Camilla be known as Queen Consort when the Prince of Wales is crowned king.

Queen Elizabeth II will leave an impressive legacy. She has given tireless support to the Commonwealth, an organization which started as a group of eight countries, including Great Britain and former colonies like Canada, India, and Australia, and now includes 54 nations containing one third of the world's population. She has managed to combine pomp and ceremony and a more modern approach which includes a royal website, a YouTube channel and a mobile phone to stay in touch with her grandchildren. Her life has not always been easy, with plenty of family crises. Most recently her favourite son Andrew was accused of sexual abuse, a case he settled out of court for an undisclosed sum rumoured to be in the millions, and her disgruntled grandson Harry and his wife Meghan left the royal household to settle in California, but she has not allowed anything to come between her and what she sees as her royal duty.

Throughout her long and successful reign, Elizabeth has kept her private views to herself. She has allowed public opinion to influence the direction of the monarchy, but has carefully preserved it as a focus for national pride, tradition and continuity, doing much to keep republican sentiment at bay. Royal executive power may have ebbed away over the centuries, and today some Commonwealth countries are making moves to replace the queen as head of state, but Elizabeth's mission to do her best by all her subjects and remain scrupulously above politics have helped make her one of the most popular monarchs in British history.

POSTSCRIPT

With each passing year speculation about the future of the House of Windsor has intensified and is bound to continue under Charles, his son William and grandson George. For seven dutiful decades the queen has skilfully avoided most controversy. In an age of damaging debate and declining deference there are bound to be more and more questions about the relevance of royalty.

Anyone our age has grown up with Prince Charles. We pasted pictures of the young prince in his velvet-collared coats into scrapbooks, watched him walking nervously into his Scottish boarding school, witnessed the ceremonial extravaganza of his crowning as Prince of Wales at Caernarfon Castle and marvelled at his "fairy-tale" marriage to Lady Diana Spencer. The vicious gossip which surrounded the disintegration of that marriage, the death of Diana and Charles's subsequent marriage to divorcee Camilla Parker Bowles in 2005 were extremely damaging. Camilla was nicknamed "the rottweiler" and many argued that she should never be called queen. As it turned out Camilla proved to be an ideal wife. Her relaxed style and sense of humour have made Charles appear happier and more in touch. In a platinum jubilee message to the nation, the queen asked that Charles and Camilla be given "the same support that you have given me" and ended years of speculation by making it clear that she wants Camilla to be known as Queen Consort. Clearly delighted by his mother's welcome intervention, Charles issued a statement saying: "As we have sought together to serve and support Her Majesty... my darling wife has been my own steadfast support."

The queen's heir is very different from his mother, unafraid to air his views on everything from architecture to alternative medicine. Although his advisers promise that, once king, Charles III will not weigh in publicly on controversial matters, it's hard to imagine him staying silent on issues like global warming and sustainable farming.

Charles is the oldest heir to the throne in history and has had plenty of time to prepare for the role of king. In recent years, he has made it clear that he wants a pared-down monarchy concentrated on him and his son-and-heir William's family. The court of King Charles will not indulge the large number of royal relations who surround his mother. But, perhaps riskily, there has been no talk of a more Scandinavian style monarchy with fewer royal palaces or a reduced number of servants.

Future heir Prince William has walked his own path, as far as he has been able. After witnessing the break-up of his parents' marriage and the shocking death of his mother Diana, William married his university sweet-heart Catherine Middleton who has no aristocratic connections. They spent their early married life as far from prying eyes as possible. William worked as a search and rescue helicopter pilot on the Welsh island of Anglesey. His charitable interests reflect many of his mother's concerns: the homeless, mental health and vulnerable children but he also champions 21st-century issues like conservation and climate change. Like his father, who set up The Prince's Trust to help disadvantaged young people get jobs, William started the Royal Foundation to support addiction, early years learning, and other issues that he and his wife endorse.

There are those who believe that William should become the next king instead of his ageing father. He shows no sign of wishing to trade his happy family life for the throne. For the time being he seems content to stand well behind the queen and his father. But he has taken on more royal duties, particularly since his brother Harry left the royal household, and accepts that one day it will be his turn to rule. William was once asked if he wanted to become king and gave this telling reply: "It's not a question of wanting to be, it's something I was born into and it's my duty."

The royals know all too well how severely they've been beset by troubles in the last few years, largely of their own making. Today with social media, tabloid newspapers and 24-hour news every royal grimace and each mistake makes headlines around the world. A family dispute causes Prince Harry and his wife Meghan to move to California. Sexual abuse charges are brought against Prince Andrew. An aide of Prince Charles promises honours for money. What used to happen behind firmly closed doors is now common knowledge, tarnishing the royal family's all-important image.

In his book *The English Constitution* (1837) Walter Bagehot warned that "We must not let daylight in upon the magic" of the British monarchy. The royal family have to retain the mystique that is in danger of crumbling at the end of the second Elizabethan age as well as modernizing and adapting to rapidly changing times. Throughout her long reign, Queen Elizabeth II has carefully remained above reproach and retained the love and respect of her subjects. Whether her successors can follow her example will prove the modern monarchy's greatest challenge.

A NOTE ON SOURCES
AND FURTHER READING

Throughout our research for this book we found valuable material in a number of works by chroniclers and historians. Sources with a vast amount of information on all the English monarchs are the volumes of the *Oxford History of England*, the first-class series of Penguin *Monarchs*, the always reliable *Oxford Dictionary of National Biography*, and the colourful *Oxford Illustrated History of the Monarchy*. Wikipedia supplied helpful links to original documents at the end of each royal entry. We also found it useful to read more general historical commentary on all periods in, among others, the histories of England and the monarchy by historians such as Keith Feiling, Simon Schama, David Starkey, Robert Tombs and Antonia Fraser.

Among other authors we turned to for our research on specific periods are:

Marc Morris whose *The Anglo-Saxons* is the best book on that era. The most contemporary source on Alfred the Great is the Welsh monk Asser and the *Anglo-Saxon Chronicle*. We also dipped into chroniclers for the period of the Norman conquest and beyond: Orderic Vitalis, William of Jumièges, Henry of Huntingdon, William of Malmesbury, Jean Froissart and Adam Usk. Marc Morris again brought King John to life, and Dan Jones did us proud with *The Plantagenets*. Charles Ross provides an objective account of Richard III aided by the independent evidence, untainted by Tudor prejudice, of Richard's contemporaries like Dominic Mancini and the Croyland chronicler.

Thomas More and the diarists Samuel Pepys and John Evelyn stand out among useful contemporary sources for the Tudors and Stuarts.

Thomas Penn's recent *Winter King* launches the Tudor family with gusto. David Starkey's and Antonia Fraser's books on Henry VIII and

Elizabeth gave us additional insight into the Tudors as well as John Guy. John Foxe's *Book of Martyrs* is a revealing commentary on Queen Mary's reign.

John Miller has excellent detail in *The Stuarts*, as do two recent imaginative accounts, *The White King* by Leanda de Lisle on the reign of Charles 1 and Jenny Uglow's *A Gambling Man* on Charles II.

Works which provided tantalizing insights into the Georgian period include *The Four Georges* by J.H. Plumb and the diary of Mirza Abdul Hassan Khan who was Persian Ambassador in London 1808–10.

A stunning source for everything you need to know about Victoria's personal life is her enormous collection of diaries which Elizabeth II made available online on May 24 (Victoria's birthday) in 2012. Stand-outs among the many books about Victoria include Christopher Hibbert's *Queen Victoria* and Judith Baird's *Victoria the Queen*.

Bertie by Jane Ridley sheds fascinating light on King Edward VII. Kenneth Rose's *King George V* is a wonderful read as is Philip Ziegler's *King Edward VIII*. *George VI* by Sarah Bradford and *Elizabeth the Queen* by Sally Bedell Smith bring father and daughter to life.

This is just a small sample of the scores of books we have consulted about the royal family and the impact the kings and queens have had on British history over the centuries.

INDEX

Page locators in **bold** refer to sovereign's chapter, *italic* to royal family tree.

IMAGE CREDITS

Archive/Alamy Stock Photo, 51. Library of Congress, Washington, 52. GL Archive/Alamy Stock Photo, 53–54. Bridgeman Images, 55. Classic Image/Alamy Stock Photo, 56. Pictorial Press Ltd/Alamy Stock Photo, 57. Lebrecht Music & Arts/Alamy Stock Photo, 58. Prestor Pictures LLC/ Alamy Stock Photo, 59. PA Images/Alamy Stock Photo, 60. Ian Dagnall Computing/Alamy Stock Photo, 61. CBW/Alamy Stock Photo, 62. Central Press/Getty Images, 63. Pictorial Press Ltd/Alamy Stock Photo, 64. Tim Graham Photo Library via Getty Images, 65. Julian Parker/UK Press via Getty Images, 66. Samir Hussein/WireImage/Getty Images

Every effort has been made to acknowledge correctly and contact the source and/or copyright holder of each picture and Welbeck Publishing Group apologizes for any unintentional errors or omissions, which will be corrected in future editions of this book.